D1617032

SOUTHERN CROSSINGS

Daniel Cross Turner

Southern Crossings

·

Poetry

·

Memory

·

And the

·

Transcultural

·

South

The University of Tennessee Press · Knoxville

The paper in this book meets the requirements of American National Standards
Institute / National Information Standards Organization specification Z39.48–1992
(Permanence of Paper). It contains 30 percent post-consumer waste and is certified
by the Forest Stewardship Council.

Library of Congress Cataloging-in-Publication Data

Turner, Daniel Cross.
Southern crossings: poetry, memory, and the transcultural south /
Daniel Cross Turner. — 1st ed.   p. cm.
Includes bibliographical references and index.
ISBN 13: 978-1-57233-856-2 (hardcover) — ISBN 10: 1-57233-856-3 (hardcover)
1. American poetry—Southern States—History and criticism.
2. Southern States—In literature.
I. Title.

PS261.T87 2012
811'.5409975—dc23
2012005297

To my wife Keaghan:
Our love divides, is made complete

To our sons Rangeley and McDaniel:
We gave you life, and you return the favor

To my father Noel (1928–2011):
For the love of story and song

CONTENTS

ACKNOWLEDGMENTS

I wish to thank the members of my dissertation committee at Vanderbilt University—Michael Kreyling, Vereen Bell, Mark Jarman, Sean X. Goudie, and Larry J. Griffin—who helped to shape this project from its earliest stages. Funding for archival research and for dedicated writing time was provided by a dissertation enhancement grant as well as a dissertation year fellowship by my chair at Vanderbilt, Jerome Christensen. Thomas F. Haddox and Casey Clabough merit acknowledgement for dutifully reading and astutely commenting on various sections of the manuscript. I would also like to thank John Lang and Robert West, the two readers for the University of Tennessee Press, as well as the anonymous member of the press's editorial board who read and recommended the manuscript for final approval. I offer many thanks especially to acquisitions editor Kerry Webb, whose attentive counsel and guidance carried this project deftly from manuscript to book, and to the other first-rate professionals at the University of Tennessee Press, including Gene Adair, who carefully copyedited the manuscript, and press director Scot Danforth, who generously aided with permissions costs for the book. John Beard, my dean at Coastal Carolina University, also provided much-appreciated financial support to cover permissions costs.

Many thanks also are in order for those poets who offered valuable perspectives on their own work and on southern poetry in general through our fine conversations, including Kate Daniels, Yusef Komunyakaa, Natasha Trethewey, and Charles Wright. I extend my gratitude to Charles, Yusef, and Natasha, who graciously allowed me to formally interview them, providing me with some excellent insights.

I am thankful for the love and encouragement of my family of origin: my father, Noel; my mother, Margery; my sister, April; and my brother, Noel. I am most grateful to Keaghan, my brightest love and hope through all, and our sons, Rangeley and McDaniel, with whom we are well pleased . . . most of the time.

• • ● ●●● •

For permission to reprint selections from copyrighted material, I also wish to acknowledge various rights holders:

"Old Mansion" from *Selected Poems* by John Crowe Ransom, copyright © 1924 by Alfred A. Knopf, a division of Random House, Inc., and renewed 1952 by John Crowe Ransom. Used by permission of Alfred A. Knopf, a division of Random House, Inc.

"Fog Envelops the Animals," "The Heaven of Animals," "The Sheep Child" from *The Whole Motion: Collected Poems 1945–1992* ©1992 by James Dickey. Reprinted by permission of Wesleyan University Press. www.wesleyan. edu/wespress.

"Departure," "Eastward in Eastanelle," "Spring," and "For My Brothers," from *Tellico Blue* by George Scarbrough, copyright © 1949, 1999 by George Scarbrough. Used by permission of Iris Press.

"Signal Fires," "The Blue Hole," "Hearth," "Outbuildings," and "Atomic Age," from *Topsoil Road* by Robert Morgan, copyright © 2000 by Robert Morgan. Used by permission of Louisiana State University Press.

"Poem," "Vague Memory from Childhood," "The Miami of Other Days," from *Collected Poems of Donald Justice,* copyright © 2004 by Donald Justice. Used by permission of Alfred A. Knopf, a division of Random House, Inc.

"New South," "Penumbra," "Final Cut," and "January," from *Intervale: New and Selected Poems* by Betty Adcock, copyright © 1975, 1983, 1988, 1995, 1998, 1999, 2000, 2001 by Betty Adcock. Used by permission of Louisiana State University Press.

"Heartburn," "Sick in Soul and Body Both," "Barbed Wire," and "Landscape with Tractor," from *The Flying Change* by Henry Taylor, copyright © 1985 by Henry Taylor. Used by permission of Louisiana State University Press.

"Photograph of a Confederate Soldier Standing on Rocks in the James River at Richmond," "Caravati's Salvage," and "Night Traffic Near Winchester, Virginia," from *The Wick of Memory: New and Selected Poems, 1970–2000* by Dave Smith, copyright © 1973, 1977, 1979, 1981, 1983, 1984, 1985, 1989, 1990, 1991, 1992, 1994, 1995, 1996, 1997, 1998, 1999, 2000 by Dave Smith. Used by permission of Louisiana State University Press.

"All Landscape Is Abstract, and Tends to Repeat Itself," "Tennessee Line," and "Chickamauga" from *Negative Blue: Selected Later Poems* by Charles Wright.

INTRODUCTION

"How sweet the past is, no matter how wrong, or how sad." This sentiment from one of Charles Wright's most well-known poems, "The Southern Cross" (1981, *World of the Ten Thousand Things* 43), allows something of the scope of the ways in which contemporary southern poets—and perhaps, more broadly, those who self-identify as contemporary southerners—view the strands of the past. *Southern Crossings: Poetry, Memory, and the Transcultural South* attempts to make concrete the cultural realities projected through Wright's evocative notion, beautiful and intact in its abstraction, that the past commingles disparate strains, ranging from sweetness to wrongness to sadness, as the remains of our experience demand response from the present. The title of Wright's poem most obviously cites the navigational constellation of the southern hemisphere as well as the Christian iconography of the Bible Belt, the poet's native territory. But it is also suggestive of the famous and infamous battle flag of the Confederate States of America, implying the darker impulses of southern history in the use of the Southern Cross as a symbol for white supremacy and opposition to the civil rights movement. Thus history returns obliquely to the evanescent surface of Wright's work, which gestures toward other forms of southern crossings, other indications of a time and region in flux, careful to note that absence, like the silences between musical notes, can be as revealing as the remembered presence of the past: "It's what we forget that defines us, and stays in the same place, / And waits to be rediscovered" (54). Contemporary southern poetry, steeped in memory, both personal and communal, awaits critical rediscovery.

Southern Crossings interprets the work of a diversity of poets as responses to cultural modes—political, social, economic, and aesthetic—of the contemporary South. The following chapters incorporate specialized approaches that connect each poet's use of form to a specific model of social memory. To test the claims of region and nation on cultural memory, I develop intersections between culturally trenchant forms of poetry and collective remembrance in relation to a particular historical and geographic locus: the changing U.S. South from the early 1950s until the present, a time when what was construed the nation's most distinct region is in process of becoming increasingly "Americanized," even globalized. This book therefore encompasses a cultural history that spans the rise of the civil rights movement and federally mandated desegregation, the lasting conflicts of the Cold War and the U.S. war in Vietnam, the spread of industrial and postindustrial forms of capitalism as well as urban and suburban zones, the advent of national and international transportation networks, and the current politics of identity formation. Combining analysis of poetry as a historically responsive medium with developments in the fields of memory work as well as regional studies, *Southern Crossings* illustrates how the creative range of southern poetics helps to reevaluate theories of collective remembering on regional, national, and transnational levels. It does so while also presenting original perspectives on a spectrum of contemporary southern poets: Betty Adcock, Kate Daniels, James Dickey, Rodney Jones, Judy Jordan, Donald Justice, Yusef Komunyakaa, Robert Morgan, Harryette Mullen, George Scarbrough, Dave Smith, Henry Taylor, Natasha Trethewey, Robert Penn Warren, and Charles Wright. Most of these poets have achieved prominence on a national scale, and their considerable reputations are reflected in myriad poetic awards as well as in the fact that six out of these thirteen writers have earned a Pulitzer Prize for poetry, arguably the highest honor given to a U.S. poet.

In addition to analyzing regional emanations of trauma and nostalgia, this study offers a more complex, multivalent vision of cultural remembrance by also exploring lesser-known, yet equally compelling uses of the past, such as historiophoty (the recording of history through visual images), primal memory (a hoped-for return to the level of archetypal memory and integration with instinctual nature), cartographic simulation (an abstract vision of memory as pure process through poetic mappings of remembered landscapes), and countermemory (resistant strains of collective memory that disrupt the continuity of the official historical record). This multiplicity of critical paradigms is commensurate to the sheer multitudinousness of contemporary southern culture, its nuances and complications, and parallels the diversity of forms and ideas engaged by the poetries under scrutiny. The variety of critical approaches demonstrates that "southernness" is not a unitary, homogenized essence, but a cultural mode that generates overlapping and conflicting levels of identification.[1] The South is understood, then, not as a mimetic constant outside the purview of representation but as always in some measure a product of mediation. What counts as southernness is a culturally created affiliation, yet one that is power-fully imprinted through representational modes. Even in terms of the geograph-ical demarcations of the South, my project calls attention to cross-regional exchanges and transitions as well as to various subregions within the region's traditional borders (Appalachian, deep South, urban South, and so on), reflect-ing the permeability of such boundaries.

As Lewis Simpson notes in *The Fable of the Southern Writer* (1994), modern southern poetry has its own mythos attached to it, the illusion of having sprung from a cohesive southern culture bound together by a seamlessly integrated, spontaneous, and vital form of collective memory—what Donald Davidson con-ceived as the "autochthonous ideal" (literally "earth-born") of southern heritage. Fred Hobson provides the following gloss on Davidson's phrase: "By the term he meant a condition in which the writer was in a certain harmony with his social and cultural environments, was nearly *unconscious* of it as a 'special' envi-ronment, quaint or rustic or backward, and thus was not motivated by any urge to interpret or explain" (80).[2] Such an arrangement exemplifies Scott Romine's definition of a "community of rhetoric": a social hierarchy that appears unified because the cultural codes of value have been so deeply naturalized that they are asserted without self-consciousness—they go without saying—thus creating the illusion of a strict and absolute referentiality.[3] The poetry of the Vanderbilt Fugitives, especially that of Davidson, Allen Tate, and John Crowe Ransom, comes with its familiar list of modes and themes, which critics have described as natural outgrowths of this coherent social environment: a distinctively (white) southern voice, the rhythms and language of the Bible, an emphasis on com-munity and family ties, an attention to the past (sometimes rising to the level of ancestor worship as well as remembrance of the Lost Cause of the Civil War with its glorified pathos of defeat), and an unparalleled devotion to place. The Fugitive poets often strove to enshrine a collective past by positing an essential economic and historical connection to the land. Their ideologically construed remembering of the South as pastoral enclave and their angst over the perceived loss of a more dynamic past devalued in the wash of modernization have be-come important, if not dominant motifs of southern literary mythopoesis since the founding of *The Fugitive* magazine in 1922. These interrelated strands forge the most visible genealogy of modern southern poetics, supplying the founda-tion of southern "renascence" literature and casting a wide shadow on postwar southern poets, whose work often expresses opposition to Fugitive poetics and politics.[4]

The southern renascence–induced fable of a constant southernness has had a powerful hold on critics and poets alike; it has been no less powerful, and perhaps more so, for having been just that—a fable.[5] Southern poetry "after the renascence," on the other hand, has existed mostly in a critical void and requires a fuller account of its value to southern literary studies as well as American literary criticism.[6] Most southernist critics have concentrated their work on literature after World War II almost exclusively on fiction, rarely mentioning poetry. Besides the occasional survey of the state of contemporary southern poetry, typically provided by one of the poets themselves, the bulk of the criticism resides in reviews and single-author studies.[7] There is a need for a critical reassessment of the poetry and poetics of the contemporary South, one that takes into account its cultural and historical value. *Southern Crossings* serves to delineate, often to redraw, the borders of southern poetry by examining the ways in which it has revised and expanded particular visions of southern culture, ones that help to reinvent southern literature after the dying away of the illusion of autochthonous collective memory. The Fugitives' faith in the seamless conjunction of history and place is shaded, ironized, abstracted, and contradicted outright by the more contemporary representatives of southern poetry. The venerated southern condensation of the past and the land—the idea that, as Wyatt Prunty phrases it, "where something occurred stands for what occurred" (747)—gives way to a contemporary displacement; the remembered meaning of the southern landscape is no longer a cultural given, but subject to challenge.

This book considers the implications, both within and without the traditional territorial boundaries of the South, of this extensively altered investment of collective memory into particular geographic sites, such as Warren's antebellum Kentucky frontier, Dickey's primitive otherworld, Komunyakaa's racially splintered Louisiana, and Wright's ethereal Appalachia. The southern terrain has been reconceptualized as a locus of the primitive as well as the surreal, the banal as well as the grotesque. In placing memory along an axis from the nostalgic to the traumatic, the personal to the collective, and the ephemeral to the monumental, I consider how, as Martyn Bone has argued,[8] the landscape has been reconstructed from being a purported outpost of agrarianism to becoming a cultural geography shifting under the pressures of late capitalism as well as the collisions and cohesions of burgeoning transregional contexts.[9] And yet the South still has a metaphoric and moral role both inside and outside its traditional geographic demarcations. As Jennifer Rae Greeson notes, the American Southeast has served ideologically as a "principle of exclusion" for conceptualizing the nation, for "'our South' aligns with and diverges from 'the United States' writ large, creating a symbiotic *ideological juxtaposition* in which each term is defined by reference to the other" (1). In literature and other cultural texts, "our South" appears to embody both sides of the disavowed binary: simultaneously colonial and colonized, it diverges from the nation writ large on the basis of its *exploitativeness*—as the location of the internal colonization of Africans and African Americans in the United States—and on the basis of its *exploitation*—as the location of systematic underdevelopment, military defeat, and occupation (3). The South appears as a knotted mass of ideological self-contradiction that both weaves and frays the narrative of American exceptionalism; while complicit in past structures of oppression and imperialism, particularly through the exploitation of Native and African peoples, our South "also holds out the potential of making something new, of getting beyond the inherited power binaries by seeing from both sides and drawing syntheses out of oppositions" (289).

Traditional southernism of the kind generated by the Fugitive poets espouses a faith in the constantness of southern identity as a means of directly connecting the past with the present. Postsouthernism stays within the frame of the past, parodying it from the inside out and revealing the ultimate contingency of its codes.[10] If, in the post–World War II era, the South's "familiar way of making and maintaining meaning, its orthodoxy or consensus, had ceased functioning, as it were, on involuntary muscles and had become a kind of willed habit" (Kreyling, "Fee, Fie, Faux Faulkner" 1), then the fable of the postsouthern poet reflects the plight of the self-conscious amnesiac. Cohesive social memory becomes a phantom pain—inoperable, though its lack is persistently felt. Confronted with the acceleration of history in the contemporary world, the postsouthern writer only simulates the presence of unmediated communal recall, while generating a stream of memory sites that serve, paradoxically, all the more to reiterate the absence of collectively remembered values. In this regard, it is fair to ask, in Bone's formulation: "Is there a danger that the parodic poetics of postsouthernism are neutered, even co-opted, by a socioeconomic system that has derealized the foundational sense of place more than hyperreal fiction ever could?" (46) Such fluidity of placelessness, of aregionality, could lead to formlessness, to a sense of never belonging, except as a consumer-citizen.

The matter of this potential derealization is translated into a third idea, which I term *transouthernism*. This concept draws attention to the nexus of identifications that are currently being circulated within and across the physical and conceptual spaces of the South. Under the mark of transouthernism, region still constitutes a crucial site for social, economic, political, and cultural allegiances and exchanges; however, it is no longer viewed as all encompassing since it becomes one of multiple levels of affiliation, which are not bound exclusively to locality but take on cross-regional qualities. The transouthern mode moves us away from the postsouthern void of "virtual southernness" (Kreyling, *Inventing Southern Literature* 153) and into a cultural space where regional identification still matters, but is placed in circulation with other modes that make significant claims on identity construction, including race, class, and gender. Transouthernism replaces postsouthernism's stress on a temporal model—the postsouthern is what comes *after* traditional southernism—with an emphasis on the way that history is formed not merely through time but also through space: "post" entails temporal loss, something left behind, whereas "trans" involves continuing transition, invoking a sense of the contemporary spatialization of history.[11] As Romine argues in *The Real South* (2008), the impulse toward multiplying, overtly "inauthentic" versions of southernness should not be seen as reflecting a devastating cultural lack (the pained loss of a once "real," deep South), but should be taken as multivalent (not broken) signals of the persistent desire for local identifications in an increasingly deterritorialized world. While Romine focuses on interpreting pop-culture artifacts of self-consciously "faux" Souths (for example, the post-*GWTW* Tara Club Estates outside Atlanta, southern-style theme restaurants, popular southern magazines and television programs) in conjunction with fictive works, poetic texts also spark productive reconstructions of heterogeneous "pockets" of multiple southernnesses under the influences of transregional, global dynamics. The transouthern implies the self-conscious appropriation of contingent identifications *as if* they were grounded identities in part to create a level of cohesive agency so that individuals and groups might operate strategically in the service of specific socioeconomic, political, or cultural ends. Akin to James Peacock's concept of "grounded globalism," the transouthern mode intersperses more diverse cultural traditions within the context of southern history, generating both fusion and friction through these translocations of encoded identities. Even—or especially—in an increasingly global world, the complexities of regional ideology remain; in fact, localism provides one of the foremost sites of social, economic, political, and ethnic difference amid the spread of transnational cultures.[12]

I augment this analysis of regionality by including specialized methodologies that connect an intensive focus on poetry to forms of cultural memory. Merging current theories of poetics with work in the emergent field of memory studies, *Southern Crossings* makes a claim for southern literary studies as an integral part of any full account of U.S. literatures, and it does so in a unique manner by interpreting poetry and poetics in connection with its contemporary social and historical contexts. There is currently a scholarly bias against poetry in favor of genres that seem to reflect historical conditions more "transparently."

In "What We Don't Talk about When We Talk about Poetry" (1998), Marjorie Perloff calls for studies that will investigate intersections between lyric poetry and critical theory, and read current poetics according to historical contexts: "a sense of history and a sense of theory: these are the twin poles of criticism missing from most poetry discourse today" (182). Perloff rightly asserts, *contra* Bakhtin's famous dictum against the supposedly monologic quality of lyric poetry, that "poetic language is never simply unique, natural, and universal; it is the product, in large part, of particular social, historical, and cultural formations. And these formations demand study" (183). Perloff's call has not yet been wholly answered.

Working in postcolonial studies, Jahan Ramazani describes this prejudice against poetry's capacity to signify social and political history: "since poetry mediates experience through a language of exceptional figural and formal density, it is a less transparent medium by which to recuperate the history, politics, and sociology of postcolonial societies" (4). Poetry is often considered such a formally dense and complicated genre with its added set of rules (radically compressed imagery, stanza and line structures, rhythm and rhyme schemes) that it is seen as resistant material for interpreting it in relation to its cultural situatedness. Although the poetic medium is thus "harder to annex as textual synecdoche for the social world" (4), poetry is deeply connected to the circumstances of its cultural production precisely because of its intensive focus on the form of its message, and by extension, on the shaping forms of our lives and histories. In addressing the question of poetry as a profoundly and uniquely historicized genre, my study makes a claim for the particularity of poetry as an art form. While avoiding an essentialist conception of genre, I utilize a pragmatic definition of poetry as a specialized kind of linguistic expression.[13] In its emphasis on symbolic compression and lyrical value as well as its lineated form, poetry has a propensity to make words appear to count more than in narrative fiction and dramatic dialogue. Because of the relative compactness of poetic form, typically verse exhibits a heightened imagistic density that distinguishes it from other literary modes and demands a greater emphasis on "specifically literary modes of response and recognition—of figurative devices, generic codes, stanzaic patterns, prosodic twists, and allusive turns" (4). But this is a difference in degree, not in kind, since other genres also may elicit such close formal analysis, though perhaps not in as much detail.

The defining feature of poetry is not simply its heightened tendency toward compact expression and lyrical play, but its focus on the rhythmic capacity of language. As recent work in the area of historical poetics and the lyricization of poetry suggests, what count as the "salient characteristics" (Culler 203) of lyric poetry are no doubt conditioned by historical formations.[14] Even so, poetic rhythm offers a means for the new lyric studies to "not only explore different historical manifestations of lyric but also propose new normative models of lyric, emphasizing features that can become the basis of new typologies" (205). My reading of rhythm as the basis for describing the medium specificity of poetry reflects the proposition set forth by Perloff and Dworkin that what we name poetry "inherently involves the structuring of sound" (749). *Southern Crossings* makes a claim that poetic forms address philosophical and historical pressures, precisely through their concentrated attention to sound patternings. Simon Jarvis describes how the technics of poetry presents a distinct formulation of cultural history:

> Philosophical poetics is historical insofar as it takes technique to be at once the way in which art thinks and the way in which the work of art most intimately registers historical experience. . . . [T]he pressure point, the point of historical formation and action in the poem, is always that of technique, because this is where the poem gets made, the point at which the voices of the many living and dead (S. Stewart) that are the poet's repertoire or material are selected from, cut into, distorted, twisted, and precipitated into this or that composition—where their natural-historical antagonisms are exposed, concealed, exacerbated, or fudged. (931–32)

Focusing on meter and rhythm, Jarvis contends that "poetics does not get more historical by tying cultural-political labels onto whole meters. The historical force of verse thinking may at a particular juncture depend upon the rendering the metacommunications of verse less immediately legible" (932). The rhythmical density of verse gives words an aural opacity set against their communicative legibility. Preventing verse effects from "shrinking to no more than a series of mere badges of belonging, of social, political, cultural, or poetical affiliation" (932), rhythmic technique allows poetry to be "reanimated as a repertoire of historically and affectively saturated paralinguistic gestures" (932). The nonverbal intonations of rhythm coursing through poetic lines are arational, gestural. Such acoustic effects distinguish lyric from prose in that "rhythmic recurrence or, minimally, segmentation are not 'constructive' factors" of prose (933). The performative affect of poetic rhythm, the way its movements shadow and shape responses in the readerly body, becomes a dramatic site for uncovering cultural "habits and practices of thinking and making that have in many cases become lost" (932).

The argument for the centrality of poetic rhythm has a long history—comparable, for instance, to Edgar Allan Poe's assertion in "The Poetic Principle" (1850) that poetry is "the rhythmical creation of beauty" (175)—and has enjoyed a critical renaissance in the past decade in debates over "historical prosody": whether poetic form fosters a unique purview into cultural and historical contexts, or, conversely, whether poems are no different from any other texts and so analysis of poetic forms should concentrate almost exclusively on how different historical periods and milieus have defined texts as "poetry." My analysis makes connections between aesthetic and cultural formations; I view the irreducible quality of rhythm in conjunction with a historicism of specific forms. Poetry's attention to form is most evident in its redoubled focus on rhythm, for the rhythmic structure of poems underscores the materiality of words in themselves. The acoustic impulse of rhythm creates a compelling experience of language as pure physical sensation momentarily separated from the conditions of meaning.[15] According to Amittai F. Aviram, "the sublime power of rhythm in connection with the body" (7) approximates, by turn, Nietzsche's Dionysian reality, Freud's drive, Lacan's order of the real, and Kristeva's *sujet en procès*. Charles Bernstein argues similarly in *Close Listening: Poetry and the Performed Word* that "it is precisely because sound is an arational or nonlogical feature of language that it is so significant for poetry—for sound registers the sheer physicality of language, a physicality that must be the grounding of reason exactly insofar as it eludes rationality" (21). Like the music (rhythm) beyond the notes (words), poetic rhythm stresses sound divided off from sense; the driving, unconscious flow of rhythm allows primal sensation to counterbalance abstract sense. Poetic rhythm thus offers the participant a feeling of liberation from strictures of socialized codes of value. Reveling in the driving momentum of language as meaningless sensation, we experience a momentary stay against confusion: we avoid confusion not by outthinking it (a matter of a poem's content, its sense), but by unthinking it (the sublimely negating effect of a poem's form, its sound). The thingness of the poem—embodied most deeply in its insistent aural repetitions—speaks directly to physical being, an experience that we can only describe indirectly. The sublime energy of rhythm "does not transcend the world of the physical senses. On the contrary, it *is* the world of physical sensation unmediated by imaginary and symbolic constructs" (Aviram 239).[16]

Since the percussive quality of verse is intrinsically without meaning, we are called to allegorize the ineffable power of these aural reiterations, and the freeplay of indefinable rhythm takes on multifaceted values when considered in particular historical contexts. Because of its heightened awareness of the performative quality of language, poetry can register—and critique—political and historical pressures in a manner distinct from other genres. Since poetry bends specific, culturally conditioned contents through the prism of inherited rhythms, my work also considers the history of particular forms in addition to reading a poem's content as a sign of its social meanings. Poetry offers an intermixture of what are often culturally specific meters, incorporating complex fusions at the level of rhythm. In its most basic form, poetic rhythm represents a means of making language more memorable as a method of cultural transmission and is therefore deeply implicated in models of collective memory. These forms carry the weight of tradition, of cultural significance, even as some of the southern poets discussed in the following chapters appropriate them toward making transcultural adaptations, hybridizations on the level of form.

My exploration of poetry as a historically responsive medium is supplemented with recent developments in the expanding field of memory studies. Memory work provides a valuable critical framework for investigating the transformations of the contemporary South as perceived through the lens of various poetries. A theoretical approach that explicitly opens up questions of the ideological dimensions of the past, cultural memory denotes acts of remembrance shared by a discrete social or ethnic group and experienced apart from the auspices of the official historical record. "Discrete" should be understood here not as absolute or essentialist, but as culturally marked according to shifting boundaries—a matter of identification, not identity. Developing from Maurice Halbwachs's conceptualization of collective memory in the 1920s and his argument that memory is never merely personal, but always carries a social facet, memory work has undergone a resurgence in the last two decades, taking on interdisciplinary implications by incorporating a spectrum of areas, such as anthropology, sociology, philosophy, cultural studies, and literary criticism. Common repositories of cultural memories include places and objects, as well as discourses and customs. To translate into a traditional southernist context, sites of collective memory might include the veneration of the family homeplace, the salvaging of Civil War mementos, and the nuances of southern dialect. As opposed to ostensibly objective historical accounts, cultural memory is never a fait accompli, but is always in process of potential alteration and reinvention. It can support dominant historiographic patterns, but can also develop contrary strains that challenge the authority of a reified tradition. The issue of cultural memory is interconnected with that of region, since southern society is often described as particularly laden with the burden of not forgetting:

No culture, of course, exists only in the present: all draw on,
hark back to, a past significant precisely because of its continued

moral, identity, and emotional utility. In this the South is no dif-
ferent, but what is unusual is how explicitly, how routinely, and
how pervasively the region's history, that very particular southern
past, is evoked in the present: the South of *then* is recreated and
oddly memorialized, concretized in a sense, in the South of *now*.
(Griffin 48)

Historically, the South has been construed as a site of exceptionalist discourse,
this marked interpenetration of the past in the present typifying southern cul-
ture as distinctively time-bound. As a consequence, the region yields fertile
ground for testing current theorizings of forms of cultural memory and gauging
the ways in which contemporary southern poetries evoke and refashion specific
models of collective remembering. This is particularly important as the region
seems in process of shedding traditional versions of cultural memory—not
merely detaching from specific accounts of "the past" (e.g., re-remembering the
Civil War via the mythos of the Lost Cause), but also the stereotypical devotion
to "pastness" that Griffin describes.

Because of their centrality to modern southern poetry, the effort to ana-
lyze the output of those poets who have come after the Fugitives is obliged
to assess this literary historical legacy. While the Fugitives are not the only
group of intellectuals to claim influence over the course of twentieth-century
southern literary history, they certainly have had the most lasting impact on
southern poetry as well as on American literature more generally. Ironically,
they established a new form of tradition-bound orthodoxy for the literature
of the modern South, one that valued the "hyper-intellectuality, verbal com-
plexity, and allusiveness" (Rubin 665) of modernist poetry, while imbuing this
avant-garde poetics with a reactionary bent by using it to venerate the time-
honored places and objects of southern memory, especially the remnants of
an older, agrarian South.[17] Their influence, of course, took different shapes,
moving explicitly into social, economic, and political spheres by providing the
core of the Vanderbilt Agrarians as well as their manifesto, *I'll Take My Stand*
(1930), and then returning to the literary field by concentrating their interest
on developing the New Criticism. The Fugitive poets' fierce nostalgia for the
autochthonous ideal of southern memory represents an elegiac shoring up of
the fragments of a pastoral South against our ruins, that nothing be lost of a
cohesive culture that never fully existed in the first instance. Even though Tate
and Warren would later admit that the Fugitive-Agrarian vision of a constant
southernness was indeed a mythopoetic production, it was nonetheless a power-
ful enabling fiction in its time and continues to exert influence on the current

generation of southern writers. Proposing a view of the South as a naturally coherent culture, though one that is apparently in peril of unraveling under the pressures of modernity, the poems of Ransom, Tate, and Davidson practice a form of monumental history reflected in the Fugitives' veneration of the lost vitality of a once-great South.[18] Much of their poetry is marked by a sense of the past as a site of holy pilgrimage, as they return in verse to some of the sacred places of southern history, recollecting themselves and their cultural inheritance in the contemplative space of hallowed grounds, such as Ransom's old mansion, Tate's Confederate cemetery, or Davidson's return to Robert E. Lee's final resting place among the Virginia mountains. Doomed pilgrims, the Fugitive poets pay zealous homage to a monumental and sacred past that has left them behind.

Although Ransom's "Antique Harvesters" (1927) is his most well-known elegy for "our Lady" of the pastoral South, "Old Mansion" (1927) offers a more emphatic view of a traditional southernness still grandiose and stately even in decay. The old mansion serves as a symbolic construction on at least two interlocking levels: as a cultural icon and as a made poetic thing. The traditional South as embodied in the old mansion appears in danger of falling to ruin, its "grave rites" losing their meaning, and before this epic structure, the narrator feels as if he is little more than "an intruder" who exhales his "foreign weed on [the old mansion's] weighted air" (70):

> It was a Southern manor. One hardly imagines
> Towers, arcades, or forbidding fortress walls;
> But sufficient state though its peacocks now were pigeons;
> Where no courts kept, but grave rites and funerals. (70)

The past literally reappears in this vision of the southern manor that provides a sufficient state of monumentalism, the very air around it "weighted" with eminence, for "Stability was the character of its rectangle" (70). Though imposing, the old forms are threatened with corrosion ("Decay was the tone of old brick and shingle" [70]), and "one had best hurry to enter it if one can" (70). Entrance into this symbolic structure is a sacred rite, one that had better be enacted soon, for the door is closing on the ritualistic South. In fact, the narrator discovers that admission into this distinguished past has been denied him; though he "clangs their brazen knocker against the door" (70), it comes to nothing, since

> The old mistress was ill, and sent [his] dismissal
> By one even more wrappered and lean and dark

> Than that warped concierge and imperturbable vassal
> Who had bid me begone from her master's Gothic park. (71)

The manor houses the remnants of a more authentic time, but one that seems destined to crumble under an ever-advancing modernization:

> Emphatically, the old house crumbled; the ruins
> Would litter, as already the leaves, this petted sward;
> And no annalist went in to the lords or the peons;
> The antiquary would finger the bits of shard. (71)

Though he attempts to retreat into this antique realm, the narrator must return, sadly, into the "unseemlier world" of modernity:

> But on retreating I saw myself in the token,
> How loving from my dying weed the feather curled
> On the languid air; and I went with courage shaken
> To dip, alas, into some unseemlier world. (71)

The matter of racial divisions is referenced opaquely in Ransom's dressed-up rephrasing of black servants as the "concierge," "vassal," and "peons" of the Old Mansion. Though, as always, there is irony in his tone, the overall nostalgic bent of the poem turns a blind eye to the racial inequities of both the Old and the modern Souths.

Tate's "Ode to the Confederate Dead" (1927) provides the Ur-text for the Fugitive movement as well as for modern southern poetry in general. Compared to Davidson, Tate, like Ransom, takes a more self-aware ironical stance; however, he is intensely nostalgic not for the Lost Cause per se, but, on a deeper level, for the lost cause of southern monumentalist history—the belief that the past is there, essentially, if only we had myths strong enough to recapture it. Tate provides a distinctly southernized brand of modernist mythopoesis: his jaded and bitterly self-conscious record of the current state of the southern wasteland only invokes the more sorrow for the loss of the glory-bound past. His Confederate cemetery is the apotheosis of Fugitive remembrance, conflating the dual impossibilities of recovering a genuinely agrarian South and of reliving the vibrant essence of Civil War history. As his narrator makes this most famous of Fugitive pilgrimages to the hallowed cemetery that memorializes the now nameless Confederate dead, Tate comes to praise "the arrogant circumstance" (21) of those who have fallen in a defeated, but honorable cause:

"Row after row with strict impunity / The headstones yield their names to the element, / The wind whirrs without recollection" (20). Dividing this sacred site of the Lost Cause from any association with the issue of slavery and race, the ode allows the South a too-easy impunity. This longing to return to "the immoderate past" that spurred white southerners to rebellion washes the blood of chattel slavery—the most intensive sign of the South's "immoderacy"—from the Confederacy's collective hands, as the salt of the soldiers' blood now "Stiffens the saltier oblivion of the sea" (22):

> Turn your eyes to the immoderate past,
> Turn to the inscrutable infantry rising
> Demons out of the earth—they will not last.
> Stonewall, Stonewall, and the sunken fields of hemp,
> Shiloh, Antietam, Malvern Hill, Bull Run. (21)

Unlike his more immoderate gray-clad ancestors, the modern white southerner is left "Cursing only the leaves crying / Like an old man in a storm" (21), forlornly chanting "Stonewall, Stonewall" as if praying for saintly intercession. In contrast to the monumental ethos of Civil War history, the present is a mere mummified version of this once-dynamic past and points to "the silence which / Smothers you, a mummy, in time" (21). So that the grandeur of the past is not lost to oblivion, it is the southern poet's task to remember the sacrifice of the forgotten Confederate dead, and if we cannot live a meaningful present, we can at least write about a storied past so that its legacy, and not its anonymity, will grow:

> What shall we who count our days and bow
> Our heads with a commemorial woe
> In the ribboned coats of grim felicity,
> What shall we say of the bones, unclean,
> Whose verdurous anonymity will grow? (22)

The "we" here signifies the white southern artist's status as part of a like-minded community of rhetoric, one that collectively bows its head with a "commemorial woe," not because "we" fought an unjust war, but because "we" lost it.

Similarly, Davidson's "Lee in the Mountains, 1865–1870" (1938) exhibits a pained nostalgia for a past that is automatically more essential and cohesive than modernity's assumed chaos. The poem elides all sense that slavery may have had anything to do with the Civil War.[19] In commemorating the fiction of a stable and stabilizing Civil War South and intermingling this with a political call to remain willfully unreconstructed, Davidson marks off an ineradicable dividing line between South and North, desiring to remain, as the title of one of his essays on regionalism suggests, still Rebels, still Yankees. "Lee in the Mountains" poetically reincarnates the iconic figure of Robert E. Lee after the War. In composing a biographical essay about his father, Lighthorse Harry Lee, for the third (1869) edition of his father's memoirs, Lee remembers the lost vibrancy of his own sacrificial service to the principles of the Confederacy:

> What I do is only a son's devoir
> To a lost father. Let him only speak.
> The rest must pass to men who never knew
> (But on a written page) the strike of armies,
> And never heard the long Confederate cry
> Charge through the muzzling smoke or saw the bright
> Eyes of the beardless boys go up to death. (4–5)

Robert E. Lee has taken part in a monumental historical struggle that the succeeding generation of southern men shall never experience, except at secondhand from the remove of a poetic revision of the past "But on a written page." The latter-day sons of the Confederacy represent a generation that descends, in both senses, from a monumental past; in a version of the Quentin Compson complex—the inability to escape the woeful weight of the fathers' past—they can never live up to their fathers. Davidson invokes a vision of Lee after Appomattox, when the defeated general entered into the academic trade, accepting the presidency of Washington College (now Washington and Lee University) in Lexington, Virginia, where he would remain until his death in 1870. The opening lines present a vision of Lee physically and symbolically walking into the shadows:

> Walking into the shadows, walking alone
> Where the sun falls through the ruined boughs of locusts
> Up to the president's office. . . .
> Hearing the voices
> Whisper, *Hush, it is General Lee!* And strangely
> Hearing my own voice say, *Good morning, boys.*
> (*Don't get up. You are early. It is long*
> *Before the bell. You will have long to wait*
> *On these cold steps. . . .)* (3)

Like Tennyson's Ulysses, this retired warrior is "spent with old wars and new sorrow" (3). The poem operates as a metaphoric pilgrimage to a sacrosanct place of the Confederacy, where the remnants of a now shattered past can be recollected in tranquility. Davidson himself made a literal pilgrimage to the campus of Washington and Lee in order to walk in his hero's footsteps, counting the very steps the old soldier would have taken from his residence to the college president's office. Indeed, Lee Chapel has become something of a shrine to the canonized general, who for many white southerners still embodies the ideal of the Christian knight—an ideal brutally inverted by the "knights" of the Ku Klux Klan. Even the land has suffered a tragic diminishment from the loss of the epic past: "The Blue Ridge, crowned with a haze of light, / Thunders no more" (5). The Cult of the Lost Cause is fully enshrined by Davidson's poem, as it rhetorically asks whether the South should have kept on fighting:

> Was it for this
> That on an April day we stacked our arms
> Obedient to a soldier's trust? To lie
> Ground by heels of little men,
> Forever maimed, defeated, lost, impugned? (5)

For Davidson, it is a shame that Lee lived long enough to see the incapacity of the fragmented present to live up to the mythological past, since under the stifling inconsequence of his academic position, the general is finally "alone, / Trapped, consenting, taken at last in mountains" (6).[20]

The remainder of my analysis is divided into six chapters, according to the prevalent mode of cultural memory at work in the particular poet's representation of regional and natural cultures. Chapter 1 considers Robert Penn Warren's 1969 masterwork *Audubon: A Vision*, which recasts the history of the brutal settlement of the southern and American frontier through filmic sequences of violent spectacles. Warren's poem combines two of the nation's most ideologically cathected regions, the South and the West, in a thoroughgoing critique of Cold War policies in the midst of what *Audubon* famously calls "this century, and moment, of mania" (267). Drawing on Jean Jacques Audubon's historical account of his wanderings on the early 1800s Kentucky prairies, Warren creates a poetic version of what historian Hayden White terms historiophoty: the recording of history through visual images. Exploiting a cinematic poetics—one that places intense emphasis on the filmic modes of spectacle, kinesis, and seriality—in conjunction with an invocation of the traditional motifs of the Western genre, *Audubon: A Vision* exposes the political dynamics of the violent conquest of the southern/western frontier. Warren's exercise of filmic memory reflects the unresolved tensions of manifest destiny by recasting these in the context of an intensely cinematic regional as well as national ethos: in *Audubon: A Vision*, he reconstructs Audubon's dark encounters in the uncivilized space of the wilderness as a southern version of the Cold War Western film.

Where Warren's cinematic technique confronts historical conflict directly, James Dickey's exercise of primal memory, the subject of chapter 2, responds to contemporary pressures of urban industrialism by retreating into a primitive otherworld, where the human merges with the instinctual order of nature. Dickey's early poems embody an archetypal desire to return to this level of undifferentiated consciousness. However, in a crucial turn not only for Dickey's canon but for the literary history of postwar southern poetry more generally, he loses his faith in the power of primal memory, and the publication of *Falling, May Day Sermon, and Other Poems* in 1967 initiates a parody of his primitivist poetics that moves away from an escapist vision of brute nature to a historically situated engagement with contemporary culture. The avoidance of historical conflict through a hoped-for return to archetypal origins ultimately collapses and yields to the deconstructive power of cultural parody, as his later work confronts the ethnographic dimensions of primitivism. This ideological shift is paralleled on the level of form, for Dickey's early use of "primal" anapests is replaced by a sprawling "wall of words" technique in his mid-career poems. This watershed in his career results in part from literary skirmishes with Robert Bly and Allen Ginsberg, members of what Dickey acerbically referred to as "the New York literati," over regional differences, racial politics, and the Vietnam War.

Picking up on Dickey's effort to reenter the primitive cycle of nature as a form of deep-structured longing for a past stripped of historical influence, chapter 3 investigates the cultural ethos of nostalgia in a range of current southern poets, including George Scarbrough, Robert Morgan, Donald Justice, Betty Adcock, Henry Taylor, and Dave Smith. These writers, all of whom practice some measure of traditional poetic formalism, explore nostalgia in its literal meaning of "homesickness"—from the Greek *nostos* ("to return home") and *algia* ("a sorrowful or distressing condition or illness")—balancing a desire to return to a more comforting, centered past with an awareness of the pained inauthenticity surrounding these repetitions. Some of the contemporary poets of nostalgia adopt the southern tradition in uncritical ways, while others of this group adapt this mode into inventive revisions that are more responsive to the conditions of the current South. To reflect the intricate range of the current southern poetics of nostalgia, this chapter is organized according to the primary form of nostalgia at work in these six representative poets: 1) restoration (a transhistorical desire to reinhabit a more stable past), 2) metanostalgia (nostalgia for the process of nostalgia itself), and 3) critical memory (nostalgia as a socially vested means of critique that reenvisions the present by basing it on a new understanding of past codes).

In chapter 4, cartographic theory serves as the specific framework for understanding the effects of cultural memory in Charles Wright's poetic cartographies. His simulated landscapes appear to dissolve the geopolitical boundaries of the historical South by abstracting the terrain into self-reflexive images that disengage the traces of distinctive regional culture. Wright's poems suggest Jean Baudrillard's thesis in *Simulacra and Simulation* that contemporary culture is characterized by an overwhelming proliferation of simulacra—subjective models unloosed from the illusion of reference, images of images, "the generation by models of a real without origin or reality: a hyperreal" (Baudrillard 631). Wright's poetic landscapes reflect a sense of memory as pure process, where art no longer mimetically *represents* the past in a Platonic sense nor creatively *imitates* the past in an Aristotelian manner, but *simulates* it, producing its own objects of memory in a *mise en abîme* of abstract and repetitive glimpses. Wright's re-creations of bypassed southern roadways—his "lost highways" and dematerialized vistas, his "ethereal landscapes"—reveal the ultimate contingency of such cartographic overlays of the South, which are not only falsely cohesive (they map over sites of social conflict and transition) but coercive (they are part of a nationalist projection of identity). Though these seem to operate at a further remove from a sense of referential history, this chapter argues that Wright's conceptual cartographies, ephemeral as they seem, nevertheless bear the imprint of cultural memory. These work in conjunction with his ecclesiastical forms and staggered lineation—his poetics of "the negative sublime"—to record and critique the potential disappearance of traditional regional markers under the flux of consumer capitalism.

My argument then shifts from Wright's view of the South as simulacrum, region as pure idea, to Yusef Komunyakaa's haunted vision in chapter 5. Komunyakaa's work parallels the racial violence of the Jim Crow South with the atrocity-laced landscapes of Vietnam in verse that embodies a surrealistic commingling of the aesthetic and the grotesque. Interposing the racial divisions of the segregated South with the brutally uncanny terrain of Vietnam, he explores two intensive loci for "the reconfiguration of lyric as speaking, once again, not for the hypothetical 'sensitive' and 'authentic' individual . . . but for the larger cultural and philosophical moment" (Perloff 185). Komunyakaa's reconstructions of traumatic memory are made even more compelling through his expert manipulation of the indefinable, repetitive force of poetic rhythm.

Because of its unconscious power, its stress on performative affect over communicative sense, rhythm functions in his poems as a nonverbal allegory for the inassimilable nature of the traumatogenic past. In describing episodes of racial and combat trauma through striking, even beautiful images broken across insistent rhythms, his poems demonstrate the potential danger of aestheticizing violence. And yet his works are highly self-conscious about the risk of poeticizing bloodshed; as a result, his use of rhythmic reiterations strengthens, not saps, his poetry's critique of the prevalent definition of trauma as fatalistic repetition without hope of productively redressing the splintered past.

The transregional dynamic of Komunyakaa's verse, which traverses national boundaries from the Deep South to Vietnam and back again, is expanded in chapter 6. This final section of *Southern Crossings* examines the work of five current poets—Kate Daniels, Judy Jordan, Rodney Jones, Harryette Mullen, and Natasha Trethewey—who set their work squarely in the domain of social history. Their poems foster poetic countersites of memory—such as Daniels's working class Richmond, Jordan's unmarked sharecroppers' graveyard, Jones's multinational Nashville as well as DDT-laced fields, Mullen's liminal spaces, and Trethewey's early-1900s New Orleans brothel—that construct new, politically engaged visions of the contemporary South. Moving past the Fugitives' one South, indivisible, these writers intersect the claims of region with other powerful identifications in volatile ways, reflecting the increasing hybridity of southern life. In so doing, they expertly inscribe a transouthern ethos. Exploiting a spectrum of poetic forms, from Daniels's extenuated lines and new narrative technique to Jordan's eerie abstractionism and Jones's contrapuntal use of dialect, and from Mullen's blues-based meters and radical linguistic play to Trethewey's ekphrastic poetics and revisionary sonnets, these poets provide counternarratives of overlooked southern subcultures that redefine the region as a nexus of crossregional affiliations. In crosshatching a strong sense of locality with larger influences, these poems enact a form of grounded globalism, gesturing toward transregional interconnectivity while maintaining the local as a primary node where globalism happens. Their poetic constructions of natural and built environments act as pluralistic "force fields," where "sense of place becomes both more dynamic and more insecure and broadens in scope toward a global compass" (Peacock 132).

The chapters that follow thus examine significant writers whose work moves contemporary southern poetry beyond the Fugitives' influence, offering visions of the enduring, yet changing functions of the South as a critical cultural space on regional and transregional levels.[21] At a time when critics have argued that the U.S. South is more like other places than ever, this project offers new paradigms for understanding the significance of southern culture, not separately but in connection with other regions and cultural spaces. At the close of *Inventing Southern Literature,* Kreyling provides a trenchant account of why southern literature and culture are still vital elements, conceptual and experiential, in the construction of a (trans)national imaginary when he insists that it is the contemporary South's status as a site of "constant movement, struggle, and negotiation" (182) that gives southern culture its ongoing value "for the study of and participation in the reinvention of culture" (182). This claim is fulfilled forcefully, I argue, in the diverse views offered by the poetries under scrutiny, whose reinvention of the materials of collective memory generates a range of models for interpreting the literary and social modes coursing within and across contemporary cultures.

Chapter 1

Poetic Historiophoty: Filmic Memory
in Robert Penn Warren's *Audubon: A Vision*

History is blind, but man is not.

—Robert Penn Warren, *All the King's Men* (1946)

Robert Penn Warren's[1] concerns with the limits of literary modernism and the need for a "new language" to match "the new world around us" (2) are made clear in his 1966 Lamar Lecture, *A Plea in Mitigation*.[2] It is the visual register of film that provides him with this new language in *Audubon: A Vision* (1969). In invoking a cinematic frame for his long narrative poem, Warren presents a historical picture of the early 1800s South that imparts a forceful analogue for the post–World War II United States struggling to redress its inheritance of "civilizing" (i.e., democratizing) the continent and the world. Interpreting *Audubon* as a poetic form of "historiophoty," the "representation of history and our thought about it in visual images and filmic discourse" (White, "Historiography and Historiophoty" 1193),[3] offers a new method not only for reading Warren's poetic sequences but also for considering the relation of the poetic medium to that of film in general.[4] Despite its historical subject, critics have had little to say about the poem's engagement with history, preferring to untangle Warren's philosophical declarations, some of which seem to tout the archetypal timelessness of his tale over and above a sense of its historical embeddedness. This chapter strives to turn critical discussions of *Audubon* away from myth and toward history, toward the ways that history often contradicts myth.[5]

One of several of Warren's works that revisit relatively obscure events in the history of his native state, *Audubon: A Vision* tells the story of Jean Jacques Audubon's wanderings on the early-nineteenth-century Kentucky frontier,[6] where the famous ornithologist hunts and kills birds, paradoxically, in order to preserve their aestheticized likeness in his paintings. Warren focuses on a particular encounter recorded in Audubon's account of his American wanderings.[7] In Warren's retelling, just before nightfall Audubon approaches a run-down cabin in the midst of the forest to ask for a place to spend the night. A woman, with a face that is "Large, / Raw-hewn, [and] strong-beaked" "under the tumble and tangle / Of dark hair" and with eyes that "glint as from the unspecifiable / Darkness of a cave" (256), allows him in for the night, provided he can pay. Inside the cabin, he encounters a wounded Indian sitting by the fire who has apparently lost an eye when his "arrow jounced back off his bowstring" (256). The Native American silently informs Audubon that the woman and her two absent sons mean their guests harm as he draws a finger "in delicious retardation, across his own throat" (256). Once the sons return, Audubon pretends to sleep, all the while ready to spring into action with his gun "by his side, primed and cocked" (257). Even as the woman and her sons move menacingly forward, he cannot respond, not comprehending "what guilt unmans him, or / Why he should find the punishment so precious" (258). In the nick of time, a posse of regulators bursts through the door—"Three men, alert, strong, armed" (258)—and rescues Audubon and the Indian. The regulators apprehend the woman and her sons, and at dawn the accused, already condemned, are summarily hanged from "the long, low bough of the great oak" (259). This all makes Audubon think about weighty matters, such as mortality, justice, fate, identity, love, and knowledge.

The very title of *Audubon: A Vision* underscores the visual dimension of Warren's technique, as he amended its working title, "Audubon and a Question for You." *Audubon*'s foregrounding of ekphrasis is apparent from the poem's opening description, yet the movement of the piece is less painterly or photographic than cinematic, providing a filmic arrangement of slow-motion sequences and time shifts. Warren described *Audubon* as a "series of snapshots"; however, these snapshots are not merely still frames, but move, forming a series of kinetic images. That *Audubon* is involved deeply with filmic technique is suggested by its pervasive concern with temporality, especially with the process of representing movements in time. In contrast to painting and photography, which both constitute still forms frozen in time, poetry, like film, is kinetic, carrying with it a sense of unfolding through time in its rhythmic pulse. In conjunction with its focus on modes of vision and spectacle, *Audubon*'s emphasis on the process of temporal ellipsis and extenuation connects its complex manipulations of poetic rhythm to a cinematic framework. Presenting a visually intense storyline that is elliptical and disjunct, the model the poem seems most consonant with is filmic representation. The thoroughgoing stress on spectacle, the sequencing of discrete scenes with analogous closing cuts and the serial repetitions of images within and between these sequences, as well as the heightened attention to unrealistic motion, all speak to Warren's poetic appropriation of characteristic conditions of film. His cinematic technique reveals a further connection between the two media: both tend to be narrative in a lyrical manner. Poetry relies less heavily on narrative structure for its force than on rhythm as its driving pleasure point, just as the moving image, not storyline, is typically the basis of cinema's spectacular power. Lyric's concern with the compressed image—an issue intensified in *Audubon*—comes to resemble film's emphasis on spectacle. Warren commingles the visual pleasures of cinema with the aural *jouissance* of poetic form, demonstrating that, like film, poetic rhythm is capable of analogous cuts and edits, its own extenuations and omissions of the established time frame. Like cinema, poetry also "makes itself sensuously and sensibly manifest as the expression of experience as experience" (Sobchack 3) on account of rhythm's visceral power, which enables us to experience words as physical sensations temporarily stripped of meanings.[8] *Audubon* exploits iambic structures, but takes pains to break, compress, or prolong the rhythm across variable lineation, fostering a range of rhythmic performance through enjambments or extensions of lines as well as anapestic and spondaic oscillations. Like Audubon and his most famous artistic subjects, the birds, Warren realizes the necessity of killing time to preserve it and in the process enacts a poetic mode of historiophoty.

Warren's late poetry is marked by an increased interest in poetic sequences,[9] yet the episodic segmentation of *Audubon* resembles less the filmic practice of montage than that of découpage, "the parceling out of images in accordance with the script, the mapping of the narrative action onto the cinematic material" (Bordwell 60). Warren's "script" was supplied by Audubon's account of his travels to collect specimens of American birds. Though he rewrote his source material, the significant moments, which typically involve some instance of spectacular bloodletting, have been carefully segmented into particular scenes. These sequences are announced by the poem's numbered sections and lettered subsections, each of which contains a series of related shots that develops a single phase of the overall story and that often ends with a visually arresting moment, a closing shot (e.g., section II [E] ends with the image of the frontier woman rising, knife in hand; the final shots of sections II [K] and

II [L] are graphic frames of the woman's hanged body, postmortem). Moreover, between particular segments there is serial repetition of related images, creating a sequence of visual echoes across episodes (e.g., the repeated vistas of sunrises and sunsets, images of spitting/sputum, visions of things hanging). This technique approximates the filmic mode of parallel cutting, a style of editing that foregrounds "logical relations rather than causality and chronology" (Bordwell 48). In contrast to crosscutting, which emphasizes simultaneity and narrative order, parallel editing "makes abstract analogies" between scenes (48), visual alliterations that are not bound to chronology. Such parallel sequencing produces a sense of memory as a recurring series of visually impressed events. By continuously redisplaying spectacular moments, the poem forces us to *re*-view like images in dissimilar contexts, a defamiliarizing process that evokes metonymic connections between remembered spectacles, as we find ourselves recognizing the image but losing its meaning.

This shifting within and between sequences reveals another aspect of filmic technique: a cinematic succession of images and scenes is not static, but expresses movement. This kinetic property is highlighted by the slow-motion sequencing of crucial scenes in *Audubon* that draw focus to movement for movement's sake, lending Warren's poetry a degree of the moving power of film. The slowing of kinesis brings into relief the suspension of movement as a grotesque phenomenon (e.g., repeated spectacles of things—and bodies—hanging). The emphasis on exaggerated forms of motion is often preceded or accompanied by an approximation of deep-focus or close-up shots on critical objects that exhibit a heightened attention to angle of perspective (e.g., the gold watch hanging on a chain before the hag-woman's enthralled gaze). Warren's invocation of a type of motion associated with cinematic form suggests an understanding that film provides a novel experience of time and of history, one that foregrounds the potential for radical compression or prolonging of lived and remembered time.[10]

The cinematographic aspect of *Audubon* not only points up a poststructuralist concern with framing, but also dovetails with Warren's invocation of a specific, and specifically American, genre: the Western. Although Warren enters the Western mode outright in another late long narrative poem, *Chief Joseph of the Nez Perce* (1983), *Audubon* offers a more subtle and complex interrogation of the genre's trademark means of representing history. It sets up Jean Jacques Audubon as a figure for exposing the power dynamics at work in the continuing project of manifest destiny, commingling the memory of the lost frontier—the early-nineteenth-century Kentucky wilderness—with the exploitation of Cold War paranoia in the postwar era. Warren ironically reinscribes the representative motifs of the frontier film. Audubon fills the role of the gun-toting, moccasin-clad pioneer, alone and drifting in the open wilderness. Alongside the frontiersman are the stock figures of the broken Indian and degenerate backwoods dwellers. The poem contains the memorable image of an abortive shootout "in delicious retardation"—a bungled quick-draw contest drawn out in excessively slow motion—and presents a grotesque vision of frontier justice as the regulators ride in to save the day and stage the triple hanging of the outlaws from a low bough. The panoramic vignettes of the natural world, particularly the repeated images of sunrise and sunset, suggest the Western motif of using the landscape as a primary character.[11]

Appropriating major elements of filmic discourse—spectacle, seriality, and kinesis—into the poetic sequences that make up *Audubon*, Warren integrates these into a recasting of the postwar Western that draws on southern history as a microcosm of the tensions confronting U.S. politics and policies at large. Set "out west in Kentucky," the poem merges two of the United States' most ideologically charged regions, at least according to the narratives spun about them.[12] Doing so gives added weight to Warren's critique of the American nationalist and internationalist drive toward controlling the geopolitical direction of the continent and the globe. Primitive lawlessness is familiar conceptual terrain both south of the Mason-Dixon and west of the Mississippi; indeed, there is a strong cinematic tradition of Westerns that contain relocated southern motifs, and these often use their doubled sense of location as a means of displacing contemporary pressures of social and political unrest in the South to an antiquated Western wilderness.[13] The Western genre is often, almost always, involved in veiled conflicts over definitions of gender identities (especially figures of rugged masculinity), in the history of manifest destiny (usually centering on the genocide of Native Americans), and in Cold War politics (often translating anxieties over contemporary international power imbalances and the threat of nuclear holocaust into the "simpler" time of more "honest," outright battles—raids and shootouts between heroic cowboys and savage Indians).[14] All of these historical contents are seen in Warren's poetic revision of the postwar Western. The poem undercuts the codes of raw masculinity associated with the figure of the frontiersman out to civilize the wilderness. Our hero appears rather unheroic, induced into "the manly state" (259) only through his voyeuristic and necrophilic pleasure in the spectacle of the hangings, hardly a manly man by Western standards. *Audubon* equally reflects the unstable stasis of Cold War politics. In contrast to many postwar Westerns, which provide the fantasy of the square-jawed, steely-eyed stoic hero saving the day by unleashing his powers of hypermasculine violence, here masculinity unravels under the pressures of immediate violence as Audubon is moved to *inaction*. The scene of the aborted showdown serves as the perfect figure for Cold War political and military stalemate (the deadlock of Korea, the nonbattle of the Cuban missile crisis, the unvictory of the Bay of Pigs, and the quagmire of Vietnam), obliquely reproducing the politics of impasse in a kind of slow-motion *tableau vivant* of brinkmanship. In southernizing the West and westernizing the South, Warren's poem redoubles its criticism of U.S. domestic and global political dogma.

The volume's opening section offers a filmic sequence of Audubon's visions of the Kentucky wilderness at dawn, evoking at once the pervasive motif of the Western sunrise:

> Saw,
> Eastward and over the cypress swamp, the dawn,
> Redder than meat, break;
> And the large bird,
> Long neck outthrust, wings crooked to scull air, moved
> In a slow calligraphy, crank, flat, and black against
> The color of God's blood spilt, as though
> Pulled by a string.
>
> Saw,
> It proceed across the inflamed distance.
>
> Moccasins set in hoar frost, eyes fixed on the bird,
> Thought: "On that sky it is black."
> Thought: "In my mind it is white."
> Thinking: "*Ardea occidentalis*, heron, the great one."
>
> Dawn: his heart shook in the tension of the world.
>
> Dawn: and what is your passion? (254)

The repetition of "saw" immediately signals the volume's emphasis on spectacle. The initial sequence contains the first of a series of single words excised from the normal lineation to form lines unto themselves, as the word "Saw" constitutes an entire line twice over in the opening section. Such extricated words/lines bring the rhythm to a dead stop by consolidating unwarranted stress on themselves. Often these serve a function analogous to a cinematic cut, as we shift perspective to a distinct line of vision, the rhythmic switch approximating a filmic edit to a different shot. The truncated style and omission of the subject for the verbs "saw," "thought," and "thinking" embody a suppression of interiority, as subjectivity literally drops out of the grammatical formulation. Audubon thus becomes a model of passive spectatorship, the subject elided by the clipped syntax.[15] All of his comments and reactions occur at the level of description. His thoughts are typically rather unthinking: he merely watches and records. The economy of language allows for a projection of Audubon's feelings onto the external view, a mode consonant with the Western technique of having the landscape function as the symbolic expression of inner character, serving as a screen for an unspoken or nearly inarticulate interior state. The verbal compression of the initial lines is consistent with the standard taciturnity of the Western male hero, whose "silence symbolizes a massive suppression of the inner life," though this restraint of speech may "stand as well for inner confusion. A welter of thoughts and feelings, a condition of mental turmoil that is just as hateful as the more obvious external constraints of economics, politics, and class distinctions" (Tompkins 66).

Indeed, Audubon's vision of the heron provides a filmic negative of internal consciousness (vision of the heron as black) in relation to external "reality" (knowledge of the white heron) that is paralleled on the level of poetic rhythm: the monosyllabic phrasing and twofold anapests of "On that ský it is bláck" are repeated in the logical and ocular inversion supplied in the succeeding line, "In my mínd it is white." Even the zoological encoding of the bird as a specimen of "Ardea occidentalis" puns on the Western framework. In his typescripts for Audubon, Warren had originally written, "Thinking: casmerodius albus, heron, white" (Robert Penn Warren Papers: Box 115, Folder 2124). That he decided to replace this phrase with a play on "occidental" is suggestive: the Western format is literally written into the text. Audubon is seen picturing a moving reality, and the bird's "slow calligraphy" across the sky reveals an intersection between the kinetic qualities of poetic rhythm and film: the vision of the heron embodies the moving language of cinema, its slowness emphasizing the property of motion itself, which coincides with the polysyllabic phrasing and "l" alliterations that slow down Warren's own rhythmic calligraphy on the page. The Western motif is further suggested by Audubon's dress, his moccasins showing that he, like so many frontier heroes, has passed the boundaries of civilization and is going native out in the territory. Set against the panorama of wild, open space is the imagery of Audubon tracking and shooting birds. He does this not for sustenance but purely for use in his art, which implies a level of control over the wilderness as it is converted into frontier and then settlements.

The opening section begins a series of images of sunrise and sunset that repeats throughout the work. The interspersion of prismatic scenes of dawn and dusk intensifies the experience of spectacle over narrative, providing almost fetishized descriptions of the landscape in all its scenic glory. Displaying an eye-catching overlay of color that suggests the way that a filmic tableau colors our vision, these reiterated sunrises and sunsets also function as visual echoes of Western conventions, in particular the focus on aestheticizing the frontier terrain, the motif of the plains drifter waking with the dawn, and the cliché of the cowboy riding off into the sunset.[16] Such vistas appear in the traditional Western to "make the land speak for itself" (Tompkins 71), offering before our eyes "space, pure and absolute" that "was here first before anything" and thereby giving us "the sense of being present at a moment before time began" (70). The serial repetition of dawns and dusks reflects the Western's claim to mythical timelessness, implying that the cycle of natural time overrides considerations of human or cultural time: the world seems forever dawning or dying. However, just like the Western, this sense of timelessness is itself historically bound, for "the West in the Western matters less as verifiable topography than as space removed from cultural coercion, lying beyond ideology (and therefore, of course, the most ideological of terrains)" (Mitchell 4). Through these serial, spectacular panoramas, we glimpse the historical dynamics of the unsettled frontier in process of being settled. In their repeated visions of landscapes, Westerns lend themselves to digressive spectacles that make us, like Audubon, stop and stare.

Section II, "The Dream He Never Knew the End Of," formulates the central action of the poem, containing the faux shootout as well as the frontier lynching, and showcases *Audubon*'s cinematic dimensions. The section begins with another shot of a frontier vista, only this time all hints of pastoral beauty have been drained from the landscape. Audubon, once more striking the pose of a weary searcher leaning on his gun, experiences the South/West in all its rawness, as a stark vision of a backwoods hovel rubs his eyes the wrong way:

> Shank-end of day, spit of snow, the call,
> A crow, sweet in distance, then sudden
> The clearing: among stumps, ruined cornstalks yet standing, the spot
> Like a wound rubbed raw in the vast pelt of the forest. There
> Is the cabin, a huddle of logs with no calculation or craft
> The human filth, the human hope. (255)

As in the opening sequence, Audubon's interiority is witnessed primarily through his external acts and through the setting itself. When his inner thoughts are expressed directly, it is in superficial descriptive phrases ("Punk-wood" and "Dead-fall half-rotten"). The lines read like stage directions for a film treatment of a silent Western, mechanically moving from one shot to next. As Audubon approaches and enters the decrepit cabin, the scene takes on an eerie, expressionistic tone. We, like Audubon, are met with the spectacle of the woman's "strong-beaked" visage (another visual alliteration of the poem's repeated bird imagery) suspended before us in the threshold space of the hovel's doorway:

> The face, in the air, hangs. Large,
> Raw-hewn, strong-beaked, the haired mole
> Near the nose, to the left, and the left side by firelight
> Glazed red, the right in shadow, and under the tumble and tangle
> Of dark hair on that head, and under the coarse eyebrows,
> The eyes, dark, glint as from the unspecifiable
> Darkness of a cave. It is a woman.
>
> She is tall, taller than he.
> Against the gray skirt, her hands hang.
>
> "Ye wants to spend the night? Kin ye pay?
> Well, mought as well stay then, done got one a-ready,
> And leastwise, ye don't stink like no Injun." (256)

The images of the woman's face hanging in midair and her hands hanging against her gray skirt pick up on the previous instance of Audubon's hand lifting and hanging before he knocks on the cabin door. This continues a series of visual repetitions of things left hanging that recurs through the poem. Indeed, after we cut to inside the hovel to inaugurate the succeeding sequence, the first sight is a grotesque vision of the Indian crouched by the fire, with blood and mucus hanging from one of his eye sockets:

> The Indian,
> Hunched by the hearth, lifts his head, looks up, but
> From one eye only, the other
> An aperture below which blood and mucus hang, thickening slow.
>
> "Yeah, a arrow jounced back off his bowstring.
> Durn fool—and him a Injun." She laughs. (256)

The gouged eye of the Indian goes beyond an autobiographical reference to Warren's own lost eye to imply the brutality latent in acts of spectatorship. The Indian's sliced eyeball recalls the stunning image that begins Luis Buñuel and Salvador Dali's surrealist film, *Un Chien Andalou* (1928), in which Buñuel, after a romantic gaze up at the moon from a balcony, takes a straight razor and slashes the eye of a woman who is seated and staring straight ahead. Warren's poem repeatedly abuses our eyes with spectacles of violence, exposing our potential pleasure in such visions. The Indian's ruined eyeball provides an image of grotesquely deformed vision, of the violence built into ways of seeing. It suggests the intensity with which filmic technique envisions the world, conditioning the spectator and making us complicit in its screened reality, however dark.

Greeted with the sight of the wounded Indian, Audubon deposits his pack and gun in the corner and immediately takes out his gold watch, which hangs from a thong-loop:

> The Indian's head sinks.
> So he turns, drops his pack in a corner on bearskin, props
> The gun there. Comes back to the fire. Takes his watch out.
> Draws it bright, on the thong-loop, from under his hunter's frock.
> It is gold, it lives in his hand in the firelight, and the woman's
> Hand reaches out. She wants it. She hangs it about her neck.
>
> And near it the great hands hover delicately
> As though it might fall, they quiver like moth-wings, her eyes
> Are fixed downward, as though in shyness, on that gleam, and her face
> Is sweet in an outrage of sweetness, so that
> His gut twists cold. He cannot bear what he sees.
>
> Her body sways like a willow in spring wind. Like a girl. (256)

The watch hanging encodes film's capacity to stop time, to manipulate and suspend our sense of temporality. The spectacle of the dangling gold watch, its splendor projected by the kinetic firelight ("it lives in his hand in the firelight"), captivates the woman's imagination, fixing her eyes as she becomes a figure of the enthralled spectator. Not yet willing to admit any connection or complicity with the woman as himself a captivated spectator, Audubon finds her pleasure in the moving image of the watch a repulsive thing to watch, unable to "bear what he sees." This episode serves as an emblem of how film can alter our perception of being in time, the way that cinematographic form hangs spectacles in air, floating them across the screen and hovering them before our transfixed eyes. The smooth transition from iambic to anapestic rhythm in the line "Her bódy swáys like a wíllow in spríng wínd. Like a gírl" connects the filmic thrall with the spectacle of moving images to the swaying motion of the line's steady, yet shifting meter. This is one instance of repeated images of suspended objects in the poem that replicate the serial aspect of film as well as its kinetic quality, since the things left hanging are often suspended in time as well as space: not just things, but time is left hanging too. This extenuation of temporality suggests the cinematic technique of slow-motion sequencing while creating a series of visual echoes—all of which involve spectacles of the grotesque—that appropriates the filmic propensity to picture motion across time. This chain of serial repetitions culminates in the central spectacle of the poem, to which I will return: the image of the woman and her two sons' being hanged in an act of frontier justice—retribution, in part, for their having robbed and killed other drifters like Audubon.

The poem's invocation of forms associated with the cinematic Western is further evident in the aborted shootout scene. The hostile "other" whom our wandering hero confronts is less the ethnic other (played by the broken Native American, who, like a classic celluloid Indian, will soon fade into the forest again like smoke) than a socioeconomic threat—the nearly impoverished, uneducated, primitive backwoods dwellers. The scene flirts with the Western's promise of providing "moral and emotional resolution in a singular act of violence" (Slotkin 352), yet frustrates this expectation through its severe time delay. As Audubon lies with his gun by his side, "primed and cocked," we expect him, per the announced Western motif, to shoot up the place and emerge still standing from the showdown against the hag-like woman and her two equally squalid sons. We count on the hero to corral the outlaws single-handedly. Three times over the course of the faux shootout sequence Audubon declares "Now," filling us each time with the immediate expectation of this culminating episode of violent encounter. Yet the moment of confrontation never comes. Instead, we are met with an overwhelming sense of duration itself. The scene arrives in slow motion, showing less the tight deadline of a dramatic showdown, than the slow drag of time itself in "delicious retardation"; in fact, the juxtaposition of these two polysyllabic words retards poetic time as well, slowing the enunciation of the rhythm. The climactic moment is therefore the very picture of belatedness, kinesis for its own sake, creating, in essence, a spectacle of film's kinetic powers. Despite Warren's throughgoing pronouncements on the metaphysical properties of time, here he gets closest to capturing a visual representation of time at work, using the protraction of poetic rhythm to draw the parabola of an extenuated moment's arc, reflexively demonstrating a physics of filmic time.

On a further level, this sequence shows Audubon to be a reversal of the Western's trademark gunslinger, since he violates the code of shooting first and damning the consequences: in stereotypical Westerns, "men acted; for better or for worse, wisely or stupidly, they acted. They didn't ponder, debate, subject their tortured souls to self-examination" (Fenin and Everson 42). By contrast, Audubon is a man of inaction who, at the very moment of crisis, subjects his tortured soul to self-examination. His self-psychoanalysis, which prevents him from acting to save himself by firing his gun, is painstaking to a masochistic degree, for even as the moment of (in)decision unfolds, "He cannot think what guilt unmans him, or / Why he should find the punishment so precious" (258). The image of Audubon as ineffectual gunfighter literalizes "the central paradox of America's self-image in an era of Cold War, 'subversion,' and the thermonuclear balance of terror: our sense of being at once supremely powerful and utterly vulnerable, politically dominant and yet helpless to shape the course of critical events" (Slotkin 383). The bungled shootout mirrors an age of political belatedness and highly contained military action, even to the point of paralysis. If translated from the personal to the cultural, the intrusion of the regulators and the frontier justice embodied in the summary executions coincide with Slotkin's description of how the Cold War Western bore the influence of contemporary politics:

> In both the domestic and the imperial spheres, Westerns asserted
> the entitlement of representatives of the "better" or "decent"
> classes to a privileged form of violence. The perceived imperatives
> of the Cold War would lead a series of American governments to
> assert a similar privilege for the use of armed force and to justify,
> in the name of national security, the evasion, abuse, or overriding
> of the official procedures and social institutions through which
> the American public registers its consent. (353)[17]

Audubon and the regulators serve as "representatives of the 'better' or 'decent' classes" who are permitted to exercise "a privileged form of violence" in order to contain the threat of violent subversion from their cultural inferiors. Even during all-out military assaults, containment strategy requires a thoroughly disciplined set of soldiers who are "alert, strong, armed" to carry out highly limited yet often muddled objectives, as in the cases of Korea and Vietnam. The ideal of the Cold War warrior is embodied in John Wayne's famous contrapposto stance, which is the picture of asymmetrical balance, self-discipline, and controlled motion. Contrapposto presents an apt metaphor for Cold War politics in general, which required the U.S. military to be self-contained in order to carry out the strategy of containing communism and thus bringing nations into an asymmetrical balance of power. It was the perceived failure of such discipline that created public relations disasters for the U.S. military in Vietnam.

That Audubon fails to match up to our expectations of a heroic gunfighter suggests Warren's understanding of the difficulty of forceful and coherent action in an era when pulling the trigger potentially means mass annihilation. Despite the screen iconography of a rough, untamed landscape reflected in Audubon's vision of the southern/Western frontier, in 1969 there was no such thing as wide-open space anymore. Under Cold War conditions, all space was confined, contaminated, or contested, generating a profound sense of insecurity and un-homeliness on national and international scales. John Kennedy's vision of the New Frontier projected the territorialization of the world for U.S. economic, political, and military interests at a time when the "original" American frontier—"original" from a white, not Native, vantage—was lost to all but the movies. The national boundaries established by manifest destiny seemed in danger of being subverted by the Red menace of communist operatives or shattered apart by the threat of nuclear attack.[18] The intervention of the three regulators and their swift, decisive response provides a Cold War fantasy of easy and complete resolution of conflict through unfettered savagery, an illusion of total victory in an age when there was no such thing. It is the hanging, then, not the shootout, that provides for us the Western's typical "moral and emotional resolution in a singular act of violence," thus protecting the interests of "civilized" democracy. The action of the regulators makes it plain that containment of such unruliness is necessary on this contested frontier. The abrupt lynching fulfills the requirements of the Western formula as it assuages Cold War anxieties concerning the threat of uncontainable forces. It creates a sense of narrative closure that simultaneously provides a level of ideological comfort. An unsettled and unsettling frontier has been tamed, and the South/West is now a secure area. Peaceful contemplation, in the form of Audubon's search for aesthetic beauty and the narrator's metaphysical ruminations, can resume. However, Warren's critique of the Western cliché of masculine redemptive violence does not conclude here. Audubon is quite literally not out of the woods yet.

Warren's depiction of the hanging satisfies filmic conditions on a formal level as well, supplying what is the most memorable episode of historiophotic representation in the volume. In Audubon's vision of the lynching of the de-generate woman and her two sons, the veiled pornographic quality of cinematic

spectacle tips over into an instance of explicit necrophilia.[19] As Audubon gazes
on the hag-woman's face just before she is executed, he "becomes aware that he
is in the manly state":

> And in the gray light of morning, he sees her face. Under
> The tumbled darkness of hair, the face
> Is white. Out of that whiteness
> The dark eyes stare at nothing, or at
> The nothingness that the gray sky, like Time, is, for
> There is no Time, and the face
> Is, he suddenly sees, beautiful as stone, and
>
> So becomes aware that he is in the manly state. (259)[20]

This vignette is filmic not only in its extenuation of temporality (the woman's
dark eyes stare at the nothingness that is like time) and movement (in her
forced rigidity, she becomes "beautiful as stone"), but also in its explicit atten-
tion to the nearly pornographic pleasures of spectacle. The sequence's shocking
final line emphasizes the poem's overall sense of subverted, even perverted
masculinity. By invoking the terms of what counts as *manly* on the frontier, the
scene reinforces *Audubon*'s connection to the Western frame, though it does so
through an ironic inversion of the hero's typical trait of masculine self-possession
and sexual restraint. In its grotesquely erotic display, the sequence graphically
illustrates how spectacle's effects are both unreal and yet real, illusionary and
yet visceral; the scopophilic potential of cinema is brought into deep focus,
where our pleasure in seeing takes on erotic dimensions as we convert spectacle
into an object of sexual desire. The metrical evenness of the culminating line
as it levels out into a perfect iambic flow—"So becómes awáre that hé is ín the
mánly státe"—points to the poem's motif of discovering pleasure in horror, of
aestheticizing violence. The spectacular brutality of the hanging itself further
lends a darker emphasis to the speaker's comment that Audubon "walked in
the world. Knew the lust of the eye" (263):

> The affair was not tidy: bough low, no drop, with the clients
> Simply hung up, feet not much clear of the ground, but not
> Quite close enough to permit any dancing.
> The affair was not quick: both sons long jerking and farting, but she,
> From the first, without motion, frozen

In a rage of will, an ecstasy of iron, as though
This was the dream that, lifelong, she had dreamed toward.

                                                        The face,
Eyes a-glare, jaws clenched, now glowing black with congestion
Like a plum, had achieved,
It seemed to him, a new dimension of beauty. (260)

The understated tone of Warren's diction, referring to the lynching twice as
"The affair" and to the executed as "the clients" as if it were a minor transac-
tion, is at odds with the shock value of the primal spectacle itself. The hag-
woman's dark eyes that stared at nothing are now "a-glare," as she reverses the
power of the gaze, unveiling Audubon's and the reader-viewer's complicity in
the excessive pleasures of the spectacle. In the midst of her death throes, she
glares back at her spectators, claiming some final semblance of subjectivity even
as she is in process of being converted into a pure object, her face blacken-
ing like a plum. Despite the sense that we are screened from the violence—or
because of it—we feel a degree of guilty complicity for taking pleasure in this
death scene, which resembles something like an early-nineteenth-century snuff
film. The "new dimension of beauty" Audubon experiences is that offered by
filmic spectacle in conjunction with the moving force of poetic meter. With
its connected stresses on alternating "m" and "n" sounds and its return to the
grounding rhythm of a flowing iambic pulse, "It séemed to hím, a néw dimén-
sion of béauty" reiterates on an aural level the grim aesthetics of the spectacle,
another visually arresting moment that converts an otherwise horrific vision
into a dimension of beauty. In highlighting the scopophilic draw of the spec-
tacle, in seizing our lustful eye along with our lustful ear, Warren suggests the
dangers as well as attractions of filmic art. Immersing us into a screened world
where even a corpse can be eroticized, cinematic presentation itself becomes
the object of the most intensive fetishization.

The second section of *Audubon* closes with a shot of the hanged dead.
Even though Audubon realizes that he must go, he cannot stop himself from
gawking at the forms suspended before his gaze:

He thought: "I must go."
                                    But could not, staring
At the face, and stood for a time even after
The first snowflakes, in idiotic benignity,

Had fallen. Far off, in the forest and falling snow,
A crow was calling.

So stirs, knowing now
He will not be here when snow
Drifts into the open door of the cabin, or,
Descending the chimney, mantles thinly
Dead ashes on the hearth, nor when snow thatches
These heads with white, like wisdom, nor ever will he
Hear the infinitesimal stridor of the frozen rope
As wind shifts its burden, or when

The weight of the crow first comes to rest on a rigid shoulder. (260–61)

The kinetic power of the scene will continue long after rigor mortis has set in, as the bodies will be put in motion again—just as the words themselves are equally put into rhythmic motion through the iambic-anapestic variations of the closing line—by "the ínfinitésimal strídor of the frózen rópe / As wínd shífts its búrden, or whén / The wéight of the crów first cómes to rést on a rígid shóulder." The final vision of the crow serves as a bleak visual alliteration of the poem's serial bird imagery. The figure of filmic memory is again invoked here as time is cast into the future as if it is already past, approximating a cinematographic wipe to a future already pictured. This temporal ellipsis is a final illustration of Warren's intuitive understanding of cinematic time as almost infinitely malleable, subject to compression, extenuation, and omission beyond the bounds of lived experience. As the narrator notes in the concluding section, with heavy tones of self-reflexivity, when telling "a story of deep delight" you must recognize that "The name of the story will be Time / But you must not pronounce its name" (267).

The Western is a cinematic genre that is particularly time-stained, uniquely devoted to memory. Westerns often thematize the value or even necessity of not forgetting—a motif especially prevalent in the revenger Western—and the genre's heightened attention to the memorable quality of the frontier landscape encodes a radical spatialization of memory: it seems to stop time in space, even to the point of mythopoesis. In discussing the Western as a form of cultural mythmaking and, more specifically, the mythic figure of John Wayne, Joseph Campbell makes a point about the screened and therefore divergent quality of filmic time: "There is something magical about films. The person you are looking at is also somewhere else at the same time. That is a condition of the god" (15). Yet in visually commingling landscape and memory, the Western effects a sense of deep cultural remembrance. Though there is certainly a good deal of nostalgia for the lost frontier expressed through the Western's wide open spaces, its untamed wildernesses, this spatializing of time also lays bare the darker aspects of American collective memory, past and present. Even as the well-known final section of *Audubon*, "Tell Me a Story," intersperses reminiscences of the speaker's boyhood memories of Kentucky with longings for mythic timelessness, the poem's closing lines reveal that this nostalgia is in part a reaction-formation against the military and political chaos of the contemporary world. The speaker longs for a transcendent narrative in order to escape the burdens of "this century, and moment, of mania" (267), an explicit indication of the poem's concern with current historical events. The military failure of the Tet offensive as well as the assassinations of Martin Luther King Jr. and John and Robert Kennedy all seem to lurk behind this sentiment, setting the poem's critique clearly within the frame of Cold War history. The poem's concluding sequence speaks to the loss of stable frontiers during this moment of regional, national, and international mania. Above the pastoral wreck of an upturned great tree on a mud bank of the Mississippi enters a Northwest Orient jetliner making its path cross-country from New York to Seattle. The juxtaposition of "west" and "Orient" emphasizes the connection between East and West, symbolizing how transnational networks of transportation seem to be making frontiers obsolete. In the wake of postwar industrial technology, South and North, East and West are all one, though this has led, not to unity, but to a heightened sense of disunity, to the point of mania.

Warren's poetic representation of filmic memory brings into focus distinctions as well as convergences between poetic and cinematic media. As opposed to sculpture or painting, plastic arts that merely suggest movement by the use of static forms, filmic images seem to actually move across the screen—our perception is that movement is not suggested, but *is*. In a related way, the rhythmic flow of poetry connotes a form of movement, a kinetic use of language. Like film, poetry is a nonstatic art because of the percussive pulsings and modifications involved in its exploitation of rhythm, as sound and sense come in and out of alignment with one another. Though all language can be seen as kinetic—we utter one phoneme, and then another, and then another—poetic rhythm redoubles our sense of movement, linguistic *and* bodily, through time; to cite Attridge again, "rhythm is what makes a physical medium (the body, the sounds of speech or music) seem to move with deliberateness through *time*, recalling what has happened (by repetition) and projecting itself into the future (by setting up expectations), rather than just letting time pass it by" (4).

Warren's use of metrical shifts in *Audubon* approximates the dynamic rhythm of film editing, recasting the visual movement of filmic performance in terms of the power of poetic meter. The poem's cinematic frame offers a scheme for translating the inexplicability of poetic sound into a culturally trenchant context that is presented self-reflexively by the poem's own figures. The filmic aspects of the poem—its patterns of spectacular episodes, images of kinetic movement, and repetitive sequencing, as well as the Western genre's characteristic motifs and meanings—thus provide a means for reading the otherwise unreadable power of rhythmic freeplay. Moreover, the formal process of poetry offers a remove from which to gauge the power of filmic art as well as its limitations. While film offers a means of screening history, of aestheticizing the violence of the frontier South/West, one of the main concerns of Warren's work is how we remake history in our own image. History yields to artful refashioning; as Warren put it famously in his foreword to *Brother to Dragons*, "historical sense and poetic sense should not, in the end, be contradictory, for if poetry is the little myth we make, history is the big myth we live, and in our living, constantly remake" (xiii). Through his ironic revision of the postwar Western, Warren uses the modes of cinema to create a poetic form of "de-fetishizing" historiophoty, one that ultimately works to unscreen history, self-consciously opening up debate over the relative instability of the historical referent:

> Modernist techniques of representation provide the possibility
> of de-fetishizing both events and the fantasy accounts of them
> which deny the threat they pose, in the very process of pretending
> to represent them realistically. This de-fetishizing can then clear
> the way for that process of mourning which alone can relieve
> the "burden of history" and make a more, if not totally realistic
> perception of current problems possible. (White, "The Modernist
> Event" 32)

And thus history is undone in order to be redone, this time in highly visual, sequenced, and kinetic poetry that offers a more clear-sighted and mournful accounting of the South's and America's shared burden of history in the Machiavellian contortions of manifest destiny.

Having repudiated his Fugitive and Agrarian roots, Warren writes against a stagnant southern nostalgia in his poetry of the post–World War II era, often emphasizing aspects of a brutally antipastoral South. In the final section of *Audubon*, he offers a pointed revision of "Bearded Oaks" (1942), replacing his earlier poem's emphasis on neo-Fugitive rootedness with a darkening vision of the nostalgic desire for place:

> In the Mississippi,
> On a mud bank, the wreck of a great tree, left
> By flood, lies, the root-system and now stubbed boughs
> Lifting in darkness. It
> Is white as bone. That whiteness
> Is reflected in dark water, and a star
> Thereby. (265)

The bearded oak has been uprooted, as the Agrarian South has been overturned, leaving no retreat inside the mythos of the southern landscape as pastoral enclave, which is now whittled to the bone, remnant of a wrecked past. Like the image of the "sagging gate" at the end of *Brother to Dragons*, which ironically references Tate's decomposing wall in "Ode to the Confederate Dead," Warren is again saying his farewells to the Fugitive-Agrarian past. In picturing an antipastoral southern frontier, Warren cancels out unflinching devotion to the ways of the tradition-bound South, offering instead a stark confrontation with history. Connecting the kinetic property of film with the moving power of poetic form, Warren puts cultural memory in motion in a way that countermands the nostalgic emphasis on placefulness that colors not only Fugitive verse but also much contemporary southern poetry.

The biographical and aesthetic intersections between Robert Penn Warren and James Dickey are many and deep. Both held degrees from Vanderbilt University, with Warren earning his Bachelor of Arts in 1925 and Dickey completing a Bachelor as well as a Master of Arts at the Nashville institution in 1949 and 1950, respectively. On a broader scale, both the Kentucky-born Warren and the Georgia-reared Dickey grew up in view of the general southern history of racial segregation, class tension, and purported cultural "backwardness." Both were novelists of note, with Warren's *All the King's Men* (1946) winning the Pulitzer Prize and Dickey's *Deliverance* (1970) becoming a national best-seller, and both novels being converted into successful film versions. They were also two of the most well-known and prolific poets in the U.S. during their lifetimes. Among myriad other honors, Warren earned two Pulitzers for his later poetry and was named the first poet laureate of the United States in 1986. Despite a decade-long hiatus from writing poetry in the 1940s and early 1950s, Warren distinguished himself as one of the most productive and wide-ranging poets of the twentieth century. For his part, Dickey earned a National Book Award for *Buckdancer's Choice* in 1966 and was appointed poetry consultant at the Library of Congress from 1966 to 1968; his collecting of poetry prizes dropped off after these notable early honors, but this was perhaps the result, as Ernest Suarez has argued, of Dickey's conservative political stances—though other critics have suggested that Dickey's late poems are simply not as good as his early ones. Warren and Dickey were impressed with one another's work, and each one's poetry bears the mark of the other. Each poet dedicated at least one work to his counterpart: Dickey honored Warren with "Under Buzzards" (1968)—writing his fellow craftsman that he felt "some root-deep kind of affinity with [Warren's] poetic effort" (Bruccoli and Baughman 281)—and Warren returned the favor with "Rattlesnake Country" (1973) and *Chief Joseph of the Nez Perce* (1982). Dickey read the sweeping final section of *Audubon* as the eulogy at the funeral of his first wife Maxine, explaining this choice in a 1980 letter to Warren: "I could think of nothing of my own so fitting, or so likely to last, or to hang longer in the bearded oaks of Waccamaw Cemetery, at Litchfield, where we were all together" (Bruccoli 389). Warren and Dickey shared a long personal friendship and were even filmed together in Connecticut and South Carolina as the subjects of a CBS documentary titled *Two Poets, Two Friends* in 1982.

The two most prominent southern poets of the first quarter century following World War II, Warren and Dickey shared a particular philosophical and aesthetic concern: their sustained interest in invoking two interrelated, yet distinct forms of modern primitivism. Like Dickey, whose poetic manipulation of primal memory is the subject of the following chapter, some of Warren's later verse includes a sense of the South as a privileged site of primitive sexuality and aggression. There is something of the primal in several of his later poems, such as "Rattlesnake Country" and "Heart of Autumn" (1978), as well as *Audubon* and *Brother to Dragons*. However, where Warren confronts southern history directly, explicitly unveiling the sociological dimensions of primitivism, Dickey often uses the possibility of recourse to a primal self as a form of ultra-nostalgic retreat from historical conditions. In direct contrast to Dickey's proposed ahistoricism, Warren shows a greater sense of complicity with the past, a deeper awareness of cultural and racial guilt. For him, social injustice cannot be explained away by entering a primitive netherworld. Dickey tends to view the primitive as a denial of history; Warren uses it as a means for historical confrontation. Dickey himself noted Warren's historical penchant in a 1954 letter to Andrew Lytle, suggesting parallels between the historical concerns evident in both Lytle's and Warren's work:

> Do you like [Warren's] work? I very much do. "History is blind,
> but man is not," Warren writes in <u>All the King's Men</u>. Critics
> have not said much about this side of Warren, but it seems to me
> to be the central preoccupation of all his work to define and eval-
> uate the past. That is, can we see in certain happenings behind
> us, on which we have a kind of perspective, symbolic patterns? If
> so, what are their value to us? How can this be assimilated to our
> lives? (Bruccoli 63)

The subsequent chapter argues that Dickey at first attempts to elide a sense of historical situatedness by engaging the eternal depths of the unconscious and then realizes the limits of his primal escapism, eventually falling into parody of his own earlier primitivist thematics and forms, a watershed event for contemporary southern poetics.

CHAPTER 2

Returning the "Undying Cry of the Void": The Changing Condition of Primal Memory in James Dickey's Poetry

> Nature is but an image or imitation of wisdom,
> the last thing of the soul; nature being a thing which
> doth only do, but not know.
>
> —Plotinus (205?–270?)

James Dickey's[1] early poetry, exemplified in *Drowning with Others* (1962), exhibits an essential faith in the overwhelming restorative force of merging with the natural world, a power often made manifest in scenes of primal violence and sexuality.[2] A raw, direct connection with the driving momentum of instinctual nature—if forged powerfully enough—can lead to transcendence of the material limits of human experience. This is the idea animating Dickey's invocation of primal memory that seeks to overcome our condition as time-bound both in terms of our historical situatedness and, ultimately, our mortality. The poems of *Falling, May Day Sermon, and Other Poems* (1967),[3] however, serve as a parody of this earlier conviction in the strength of primitive essentialism. Under the historical pressures of the Vietnam War and the civil rights movement, as well as personal attacks on his primitivist and southernist poetics, he exchanges a commitment to primitive values for the irruptive play of parodic reiteration. His parody falls equally on South and North: on the painful contradictions of postwar southern culture as well as on the way American haute couture marks the "backward" South as a privileged site of primal riot, on the limits of his own primitivist poetics as well as on the excesses—and excessive influence—of Beat and "confessional" poetries. In response to the anti-southernist bashing given him by Robert Bly and his fellow anti-Vietnam "New York literati" in the mid-1960s, Dickey takes on the role of redneck poet par excellence, giving them back both barrels of hyperstylized southern poetics in *Falling, May Day Sermon, and Other Poems*. In doing so, Dickey out-Dickeys Dickey.

Much of Dickey's earlier poetry can be read as a response to post-Darwinian anxiety over origins.[4] By the late 1960s, his poetic reconstruction of primal memory becomes a set of empty figures echoing back "the undying cry of the void" ("Falling" 243) in a culture teeming with urbanization, (post)industrialism, and the abstract impetus of late capitalism. Where is there space to go primitive in a world increasingly striated by the emerging forces of global culture? Even the South, a stereotypical depository of primal feelings, the R-complex of the national consciousness, appears too transregional to sustain the impulse of a regenerative primitivism. The explicitly nonredemptive critique offered by parody offers a pointed form of seizing cultural authority in such a time, for "parody . . . is power—perhaps the only type of power available (or desirable) to a writer or critic living in the post-conscious sequel to a successful age of inimitable originals" (Kreyling, *Inventing Southern Literature* 157).

Virtually all of the critical literature on Dickey's poetry addresses his presumed aesthetics of primal return to a level of undifferentiated consciousness in nature. In *James Dickey and the Politics of Canon* (1993), Ernest Suarez notes the predominance of the primitivist line in Dickey criticism, suggesting that the poetry serves—at least as far as most critics are concerned—as a reworking of what W. J. Cash termed "the savage ideal" in *The Mind of the South* (1941), his famous account of southern culture.[5] Arguing that Dickey's fall from critical grace in the late 1960s was a result of attacks, more political than aesthetic, on his penchant for (mainly southern) scenes of primal aggression, Suarez describes how Dickey was ostracized by "the New York literati," especially Bly and Allen Ginsberg, as a result of his perceived nonconformity to their liberal ideology. They were particularly offended by what they believed to be Dickey's regional failings, his presumed racism and love of violence, including warfare, especially his refusal to condemn the politics behind the U.S. war in Vietnam. According to the critical consensus, at the base of Dickey's brand of poetic primitivism lies his eerie commingling of violent victimage and mystical renewal that takes place most often in a natural otherworld, far removed in both time and space from the abstract vicissitudes of contemporary culture. This return to one's "natural" (i.e., violent) instincts recenters the self on its primal foundations. Out in the primitive netherworld, bloodletting is not traumatic or tragic, but regenerative and revitalizing.[6]

Dickey's initial version of modern primitivism presents us with a kind of ultranostalgia, a primal longing for our earliest preconscious "home" that searches for the lost vitality of the prelingual, prehistorical realm of undifferentiated consciousness. His early poems manipulate incantatory rhythms and ritualistic repetitions in order to articulate a willful denial of the ultimate contingency of human existence on individual and collective levels. Though fully aware of the existential predicament—a concept given not merely philosophical but personal significance through his experience as a bombardier in World War II[7]—he attempts to lend some temporary permanence to existence by forging an original relation of the self to the underlying rhythms of the natural world.[8] The apparent contradiction between conscious arrangement of experience (memory) and unconscious drives (instinct) forms a central conflict in his early verse, which mimics a kind of energized fugue state when intuitive nature takes over. Despite the "primal" force of his art, he is unable to dispel either the existential anxiety over death or the burden of his own cultural situatedness. His primitive mysticism offers only a momentary respite against the individual's conscious awareness of life's contingency, while his poetic reconstruction of primal memory is exposed as a culturally specific artifact. Indeed, much of Dickey's mid-career work counterbalances the primitive as a hoped-for return to instinctual memory by also showing a keen awareness of the sociocultural effects of primitivist ideology.[9] At times he longs to embrace the primitive "as an inexact expressive whole" (Torgovnick 20) that centers "our passion for clearly marked and definable beginnings and endings that will make what comes between them coherent narrations" (245). Yet once he makes the turn to parody, he shows a higher awareness of the ways in which primitivist "images and ideas . . . have slipped from their original metaphoric status" and self-reflexively reveals primitivism as a means of "handling, by displacement, the series of dislocations that we call modernity and postmodernity" (245). *Falling, May Day Sermon and Other Poems* thereby moves out of "the warmth of tradition" and "the repetition of the ancestral" and falls into the postsouthern void, where "self-consciousness emerges under the sign of that which has already happened, as the fulfillment of something always already begun" (Nora 7), where parody of past codes is a last resort. In the end, Dickey's exercise of primal memory serves as the sign of "a historical age that calls out for memory because it has abandoned it" (12), and his effort to return us to the level of instinctual knowledge via ritualized violence brings into relief the very "deritualization of our world" (12).[10]

"Fog Envelops the Animals" espouses the ritual of hunting as a means of locating the unconscious according to the Darwinian definition of it as "a separate domain, relating to the earth's movements" (Beer 73), a psychic archive that lodges the vestiges of an instinctual relation to nature. Out bow-hunting—a rifle would be too modern an implement—the speaker finds himself enveloped in a dense fog that forms a cloak of invisibility around him as he searches for his prey:

> Fog envelops the animals.
> Not one can be seen, and they live.
> At my knees, a cloud wears slowly
> Up out of the buried earth.
> In a white suit I stand waiting. (80)

As an intermediary state, between liquid and air, the fog allegorizes fusion with the elements, an impulse that Casey Clabough describes as the phenomenon of "merging": the assumption of the individual into the essence of nature. The slow-driving anapests create an aura of permanence, as if the heavy rhythmic recurrence guarantees the unchanging process of monolithic nature—"Not óne can be séen, and they líve"—thus embodying Dickey's "preference for marchlike anapests—hypnotic, compulsive, primitive" as his "rhythmic music conveys the persistent power of his principles by constituting a recurrent ground rhythm that itself seems magically independent of the speaker" (Kirschten 37).[11] The deep accent on "live" further stresses the inalterability of the natural cycle. The animals are there, implacably: they simply live, as it was in the beginning, is now, and ever shall be. The line enacts a Darwinian "teleology," emphasizing the primitive fact of existence where survival is everything, for just *living* is enough, is all.

Like the animals, the speaker-hunter himself feels the pull of the primal demand for survival, as the fog reduces him to his elemental state of being:

> Soundlessly whiteness is eating
> My visible self alive.
> I shall enter this world like the dead,
> Floating through tree trunks on currents
> And streams of untouchable pureness
>
> That shine without thinking of light.
> My hands burn away at my sides
> In the pale, risen ghosts of deep rivers.

In my hood peaked like a flame,
I feel my own long-hidden,

Long-sought invisibility
Come forth from my solid body.
I stand with all beasts in a cloud.
Of them I am deadly aware,
And they not of me, in this life. (80)

The soundless whiteness that eats the speaker's "visible self alive" (80) de-
scribes the quiet dissolution of his individuated self and his descent to instinc-
tual memory. The "untouchable pureness" that streams through his solid body
comes "without thinking," dredging up the risen ghosts of his primal self, which
has remained "long-hidden" under the accoutrements of abstract culture. The
poem ends in an approximation of regression to a primitive state:

My arrows, keener than snowflakes,
Are with me whenever I touch them.
Above my head, the trees exchange their arms
In the purest fear upon earth.
Silence. Whiteness. Hunting. (81)

As the speaker is assumed almost wholly into the fog, subject (the human
hunter) and object (nonhuman nature) appear to merge into one, since they are
connected by the most primitive, "purest" verbal forms: the poem closes with
three single-word "sentences," with no explanatory phrases to establish any-
thing more than the most basic relation between items. This Zen-like mantra
flows in three equal trochees ("Silence. Whiteness. Hunting."), the paralinguis-
tic pulsations of sound assuming, for the time being, the strictures of ratio-
nal sense. The silence and the whiteness suggest the nothingness that is there
among the animals in the fog, while the ritualistic forms of the hunt imply the
speaker's conscious effort to reconnect with this zero level of the soul. Like
the poem itself, the rites of hunting reflect an attempt to make a return to the
prelingual basis of subject-formation through a highly developed—and cultur-
ally inculcated—ritual practice. Mark Edmundson focuses on Dickey's capacity
"to learn from others, not the Other" (63), a term that he defines as "Dickey's
image of a heroic ideal-I, his self-made superego" (48). Where other poems by
Dickey show him learning from others, "Fog Envelops the Animals" reveals

that the most essential kind of knowledge comes from deep within the self, for the ritualized act of hunting embodies an archetypal drive for bloodlust. It is therefore an unconscious form that the speaker imbues with conscious content, providing a symbolic parallel for the poet's own conscious arrangement of unconscious rhythms through the exploitation of poetic structure.

"The Heaven of Animals" delivers on its titular promise by proffering a primal vision of a starkly animalistic heaven. This bestial Eden reflects a level of undivided consciousness where the Adamic power to name holds no sway. Dickey attempts through adept manipulation of symbolic language to return us to a time before symbols, when, like animals, humans were motivated wholly by instinct.[12] The poet's implicit faith in the power of imagination is ironic since it is imagination itself that condemns humans to awareness of time and death, of possibilities other than present actualities. The conscious ability to imagine a better condition (and ultimately a life without death) is exercised by the poet in this instance to create an ideal set of conditions, not for humans but for animals. Paradoxically, this heaven is marked by earthiness:

> Here they are. The soft eyes open.
> If they have lived in a wood
> It is a wood.
> If they have lived on plains
> It is grass rolling
> Under their feet forever. (78–79)

The afterworld is not a blanched-out abstraction, with disembodied souls plucking celestial harmonies on golden harp strings, but a place where the preconscious instincts of animals can "wholly bloom" (79). That the full realization of these instinctual drives involves violence and death is an inevitability, for "It could not be the place / It is, without blood" (79). Even those animals marked forevermore as prey acquiesce in full compliance with the natural order, "Fulfilling themselves without pain / At the cycle's center" (79). The essential permanence of the natural cycle is reinforced by the poem's repetition of "is" forms: "Here they *are*," "It *is* a wood," "It could not *be* the place / It *is*, without blood." There is no space for imagination, a human liability. Here, without question, whatever *is* is right. The poem's rhythmic repetitions underscore these verbal reiterations, imbuing it with a sense of heavy-handed fixity. The lines give the impression of having been rough-hewn out of stone, and the decided stresses evoke an almost shamanistic cadence. Sound and sense, like the paradisal predators and prey, seem bound together in unalterable blood marriage. The initial statement of the poem, "Here they are," announces the endless cycle of violence and renewal, as it forcefully declares the whereabouts of all the animals, leaving no place for us to imagine them to be elsewhere; we, like the animals, are stuck in the eternal present. This sense of permanence is seen again in the repetition of particular words or phrases (e.g., "The soft eyes open," "Outdoing," "It is") as well as like rhythms throughout the work.

The centrality of the phenomenon of savage violence and renewal to Dickey's primitive essentialism is evident in the utter intactness of the natural order fulfilled by the animals and in the inescapability of each animal's instinctual role, expressing "an almost feudal vision of order: The hunted are as satisfied with their place in creation as the hunters; they are part of 'the cycle'" (Gunn 14). The final stanza continues the expert merging of form to content, as the rhythmic repetition shadows the fixed repetition of the primitive cycle of predators and prey:

> At the cýcle's cénter,
> They trémble, they wálk
> Únder the trée,
> They fáll, they are tórn,
> They ríse, they wálk agáin. (79)

That all of the animals, predators as well as victims, fully embrace this pattern is emphasized by the repetition of active verbs in the final stanza. Even though it describes the victimage of the hunted animals, it contains only one passive verb ("they are torn"). The predominance of active verbs suggests that completing their instinctual role as victims is not a mark of passivity, but the active fulfillment of the primary and preordained reason for their existence. While these animals have no souls and have come here "beyond their knowing," they are later described as existing "in full knowledge" of their condition, as the prey are rewarded by walking "Under such trees in full knowledge / Of what is in glory above them" (79). This apparent contradiction alludes to the implications of the Eden myth and its fabled origin of human guilt and regret and signals that the only kind of "knowledge" the animals experience is purely instinctual. As a result, they are able to kill without remorse and to die without regret, each in its ordered place. If this arrangement is translated into the human realm, it starts to resemble, chillingly, the politics of social Darwinism. Kept safely out in the primitive netherworld, however, the poem represents a fantasy of reconnecting to the primal reservoir of our collective origin, of remembering our instincts. Yet the poem itself cannot effect such a return; it can only approximate this experience, and the reconstruction will always be tainted by the intrusion of the rational mind since this description of the heaven of animals is the product of the poet's conscious arrangement even as the poem evokes ineffable rhythms drawn from the unconscious.

In an age of anti-essentialist skepticism, it makes sense to evaluate the validity of Dickey's model of primal memory—to ask, in a paraphrase of Gertrude Stein, if there is any there there. Is there any substance behind Dickey's poetic use of essentialist paradigms and repetitive, incantatory rhythms? Or is his primitive mysticism, his attempt to return us to a preconscious state of being, purely metaphoric, little more than an extensive poetic trope? The rest of this chapter will assert a critical recalibration of established interpretations of the role of primitivism in Dickey's work. I contend that his primal vision becomes at times a willful misprision, that his use of primitive-mystical experience often carries with it an underlying sense of ironic inflation, of a poetic pitchman selling us on the idea of a transcendent union with the first things of the universe. Through ritualistic cadences and archetypal images, he tries to *make* it true through the power of the creative lie. Even if poetry could erase the divide between instinctual experience and conscious construction, it could offer us only temporary leave against the contingency of the human predicament. To cope with this gap, I argue that Dickey sometimes turns to parody—a self-conscious repetition with variation of his early primitivism that reflects aspects of Fredric Jameson's concern with the arch depthlessness and endless pastiche of "postmodern" culture. This acceptance of nontranscendence, of philosophic and cultural materialism, is suggested by Dickey himself as he recants his faith in primal memory as a form of "immortal" (read: transhistorical) revelation. In the concluding pages of *James Dickey and the Politics of Canon*, Suarez wonders whether Dickey had not been disappointed that in all his years he had not experienced "revelation, some kind of Old Testament vision, that he expected his poetry or his life to yield, and that would allow him to deliver the 'immortal message to mankind' he spoke of in *Sorties*" (157). He poses the question to Dickey, then in his late sixties, by invoking the final lines of "Circuit" from *The Eagle's Mile* (1990) and asking why the poem ends not with a confirmation of "meaning, consequence, [and] a positive assessment of the savage ideal" (158), but with an "expression of desire" (158): the hope, left unanswered, for revelation and transcendence. Dickey responds with a sincere acknowledgment of the limits of his art: "Because those things can't happen" (158). Ultimately, his primitive essentialism may be a lie, but the magnitude of the creative force with which it is told contains its value.

By the time of *Falling, May Day Sermon, and Other Poems*, Dickey seems to confess that primitive transcendence is one of those things that can't happen, that his poetic reconstruction of primal memory is a symptom, not the cure of our historical condition. He shifts to a parodic form of primitivism, where the restorative power of the natural cycle is challenged, even exaggerated outright, as the primitive becomes primarily a deconstructive as opposed to reconstructive force. In *Self-Interviews* (1970), Dickey confesses his tendency toward contrivance and absurdity: "There's a razor's edge between sublimity and absurdity. And that's the edge I try to walk" (65). At times he appears to tip over this edge, "courting the ridiculous" (65) wholeheartedly. The poems of *Falling, May Day Sermon, and Other Poems* revel in the power to disrupt, to unhinge cultural paradigms, such as the links between savagery and the South, masculinity and power, femininity and victimization, undermining Dickey's former faith in invoking the primal. In a "postsouthern" reversal, the volume parodies the region's loss of a ritualized sense of lived memory, its outliving of the autochthonous ideal. Postsouthernism hinges on pastiche and parody: it recollects the broken fragments of traditional southernism (especially those southernist clichés of place, rurality, voice, religion, overblown gentility matched by overblown violence, the past, and so on), yet does so not to honor, but to destabilize, even mock, the conservative bent of the past. Dickey seeks to leave the southern past, as well as his own poetic and biographical past, behind, and he does so by corroding the traditional codes of the South from the inside out. Where his initial primitivist poetics attempts to escape culture by retreating into primal nature, his parodic turn exposes nature as a form of culture. This thematic shift is paralleled on a formal level, as Dickey's tight, anapest-driven three- or four-beat lines fall through into more open-ended rhythmical structures, including the frenzied visual rhythms of what he termed his "shimmering wall of words" technique.

This movement is evident in "Falling," which dramatizes the story of an airline stewardess who is swept out of an airborne jetliner miles above the earth. The poem begins with an account of this bizarre but real accident taken from the *New York Times*: "A 29-year-old stewardess fell . . . to her death tonight when she was swept through an emergency door that suddenly sprang open. . . . The body . . . was found . . . three hours after the accident" (243). In his recounting of the flight attendant's fall, Dickey shows her performing a series of miraculously controlled superhuman aerobics as she plunges to her death through "the vast beast-whistle of space" (243) and confronts "the undying cry of the void" (243). The vortex-like motion is replicated on a formal level, trading Dickey's tight "primitive" anapests for this more open form. Experimenting with rhythmic structures, his work shifts into "a new condition" (244), drawing his lineation out across the page and chopping the lines into walls of words. Dave Smith describes this new technique as "a form identified by long lines and sweeping periodic sentences" ("The Strength of James Dickey"173). In Dickey's poems of the late 1960s, a single line seems to suture together two or more of his earlier, shorter lines, offering a sort of metrical pastiche of his previous poetics: in his mid-career verse, "the single poetic line carrie[s] truncated and whole his earliest two-, three-, and four-stress statement-lines" (Smith 173).[13] The effects of his changed technique can be glimpsed in the opening lines of "Falling":

The states when they black and out and lie there rolling   when they turn
To something transcontinental   move by   drawing moonlight out of the
    great
One-sided stone hung off the starboard wingtip   some sleeper next to
An engine is groaning for coffee   and there is faintly coming in
Somewhere the vast beast-whistle of space. In the galley with its racks
Of trays   she rummages for a blanket   and moves in her slim tailored
Uniform to pin it over the cry at the top of the door. As though she blew

The door down with a silent blast from her lungs   frozen   she is black
Out finding herself   with the plane nowhere and her body taking by the
    throat
The undying cry of the void   falling   living   beginning to be something
That no one has ever been and lived through   screaming without enough air
(243)

In stretching from margin to margin yet being segmented into individual blocks within each line, the lineation is sprawling yet contained, drawn out yet truncated, the rhythm giving a sense of motion that is frenetic yet directed. This give-and-pull structure dovetails neatly with the poem's content, as the falling woman discovers that "There is time to live / In superhuman health" (244) while she performs "endless gymnastics" in the air and suffers "a fall / That is controlled   that plummets as it wills   turns gravity / Into a new condition" (244). The woman's desperate attempt to will the material force of nonhuman nature "Into a new condition" begets only a temporary illusion of mastery, a stalling tactic that is eventually voided by death's final rejoinder.

    The woman's fall from air to earth, "from the frail / Chill of space to the loam where extinction slumbers" (246), from unsustaining simulacrum to fatal soil, reflects a significant aspect of Dickey's aesthetic sense, highlighting his ethos of hyperphysicality that traffics in figures of gross materiality and bodily excess. He is at times a nearly excremental poet who deals out images that show a brute fascination with bodily form in and of itself. His poetics of hyperphysicality is evident as he describes in detail the woman's sustained performance of a kind of mid-air, near-death striptease, casting off her jacket, skirt, blouse, slip, stockings, brassiere, and girdle in quick succession. Once stripped bare, she is "no longer monobuttocked" (246). If this phrase makes us cringe, it is one of a series of such full-bodied phrases in *Falling, May Day Sermon, and Other Poems* that make Dickey's self-conscious attention to physique at times almost pornographic. The woman's final act before her crash landing into a Kansas cornfield takes the poetics of hyperphysicality to the point of autoeroticism:

Her last superhuman act   the last slow careful passing of her hands
All over her unharmed body   desired by every sleeper in his dream:
Boys finding for the first time their loins filled with heart's blood
Widowed farmers whose hands float under light covers to find themselves
Arisen at sunrise (246)

The pull of the primal no longer promises any grandiose return to a more essentially meaningful state of being, but has been reduced to the level of a common erotic thrill that shoots through the blood and bodies of widowed farmers and adolescent farm boys alike. Even though the stewardess herself shares in the autoerotic impulse, passing her palms "deeply between / Her thighs," the pleasure of the passage seems distinctly masculine. She functions primarily as the object of their unconscious attention, the unseen focus of a primordial male gaze. Though the lines suggest that she has some degree of control over her own body (she is finally, if briefly, in possession of "*her* long legs" and "*her* small breasts"), there is a more disturbing undercurrent that figures her as the purely sensuous object "desired by every sleeper in *his* dream" (my italics). The woman is equally the object of manipulation by the poet, who choreographs her fall and response to it as if she were a life-size puppet.

Even as the opening lines announce an atmosphere of negation (images of blacking out into the void, "nowhere," "in no world," etc.) that seems to void Dickey's earlier primitivist faith, the poem also reasserts a measure of primal faith in an elemental merging with nature. At first, "Falling" appears to be filling in the void. Air, the most ethereal of natural elements, is made real, solidified into an elemental reality, substantial if not sustaining. There is a shift from the undying void to air as an undying element: the stewardess is "hung high up in the overwhelming middle of things" (243) and seems able to transcend, momentarily at least, the limits of the human as "the levels become more human" (243). The stewardess attempts to merge with and master the elemental air. However, the primal power of the air ultimately falls through. While she is whirling in thin air, there is the sense that her attempted primal merging holds no sustaining power, for her body "will assume without effort any position / Except the one that will sustain it" (246). The air, ultimately, is not elemental, but empty, a blacked out space. Gravity is the only higher force, and it offers no productive regeneration, just inertia that carries all dead matter equally downward. The stewardess comes down "from a marvellous leap   with the delaying, dumfounding ease / Of a dream of being drawn like endless moonlight to the harvest soil / Of a central state of one's country" (243). The pun on "central state" betrays Dickey's primary concern with parody, pointing up how the woman cannot merge transcendently with the central state of the air, but falls through to meet her death as she will literally merge into the earth of Kansas, a geographically centered state. Lest we were tempted to place too much faith in the regenerative capacity of the stewardess's encounter with the quasi-elemental air, by poem's end we see that the woman's "controlled" movement ends not in a moment of transcendence, not in some primally "dreamed eternal meaning" (247), but in the blunt failure of merging. Instead of an instant of productive reintegration, the poem concludes with images of disintegration. The woman's clothes come down in fragments, so much airborne detritus scattered "all over Kansas" (247). In ironic reversal of her earlier superhuman bodily control, her body itself cannot remain intact, but de-forms into trash as she "Lies in the fields   in *this* field   on her broken back as though on / A cloud she cannot drop through" (247). The poem's final assertion of Dickey's brand of hyperphysical poetics leaves us with a gross impression of the woman's body as itself trashed. The figure of her broken body in the field embodies an abortive act of merging, foregrounding a piercing instance of the incapacity to become one with natural elements, except in a grimly fatal, purely material "merging" with the earth:

> All those who find her impressed
> In the soft loam   gone down   driven well into the image of her body
> The furrows for miles flowing in upon her where she lies very deep
> In her mortal outline   in the earth as it is in cloud   can tell nothing
> But that she is there   inexplicable   unquestionable (247) .

"Falling" shows Dickey's primitivist poetics come falling down to earth as the motif of regenerative primitivism becomes a closed field; the stewardess's effort to productively merge with elemental nature (as air and as earth) and transcend material reality, her endeavor to outbelieve the simulacrum, is terminal.

Prior to "May Day Sermon," Dickey's primitive essentialism is gendered masculine, implying that a penchant for dominance is endemic to male nature. Typically for Dickey, it is *men* who recognize the savage ideal in the depths of the human psyche and *men* who act on their violent primal instincts. "May Day Sermon" offers a telling counterexample to such testosterone-injected primitivism, explicitly challenging the masculinization of the savage ideal. It contains a riot of primal violence, a raw splitting open of the wounds of regional, gender, and class stereotypes, one that lays bare a rather gruesome portrait not of savage masculinity, but of savaged masculinity. Furthermore, "May Day Sermon" carries specific resonance with respect to the political and aesthetic climate of the late 1960s, given that on one level, it serves as a satire of what Dickey believed were the extremist tendencies of the Beat and "confessional" schools while simultaneously setting this grim parody of his own primitive poetics within an unmistakably southern context. In his preliminary notes for the poem, Dickey suggests that he wished to invent a new "method of diction and imagery," which he termed "country surrealism" and defined as "surrealism in colloquial southernisms: 'hound dog' etc.—" (James Dickey Papers: Box 112, Item 23). His notes indicate that he was chiefly concerned with developing a specifically nonrealistic style for the poem, one that reflects the influence of surrealist art, which would seem sharply at odds with primitive aesthetics. Where primitivism seeks an ultimate reality that lurks below the layers of abstract culture, surrealism moves in the opposite direction, inventing ethereal and fantastic meanings over and above the typical modes of social being to demonstrate the absurdity and impossibility of an essential reality. Dickey's invention of "country surrealism" points up the unreality of prevailing constructions of southern identity, ironizing clichéd definitions of southern "realities," especially the idea that the South is the nation's reservoir of things backward and primeval. Dickey thus offers a potential means of deliverance from the burden of this brand of southern exceptionalism; whether this deliverance will be lasting or not is an open question that concerns the limits of parody. Above his notes on country surrealism, he considers using "A super-long line, so that they would have to turn the page around" (James Dickey Papers: Box 112, Item 23). With the extended, yet blocked-off lineation of "Falling" and "May Day Sermon," he seems to have found a toned-down form of this "super-long" line that he fills with "Very roughed-up, clunking, energetic diction here, full of workaday halting, going-forward rhythms and words" (James Dickey Papers: Box 112, Item 24), per his notes for a poem tentatively titled "The Barn," another manuscript precedent for "May Day Sermon." Form and content coincide in "May Day Sermon" to create a frenetically surreal vision that unmasks his former primitivism as an ultranostalgic fantasy.

At the same time that Dickey seems to be selling himself as the poet low-rate of the South in this poetic tour de force, he levels a satirical counteroffensive against the regional prejudices underlying attacks on his poetics, politics, and personality. The most notorious of these affronts can be found in Bly's review of Dickey's previous volume, *Buckdancer's Choice* (1965). Bly assaults Dickey's take on the southern savage ideal, vehemently criticizing Dickey's use of detached violence and his alleged racism in poems like "The Firebombing" and "Slave Quarters." A sample from the review, titled "The Collapse of James Dickey" (1967), provides a sense of its tone:

> [Dickey] began writing about 1950, writing honest criticism and sensitive poetry, and suddenly at the age of forty-three, we have a huge blubbery poet, pulling out southern language in long strings, like taffy, a toady to the government, supporting all the movements toward Empire, a sort of Georgia cracker Kipling. (79)

In "May Day Sermon," Dickey seems to give Bly and his supporters precisely what they want—and then some. He presents a rambling blood-and-guts tale of "white trash" voyeurism from a highly uncouth loudmouth-of-the-South poet with a penchant for the southern grotesque.[14] In overstating the claims of the primitive South, the poem parodically answers contemporary critiques of Dickey's poetics while at the same time satirizing the potentially self-indulgent strain and the formal qualities of Beat and "confessional" poetry.

Perhaps the most obvious example of the savaging of the southern masculine ideal is seen in the brutal male rape scene from Dickey's most famous excursion into fiction, *Deliverance*. Yet "May Day Sermon" is equally unsettling in its depiction of the ethnographically primitivized South. In the aptly (albeit prosaically) titled "May Day Sermon to the Women of Gilmer County, Georgia, by a Woman Preacher Leaving the Baptist Church," a female persona delivers a sermon that is less appropriate for a congregation of Southern Baptists than for a mob of hysterical Dionysians. She subverts patriarchal control over the Word by willfully conflating religious and erotic language throughout her sermon. Aggressive in word, the woman preacher spreads the gospel of a woman who has been equally aggressive in deed. In the culturally grounded mythic tale she constructs, a young woman serves as the purveyor of the primitive, thereby usurping the masculinized power of primal violence and sexuality, for she is a "blood beast and Venus together" (289). The young woman has engaged in an illicit affair with a one-eyed motorcycle-riding mechanic. After her fundamentalist father finds out about her tryst, he ties her to a post and violently whips her as punishment for her transgression. All the while, he quotes the Bible to her, "screaming / Scripture CHAPter and verse beating it into her with a weeping / Willow branch" (288). Once released, the farmer's daughter avenges her father's savagery by hatcheting him to death and then, in a *postmortem* act of gruesome yet artful excess, she renders him "blind" in one eye with several bloody two-handed thrusts from an ice pick, making his mutilated corpse into a bleak parody of her lover's one bad eye. Not only is the father's authority savaged, but the patriarchal power of the Word is emptied out as well. The woman preacher's brutal words and the daughter's brutal deeds make "the father / Sound" equivalent to "the Word / Of nothing" (292).

At the same time it seems to be undercutting prevailing gender roles, it plays up dominant biases according to class and region, presenting a voyeuristic gaze into the uncanny experience of the rural poor in the backcountry South. A poor farm girl victimized by her father's vehement religious fundamentalism and repressed incestuous desire, the daughter is a walking type of southern "white trash," making her resistance all the more pointed by bringing regionalist and class prejudices into play. In usurping the power of the savage ideal, the farm girl provides a deeply unsettling scene, since her act of violence unhinges the cultural equation of femininity with victimization. Making the man the victim of a bloody hatcheting and posthumous ice-picking uncovers a tear in the fabric of the dominant mythos of masculine self-possession and authority— a mythos that is supposed to have been at the core of James Dickey both poetically and biographically. The cultural frame of masculine power has been shattered by this memorable image of male victimage, of a grim and mutilating patricide. We are given an ironic reversal of the Agrarian mythos of the South, which Dickey encountered during his time as an undergraduate and graduate student at Vanderbilt.[15] The Georgia farmlands of Gilmer County serve as a privileged site for the primitivized penchant for sex and violence of the presumed lower orders. Although Dickey portrays the unleashing of primal energies as a productive, reinvigorating experience, it does not seem off the mark to read a degree of middle-class chauvinism into his linking of rural working-class southernness with the primitive.

The poem also serves as a parody of the psychological handwringing associated with confessional poetry. Alluding to Robert Lowell's verse, Dickey contemptuously noted in 1967:

> People are worn out listening to somebody else's weeping and
> sackcloth-and-ashes attitudes, breastbeating, and gnashing of
> teeth, frustration, and tearing of hair and personal grievances.
> . . . No poet should be so egotistical as to ask the reader to fasten
> onto his personality and his own confessions. (Quoted in Hart
> 376)

Dickey's vehemence here may have resulted in part from Bly's stinging comments on what he alleged was Dickey's *disuse* of persona in *Buckdancer's Choice*. Bly's caustic review suggested that in "Slave Quarters" Dickey "is not standing outside the poem. On the contrary, the major characteristic of all these poems is their psychic blurriness. There are no personae" (76). In "May Day Sermon" there is no mistaking the presence of a persona: it would be difficult to confuse Dickey with a woman preacher leaving the Baptist Church of Gilmer County, Georgia. He ironizes the confessional mode by having his female persona make confession for another female persona—confession at a double remove. In fact, "confession" is hardly the proper term since there is no admission of culpability because, according to the Dickeyesque primitive paradigm, there is no real sin in this patricide—our heroine is beyond good and evil. Both the woman preacher and the farmer's daughter revel without guilt in their transgressions. For Dickey's personae, there is no crime and, therefore, no punishment.

Dickey had drawn Bly's ire in part because of his pointed critique in *The Suspect in Poetry* (1964), skewering Allen Ginsberg as the worst of what little he felt the Beat school had to offer. Dickey satirized the confessional mode in Ginsberg's *Kaddish* (1961), arguing that "confession is not enough, and neither is the assumption that the truth of one's experience will emerge if only one can keep talking long enough in a whipped-up state of excitement. It takes more than this to make poetry. It just does" (19). The attack is made even more vehement in a copy of one of Dickey's speeches contained among his manuscripts. "Allen Ginsberg, His Audience, and the Assumption of Virtue" shows the severity of the literary skirmishing that went on between Dickey and his northern poetic rivals, as he attributes Ginsberg's popularity on college campuses to the fact that he is writing dull propaganda that reinforces his audience's own political and poetic tastes:

It should be obvious that much of Ginsberg's popularity comes from the fact that a great many members of these audiences <u>write</u> like Ginsberg. They are not imitating him any more than he is imitating them, turning out the same kind of formless exhibitionism producible by anyone who can perform the physical act of writing at all. (James Dickey Papers: Box 150, Item 1)

In fact, so talentless are both Ginsberg and his audience that he "might be called the poet of the aggressive inarticulate, the bellwether of the untalented and self-righteous" (ibid.). Dickey charges that Ginsberg and his fellow "New York literati," including Bly and Kenneth Rexroth, are more politicians than poets:

It is interesting to note that it is almost invariably the least talented writers, such as Ginsberg and the laughable Robert Bly, who take the public pose of righteousness most often and most vociferously. They must appear at every peace rally, they must speak at every read-in, every demonstration, everywhere publicity is to be found. They indulge, in fact, in a kind of image-making . . . quite closely akin to that practised by advertising and public relations firms. They also operate under the belief, whether stated or not, that an applause-worthy stand on public issues will make up in some way for their inability to say anything more than temporarily memorable. (Ibid.)

According to Dickey, this amounts to "a kind of Joe McCarthyism of the left," where "the listeners get to be publicly for and against things: things they are already for or against" (ibid.). Dickey sees this political impulse as mere posturing, for "Show biz, finally, is Ginsberg's bag. Indian prayers, a 'magnetic spiritual presence,' beards, costumes, stripteases, public weeping, onstage embraces, public 'forgivings' and 'reconciliations,' the whole bit" (ibid.). This acrimony toward the Ginsbergian milieu drove Dickey to react in poetic terms as well, turning out an ultraviolent, emphatically "southernized" response in "May Day Sermon."

The poem obviously resists the confessional model; however, to draw on Dickey's critiques of both Lowell and Ginsberg, it does go on and on in a whipped-up state of excitement while dealing out a fair share of weeping, breast-beating, gnashing of teeth, frustration, tearing of hair, and personal grievances.

The main distinctions between Dickey's sermon and confessional poetry are the celebratory tone of a persona that cannot be equated with the poet and the dominant concern with aggressive, even sadomasochistic sexuality and violence. On a stylistic level, Dickey's poem also reproduces some of the formal traits of his sworn poetic rivals, though one suspects that there may be more than a hint of parody in his replication of Beat poetics. "May Day Sermon" exploits a visionary style, full of Ginsbergian frenzy and, of course, madness. The poem's shimmering walls of words—these blocks of print that create visual rhythms—seem virtually indistinguishable from Ginsberg's "breath units." In Dickey's line, "she shrieks sweet Jesus and God / I'm glad O my God-darling O lover O angel-stud dear heart" (288), there are echoes of *Howl* (1956), with its image of "angelheaded hipsters" and strings of exclamatory interjections. To add some more Romantic visionary weight to the poem, Dickey specifically invokes Blake, parodying perhaps Ginsberg's famous imagined visitation by the ghost of Blake:

> Sisters, who is your lover? Has he done nothing but come
> And go? Has your father nailed his cast skin to the wall as evidence
> Of sin? Is it flying like a serpent in the darkness dripping pure radiant
>   venom
> Of manhood? (290)

The allusion to "The invisible worm / That flies in the night / In the howling storm" from Blake's "The Sick Rose" (1794) is injected with further irony in light of Dickey's earlier dismissal of *Howl* in *The Suspect in Poetry*: "*Howl* is the skin of Rimbaud's *Une Saison en Enfer* thrown over the conventional maunderings of one type of American adolescent, who has discovered that machine civilization has no interest in his having read Blake" (16–17). The overly transparent allusion to Blake in "May Day Sermon" suggests that Dickey is poking fun at Ginsberg's visionary histrionics, particularly at his claim to being Blake's spiritual and poetic heir apparent.

Dickey also makes use of Whitmanesque catalogs reminiscent of Ginsberg, but Dickey's rambling lists parodically expose the trope of nature red in tooth and claw, particularly down South, as the "endemic" proclivity for savagery is translated into a sociocultural context. With tongue plunged into cheek, Dickey implies that such primal violence could only take place in the southern backwoods. Included in his catalogs of the Gilmer County farm are images of "spiders dead / Drunk on their threads   the hogs' fat bristling   the milk / Snake in the rafters unbending through gnats to touch the last place

/ Alive on the sun with its tongue" (287). In a very un-Edenic reversal, God himself is shown transforming into a serpent as he puts "North Georgia copper on His head / To crawl in under the door in dust red enough to breathe / The breath of Adam into" (287). Furthermore, many of the lines in "May Day Sermon" share Ginsberg's sprawling stream-of-consciousness approach, heavy alliteration, and imagery of graphic sexuality. Some lines slip over into explicitly ironic replication, as much *faux* Ginsberg as *bona fide* Dickey. Witness, for instance, the forgettable line "her buttocks blazing in the sheepskin saddle" (295).

In the effort to demonstrate associations between Dickey's stylistic shift in "May Day Sermon" and those poetic schools he ostensibly rejected in the late 1960s, one should be careful not to elide the fact that there are significant differences. Dickey draws largely on the rhythms and rhetoric of the southern pulpit in constructing the woman preacher's sermon. Like the father figure in the poem, Dickey is "using the tried / And true rhythms of the Lord" (295). In addition, his poem's concern with violent victimage, with the savage ideal in its inalterably southern setting, makes it anathema to the anti-Vietnam poetic coalition led in part by Bly and Ginsberg. The work's macabre invocation of the southern grotesque tradition is made obvious in Dickey's campy puns on the means of death for the farm girl's father, who is "yes found with an icepick on his mind" (295) and who is the butt of the persona's crude inversion of Biblical language: "and it is easy for a needle to pass / Through the eye of a man bound for Heaven" (293). This emphasis on primitive savagery couched in the antipastoral South marks it as a parodic response to the poetry and poetics associated with the "New York literati." Yet "May Day Sermon" serves as a self-conscious critique not only of confessional and Beat poetics, but also of Dickey's own gendered primitivism. Like the snake that "takes a great breath bursts / Through himself and leaves himself behind" (291), the poem points up the constructedness of his own stylized primitive cool. In a transformation worthy of Ovid, Dickey sheds the skin of primitive essentialist, and bursts through himself, leaving critical interpretations of him as an antifeminist savage idealist behind.[16] This metamorphosis is reflected in the woman preacher's final exhortation of her "daughters" to embrace an unbounded earthy sensuality and in the closing image of a rootless barn wandering over the earth, an apt metaphor for the untethering of contemporary southern culture from its Agrarian roots:

> Listen   O daughters   turn   turn
> In your sleep   rise with your backs on fire   in spring   in your socks
> Into the arms of your lovers: every last one of you, listen one-eyed
> With your man   in hiding   in fog where the animals walk through

The white breast of the Lord   muttering   walk with nothing
To do but be   in the spring laurel in the mist and self-sharpened
Moon   walk through the resurrected creeks   through the Lord
At their own pace   the cow shuts its mouth and the Bible is still
Still open at anything   we are gone   the barn wanders over
        the earth. (296) .

In her concluding sentiments, the woman preacher allegorizes a South un-
moored from its traditional bindings in religion and the land, envisioning a
region that is now continually "Still open at anything" with a terrifying yet
exhilarating mobility. This final image gives a liberatory sense of newly form-
ing, free-floating allegiances, but it offers little sense of direction, much less
destiny. Dickey is committed to parody of the past, but provides little vision of
the future. In "May Day Sermon," he slashes and burns the outworn vestiges of
southern tradition, but seems unconcerned about what will be planted in the
fields after he is gone.[17]

The opening poem of part 2 of *Falling, May Day Sermon, and Other Poems*,
"The Sheep Child" also reflects a level of mock primitivism, bluntly nonregen-
erative. In contrast to poet James Applewhite, who interprets Dickey's exagger-
ated invocation of stereotypical southernness as sincere, expressing a "painful
admiration of a great Southern talent who seemed to believe in the Southern
clichés" (quoted in McFee 220), I read the poem as a biting pastiche of meta-
commentary on the defining structures of southern literature and culture, a
thoroughgoing postsouthern parody of the stock motifs of place, language,
oral history, kinship, and the pastoral tradition. "The Sheep Child" offers a
further example—arguably the most memorable one—of "country surrealism,"
although, on a formal level, it marks something of a return to his earlier tightly
constructed lines with heavy-handed rhythms. Yet this is certainly an instance
of a parodistic repetition with a difference. The poem describes the ill-begotten
progeny of "farm boys wild to couple / With anything" (248), especially sheep.
The opening lines immediately reverse the pastoral ideal of the South, replac-
ing this wistful vision with savage satire:

> Farm boys wild to couple
> With anything   with soft-wooded trees
> With mounds of earth   mounds
> Of pinestraw   will keep themselves off
> Animals by legends of their own:

> In the hay-tunnel dark
> And dung of barns, they will
> Say   I have heard tell (248)

The farm boys have indeed gone primitive, but with no productive (re)genera-
tion as a result. Dickey takes the idea of merging with nature to its illogical
extreme. This wild coupling is all a bit *too* primal, supplanting the myth of the
southern pastoral with the urban—and northern—legend of animalistic sexual
deviance among southern country dwellers. Traditionally, rural southern cul-
ture has served as a kind of deterrence machine for America in general, espe-
cially the Northeast, which marks the South as a site of grotesque abnormality,
the hybrid, deformed progeny of the nation. While ironically reiterating such
anti-southernist attitudes, Dickey makes it clear that these legends are also
propagated by the rural folk themselves who seem to have internalized these
attitudes, for the farm boys "keep themselves off / Animals by legends of their
own." In marking themselves as the regional incarnation of the primitive, these
backwoods southerners set up the rural South as a foil for the more progressive
New South as well as the North more broadly.

    The short-lived hybrid offspring of these anti-rustics is—as legend has
it—pickled in a jar and preserved in the corner of an Atlanta museum:

> I have heard tell
>
> That in a museum in Atlanta
> Way back in a corner somewhere
> There's this thing that's only half
> Sheep   like a wooly baby
> Pickled in alcohol   because
> Those things can't live   his eyes
> Are open   but you can't stand to look
> I heard from somebody who . . .
>
> But this is now almost all
> Gone. The boys have taken
> Their own true wives in the city,
> The sheep are safe in the west hill
> Pasture   but we who were born there
> Still are not sure. (248)

The southern oral tradition of relating stories is announced in the line "I have heard tell," though this is no nostalgic reminiscence. Dickey's brand of hyper-physicality is in play here with the repulsive figure of taboo sexuality and its deviant reproduction of deformed flesh. We get a vision of nonregenerative primitivism, of things that can't live, as the narrative of the South as pastoral enclave has been parodically aborted. The figure of this genetically deformed offspring dredges up memories of Menckenesque critiques of poor, rural south-erners as being themselves inherently inferior; for Mencken, the South was biodetermined to be a backward region as a result of its distorted gene pool. In preserving the sheep-child, Dickey's Atlanta museum collects the most hetero-geneous of cultural materials. The deformed progeny that has been preserved, yet hidden away, reflects a bad case of archive fever; the fetus is resistant mate-rial, unarchivable dead matter. It is explicitly marginalized, kept "Way back in a corner somewhere," but this is precisely what makes it so alluring, since it is the act of cornering it off, burying it away at the edges of collective memory, that serves all the more to put it on display. Dickey's museum houses the horrors of southern mythology, preserving the residual grotesqueness of the pastoral mythos that has been museumed away. The uncanny deadness of the southern past is preserved in formaldehyde solution even under the auspices of the uto-pian vision of the New South, the crown jewel of which is the slickly urban, highly commercialized Atlanta.

We then regress to a bizarre reassertion of primal memory as the sheep-child itself takes a turn at storytelling:

Merely with his eyes, the sheep-child may

Be saying   saying

I am here, in my father's house.
I who am half of your world, came deeply
To my mother in the long grass
Of the west pasture, where she stood like moonlight
Listening for foxes. It was something like love
From another world that seized her
From behind, and she gave, not lifting her head
Out of dew, without ever looking, her best
Self to that great need. Turned loose, she dipped her face
Farther into the chill of the earth, and in a sound
Of sobbing   of something stumbling

Away, began, as she must do,
To carry me. I woke, dying (248–49)

This reiteration of primitivism is parodic and nonsustaining: it wakes, dying. The mythos of instinctual memory has been replaced by the cold machinery of modern science. The sheep-child is preserved in the "*immortal waters*" (249) of his specimen jar, thus figuring science, not religion, as the source of an afterlife, though it is a darkly distilled, lifeless form of immortality. Moreover, the figure of the talking sheep-child exposes the politics of memory within the South itself in begging the question: "Are we, / Because we remember remembered / In the terrible dust of museums?" (248). This postsouthern object of memory replaces traditional nostalgic veneration with a freakish anti-nostalgia: the South as a pleasant pastoral mythos can't live. Likewise, Dickey's southernized primitive poetics can't live, but falls into self-parody. The final lines of the poem, spoken again by the sheep-child itself, are dyed in the wool with self-conscious parody, ironically echoing the closing lines of "The Heaven of Animals." The primal, essential, natural cycle foregrounded in that poem—

> At the cýcle's cénter,
> They trémble, they wálk
> Únder the trée,
> They fáll, they are tórn,
> They ríse, they wálk agáin.

—has been replaced by an artificial cultural phenomenon, an inessential and enclosing cycle, as the sheep-child speaks now of the farm boys who have grown up and moved to the cities, who marry and raise their kind:

> *Dréaming of mé*
> *They gróan   they wáit   they súffer*
> *Themsélves, they márry, they ráise their kínd.* (249)

This falling away from a dreamed eternal meaning for the natural cycle in "The Heaven of Animals" into a hollow recycling of social codes at the end of "The Sheep Child" betrays a heightened attention to artifice and self-conscious framing.

On the one hand, through parody, Dickey offers contemporary southern poetry a means of potential liberation from the past, killing off the empty signifiers of what has come before. In doing so, however, he is also made subject to the paradox of being trapped *within* past rhetorical codes. The poems of *Falling, May Day Sermon, and Other Poems* are like postsouthern buzzards picking clean the bleached bones of a supposedly once-vital past. The question the volume frames in all but words is whether Dickey can make these dry bones live. Does salvation really lie in self-consciousness, or is this merely another kind of damnation? The ethos of Dickey's own primitivist poetics is also "now almost all / Gone," as southern culture moves into the cities and bids farewell to old codes of regional exceptionalism. If both pastoralism and primitivism are now still-born, what is the region left with? While other contemporary southern poets will provide a range of responses, spanning from the nostalgic to the traumatic, from reveling in rootlessness to realigning the tracks along transregional lines, Dickey seems committed to a single answer: the negating momentum of parodic reiteration is now the main force. To turn the closing phrase of "Circuit," parody "may just be it" (434). He gambles that the energy he infuses into creating a postsouthern vortex is itself culturally regenerative. Better a living buzzard than a dead hawk.

The primitivist thrust of Dickey's early poetry is based on a deep nostalgia to return to the blissful unknowing of a preconscious state, seeking to enact the animalistic capacity "to feel *unhistorically*" (Nietzsche 62): whereas the beast is fully "contained in the present, like a number without any awkward fraction left over," the acculturated human being is overwrought with historical self-consciousness and "braces himself against the great and ever greater pressure of what is past" (61). In Dickey's later verse, the ultranostalgic drive to live unhistorically ultimately yields to the demands of the poet's cultural situatedness. The following chapter examines the work of some contemporary southern poets who hold still to the value of nostalgic remembrance, though they are not necessarily blind to the ambiguities and elisions of seeking to duplicate an ostensibly more centered past. The contemporary poetics of nostalgia sometimes returns us to a more traditional vision of southern cultural memory, reiterating the fabled checklist of "renascence" belles lettres: connection to place, emphasis on family and community, a devoted attention to the past, and a distinctively southern voice. Often they do so by reasserting poetic formalism, thereby giving us old themes in renewed forms and in a sense taking us back to the future. Although they repeat the past, the work of these poets, as we shall see, discloses the commingled possibilities of nostalgic longing as both restoring and restricting.

CHAPTER 3

Many Returns: Forms of Nostalgia in the Poetry of the Contemporary South

> The time will come, they say, when the weight of nostalgia,
>
> that ten-foot spread
>
> Of sand in the heart, outweighs
> Whatever living existence we drop on the scales.
>
> May it never arrive, Lord, may it never arrive.
>
> —Charles Wright, "Nostalgia" (2002)

Stereotypically, southerners and their literature are known for nostalgia, sometimes even defined by it, and this is one of the most prevalent paradigms of current southern poetry, though much contemporary verse resists this impulse. Nostalgia can take the seemingly innocuous form of yearning for a more peaceful and reassuring past, often centered on the longing to return to the homestead, a physical and symbolic space that merges the traditional southern staples of ties to family as well as to place, sometimes intensifying into a shrine for ancestor worship. Such pining for a more essential time and place may seem harmless enough, but it can also take on ideological import, especially in relation to racial politics. Retreating into the past can elide pressing social realities of the present, something apparent in ongoing conflicts over the politics of nostalgia for the Lost Cause, seen most vividly in the current battle over the flying of the Confederate flag on the grounds of the South Carolina statehouse. Waxing nostalgic is a politically weighted act.

Several prominent southern poets—including George Scarbrough, Robert Morgan, Donald Justice, Betty Adcock, Henry Taylor, and Dave Smith—make use of nostalgia, though not necessarily in traditional ways. Nostalgia remains a driving force in the poetics of the contemporary South even or especially as the region operates under the shifting socioeconomic and political conditions of a transregional ethos. Although at times their poetic measures can become reactionary ones, preserving a mummified past from such cultural transitions, these poets also show signs of a more jagged nostalgia, one that struggles to come to terms with a transformational South: old times there are not forgotten, but re-viewed with a different, even distrustful eye. While some of these writers display an abiding desire to shore up the remnants of a more meaningful time and place, others are more self-consciously critical of their penchant for nostalgia. At their worst, these poets long wistfully to preserve the vestiges of better days, thus practicing a form of antiquarian history.[1] However, they can also offer a more nuanced and balanced vision of the cultural uses of nostalgia, one that takes into account its escapist undertones as well as its restorative potential. Their nostalgia is often connected with the natural world; this can lead to an uncritical neopastoralism, but in the context of ecocriticism, the pastoral can also assume a dimension of cultural significance, as John Lang notes in his work on Morgan's Appalachian poetry.[2] When exploring the function of nostalgic memory in contemporary southern poetry, there are at least two interconnected levels of inquiry: 1) as a model of personal and cultural memory, what does nostalgia look like, especially at this particular historical juncture; and 2) exactly what are current southern poets nostalgic for, and why?

By definition, nostalgia's backward-glancing would seem to run counter to the continuously shifting identifications of a transouthern world, forming a conservative defense mechanism against contemporary culture's overflow of meanings by positing the singular meaningfulness of a stable, unified past. A starting point in defining nostalgia might be Michael Kammen's understanding of it as "essentially history without guilt," a sense of heritage "that suffuses us with pride rather than with shame" (688). Although nostalgia does function as a sentimental balm of homesickness and longing to salve the wounds of more divisive historical conflict, we should use this definition to press beyond a neo-Marxist condemnation of nostalgia out of hand that seems at best incomplete. Current theorists offer a range of perspectives on nostalgia as both a method of cultural retreat *and* critique. From the Greek *nostos*, "to return home," and *algia*, "a sorrowful or distressing condition or illness," nostalgia is literally a state of homesickness.[3] By the twentieth century, the concept was gradually stripped of its medical associations and has taken on pejorative meaning as "the useless yearning for a world or for a way of life from which one has been irrevocably severed" (Starobinski 101). While there is undoubtedly a good deal of truth involved in this typical definition, nostalgia is not a univocal phenomenon, but contains various, even contrary levels. Svetlana Boym proposes two contrasting impulses of nostalgic desire: restorative versus reflective. In its uncritical restorative sense, nostalgia can become "an abdication of personal responsibility, a guilt-free homecoming, an ethical and aesthetic failure" (xiv). Restorative nostalgia "stresses *nostos* and attempts a transhistorical reconstruction of the lost home" (xviii), while reflective nostalgia

> thrives in *algia*, the longing itself, and delays the homecoming—wistfully, ironically, desperately. Restorative nostalgia does not think of itself as nostalgia, but rather as truth and tradition. Reflective nostalgia dwells on the ambivalences of human longing and belonging and does not shy away from the contradictions of modernity. Restorative nostalgia protects the absolute truth, while reflective nostalgia calls it into doubt. (xviii)

Establishing a further division between what he calls nostalgia as mood and nostalgia as mode, Paul Grainge views nostalgia as historically conditioned, becoming most visible at times when there is "a sense of cultural decline, matched with a fear of widespread societal forgetting," moments when "the pace and project of modernity [have] put adverse pressure on established traditions and cultural ideologies" (4). Locating nostalgia vis-à-vis the loss of "place-bound identity" in an age of globalization, where the coherence of local communities has been intensively challenged, he defines mood nostalgia as "a socio-cultural response to forms of discontinuity, claiming a vision of stability and authenticity in some conceptual 'golden age.'" (21). Building on Fredric Jameson's significant—albeit hyperbolic—understanding of "postmodern" culture as an endless pastiche in which any object can be invested with a sheen of nostalgic feeling, Grainge develops the concept of nostalgia as mode, which "questions the ability to apprehend the past at all in a postmodern culture distinguished by the profound waning of history" (21). While it focuses on the cultural-economic implications of the amnesiac past, Grainge's definition of nostalgia as mode seems consonant with Susan Stewart's account of nostalgia as "the repetition that mourns the inauthenticity of all repetition and denies the repetition's capacity to form identity" (23).

In investigating the second level of inquiry—exactly what are current southern poets nostalgic for, and why?—it will be necessary to decide what kind of Souths their nostalgia records—or, more likely, reinvents—and to determine the ideological impulses behind such poetic reconstructions of the southern cultural landscape. Though no longer tied to the fierce nostalgia of the Vanderbilt Fugitives (especially Tate's and Davidson's forlorn desire to return to a more consequential time before the dreaded incursion of "modernization" into the South), the politics of memory expressed by contemporary poetics of nostalgia often functions to revive through repetition a vision of the southern past as a more cohesive agrarian community, a steady and steadying place. When they are less self-conscious about their pained pleasure in remembering the past, they seem to accept Fred Davis's point that "almost anything from our past can emerge as an object of nostalgia, provided that we can somehow view it in a pleasant light" (viii).[4] Frequently they do so with a knowing irony about the impossibility of repeating the past as it once was. At times their poetry resists restorative nostalgia by foregrounding a sense of the past as an internally divergent narrative; at other times, some of these poets fall to believing their own stories, yielding to wistfulness outright. When in this restorative mood, they tend to share the sentiment, in Edward Ayers's formulation, that "from its very beginning, people have believed that the South, defined against an earlier South that was somehow more authentic, more real, more unified and distinct, was not only disappearing but also declining" (69).

If the Fugitives' poetry approximates a form of cultural pilgrimage to the holy sites of the southern past (e.g., Tate's elegiac Confederate cemetery or Davidson's retracing of Robert E. Lee's footsteps on the campus of Washington and Lee University), then the uncritical forms of contemporary nostalgia poetry conduct a type of cultural tourism, showing us around the highlights of a southern history that seems little more than a museum piece. When reenacting nostalgia as mood, these poets show the past to be almost always a good thing, repressing historical pressures while reestablishing the South as a "mimetic enclave" (Jameson 54), a safe haven from the complexities of modernity. When invoking more critical forms of reflective or mode nostalgia, these poets display a higher awareness concerning nostalgic memory's potential complicity with the past, its capacity to edit out the more violent and unseemly pages of narrative history. At their sharpest, they offer a more nuanced and balanced vision of the cultural uses of southern nostalgia, even manipulating the potential for nostalgia to create reflective space for social critique. To reflect the intricate range of the current southern poetics of nostalgia, this chapter is organized according to the primary form of nostalgia at work in these six representative poets, even though these rubrics must perforce be somewhat schematic and therefore may not capture the full spectrum of nostalgia within each author's specific canon: 1) restorative nostalgia, 2) metanostalgia, and 3) critical memory.

Scarbrough and Morgan are two long-established writers whose poetry values the restorative capacity of nostalgic memory, where *nostos* supersedes *algia*. Although each of these poets reveals some ambivalence concerning nostalgia's redemptive potential, on the whole both writers survey nostalgia as a connective force in locating a recuperative vision of days gone by. They share a basic faith in recovery over reconstruction, and nostalgia is for them a vital effort to regain the past's intensity. Their desire to create a poetic world that is moveless and substantial, beyond the churning subcurrents of historical vicissitudes, leaves them vulnerable to charges of escapism. Yet their commitment to this imaginative return home leaves a deep impression, and if they are sometimes guilty of remaining on the surface-tension of history, it seems a common enough liability.

· · ● ● ● ● · ·

In his introduction to the 1999 reissue of *Tellico Blue* (1949), Rodney Jones argues that "the central pastoral imagery of [Scarbrough's] poetry was not a choice, not an occasion for the fantastic aura of language that the Romantics so beautifully indulged, nor the post-symbolist countryside that the Fugitive poets favored, but home-ground" (vii). While Scarbrough[5] surely writes something more than mere "regional pabulum" (vii), he does at times draw on nostalgia's power as a cultural palliative. Jones imbues Scarbrough's poetry with an authenticity based on experiential knowledge: because Scarbrough grew up in a family of east Tennessee sharecroppers with Cherokee roots, his neopastoralism goes beyond post-symbolist abstraction and instead creates a nostalgia that is more deeply tied to material conditions of rural Appalachia. Although his work typically engages the restorative dimension of a redemptive agrarianism, Scarbrough's self-deprecating awareness of his own tendencies toward excess nostalgia counts in his favor. He seems to offer by way of apology a line from "Several More Scenes from Act One": "A man makes only the / conjectures possible to him out of his largely / conjectural past" (NSP 29). While his poetry is characterized by the workings of a restorative ethos, it contains a set of darker conjectures as well, positing a more reflective level of restrained and effective melancholic longing, steeped in the recognition that "memory is never full recovery, that knowledge and oblivion concur" (Ramsey, "The Truth at the Door" 56). Like the majority of southern poets before and since, Scarbrough is primarily a formalist, exploiting traditional verse structures; however, he is an endless experimenter who is willing to explore the value of free verse as well. Ramsey praises Scarbrough's poetry for "the beautiful sense of place, control of line, progress of narrative, clarity with strangeness, order with passion" (61), while R. T. Smith commends the poet's "supple lines and mixture of archaic, immediate and completely eccentric diction" (9). His poems display a spectrum of different styles, yet his subjects almost always revolve around his Appalachian native country, called Tellico Blue.[6] Although his attitude toward his region shifts, he often evokes an auratic nostalgia—one that maintains an aura of authenticity and depth—in his homages to the land itself, "this / willow country mountain grove of / [his] nativity," as he terms it in the poetic dedication to his *New and Selected Poems* (1977). In his poetic reconstructions of Appalachia, the soil is typically regenerative and forgiving, "cruelly / beautiful but not cruel," like the snake that inhabits said territory in the Edenic landscape memorialized in this "Dedication to the Book."

In the prose poem, "Several Scenes from Act One," a set of associative vignettes drawn from nostalgic reminiscences of his youth in the hills of Tellico Blue, Scarbrough imbues the landscape with a stabilizing sense of placefulness, celebrating his earliest memories of his family homeplace. He provides us with a picture of nostalgic homesickness, invoking a Romantic sensibility to describe the pangs of having had to part from his comforting cabin-home:

> My first flight over the
> hills of Kentucky and Tennessee, over the green
> and yellow of lakes and land, brought back so
> sharp a memory of the cabin nursed in a hollow of
> a ridge and a pane of glass, that I closed my eyes
> tight against the prospect, sick again in heart
> and mind, as I have been many times in between
> at the hideous impracticality of my own
> romanticism. (NSP 11)

The cabin itself is figured as a natural outcropping of the land, an organic entity nurtured by the earth, "nursed in a hollow of / a ridge." The pane of glass, however, suggests awareness on the poet's part of his own immoderate romanticism, as Scarbrough implies that his own melodramatic nostalgia proves too transparent a frame. Such intimations of restoration are often balanced by darker strains, like the melancholic impulse evident in "Impasse," a poem memorializing the death of his father:

My father died
talking of grass
in a room too small
to heave a bed in,

A window too high
to let the yard in,
but perfect for
the exit of souls. (NSP 53)

This vignette records a stark moment of final absence through the ironic language of excess (a room "too small" to permit a conventional deathbed scene, a window "too high" that shuts out the analgesic view of the landscape, for the grass exists only in talk). The paucity of the setting, which stokes the consequent desire to fill the void with language and memory, is paralleled by the truncated, two-beat lines. As the terse lines simultaneously cut and spill into one another, they connote separation as well as connectedness, just as life and death here seem mutually exclusive (or at least diametrically opposed), yet inextricable. The traditional pathos associated with a fatherly deathbed scene is instilled with a high measure of restraint: the venerated nostalgia for dead fathers, exemplified in Davidson's "Lee in the Mountains" and Tate's *The Fathers*, has reached a contemporary impasse.

In *Tellico Blue*, the overall impulse is toward the sunny side of things, typically quite literally focusing on the sunny hillsides of this Appalachian enclave, as in "Departure," with its invocation of "ye saints" and "ye sinners" to turn again to the "bright green valley" where

A spot of sun washes the place of lovers

And wild quail beat their wings beside a hill
Green as an uncut field where white ducks sleep.
Turn once, ye saints, and only if you will,
But ye who loved it, turn and look earth-deep. (TB 103)

The redemptive motive is suggested by the poem's elevated and archaic language, couched in a familiar ABAB pentameter structure. The concluding imperative for "ye who loved it" to "turn and look earth-deep" marks a return to the soil, to nostalgia for a remembered landscape that is felt soul-deep, the closing spondee ("éarth-déep") soundly rooting the final image to the page. "Eastward in Eastanalle" circumvents the subregion's history of economic stagnancy with promises of a "land of cool colors," ripe fields, running rivers, "clear blue mountains" and "green corn waving"—a "tender land" that is "kind and open" to all and is "the heart's world, too lovely for bearing" (TB 4). This "indiscriminate land, green as corn, / Ripe as plums, that makes no choice among / Its people" is the "World of the lost heart on the edge of finding!" (4) The land, in being lost, is therefore restored through the poem's wealth of images and sounds, the very abundance of the land being reinforced by the meter's tender strains (e.g., the parallel structure, both grammatical and metrical, of "gréen as córn / Rípe as plúms") that work in conjunction with the pleasing color imagery to further soften the poem's nostalgic feel.

The easy color scheme of "Eastward in Eastanalle" darkens considerably in "Spring," as the season's "hypnotic green / Swirl[s] blood-red" and April's "green game" is encountered "once in black." The poem represents the contradictory streaks of nostalgic remembrance, where nostalgia is fringed with a grim consciousness of death's immediacy:

> Kenneth fell out of the wagon that day.
> We were coming home up the red clay road between
> The house and barn, and would not shut our mouths,
> Be quiet enough to see hypnotic green
>
> Swirl blood-red with his cry . . .
>
> Spring was a green game until then, a rare race.
> We sons encountered April once in black.
> We have not felt the same since, naming the leaves
> The name of the boy with the wheel-mark on his back. (TB 33)

The formalism of iambic pentameter in an ABCB rhyme scheme pulls against the disturbing quality of the content. The tension between the recognizable, steady form—its "hypnotic" repetitions—and the shocking, though shockingly understated, subject matter provides an apt corollary for the murkier reaches of nostalgia: what appears light and lively on the surface of things often masks a deeper divide, thereby showing Scarbrough's provisional awareness that nostalgia is an inherently conflicted process. The *algia* of nostalgic remembrance is stressed in the image of the fallen brother's toppled, empty chair; such pained nostalgia is "Like a wind that suffers from the breath to blow" (TB 33). In a similar vein, "For My Brothers" trots out the motifs of family and place, but does so with self-conscious reflection on the speaker's own status as hopeless nostalgic. He knows neither he nor his brothers can come to "certain country assuredly" (TB 32) as they once had done. Despite this disclaimer, he still holds some faith in the sustaining power of nostalgic memory, telling his scattered brothers

> Believe me, Reed, in the purple aster hills,
> And believe me, Spencer, though the sky be shortened
> And haunted about your shoulders in the valley
> And the wind be hushed of leaves,
> There will be memory. (TB 32)

The assertion, "There will be mémory" combines a smooth iambic meter with a hard stress on "will," accentuating the certainty of memory's intactness at the base of identity—it is there whenever sought for—but also implying the necessity of human willfulness in actively sustaining the power of the past's hold on the present. He bestows a special blessing on his dead brother Kenneth, asking him for his "promise / To vision orchid uplands under snow" (TB 32), a paradisal vision that resembles, unsurprisingly, the mountain paradise they have known in their youth. Love's nostalgic salve will provide salvation, such as it is:

> Believe me, then: this was and this will be
> And is, my brothers, walking five deep still
> Under the hills and above the valleys
> Blowing your fine, deep laughter in the wind,
> And in the white town talking your intimate talk.
> This is, for love is not lost with the leaves,
> Nor the lovers lost by reasons of departure or arrival. (TB 32)

These final lines display arguably the most telling instance of Scarbrough's faith in the redeeming power of the past to sustain us in the present and future through the exacting repetitions of nostalgic longing: with such deep memory, there is never any love lost "by reasons of departure or arrival." There will be memory, forever and intact. While his tendency toward elegiac nostalgia can sometimes devolve from controlled pathos into bathos, as melancholia turns maudlin, the best of his poems offer a reflective distance that prevents them from degenerating into an uncritical and cloying bittersweetness. In this manner, his verse imbues Tellico Blue with darker bands, ones that gesture meaningfully toward the gray area of nostalgia's twinned purpose.

Although his poetry shows stylistic range—his first two books, *Zirconia Poems* (1969) and *Red Owl* (1972), are characterized by condensed, impressionistic poems that "sometimes eschew complete sentences in favor of staccato fragments" (West 78)—with the publication of *Topsoil Road* (2000) Robert Morgan[7] embraces the mantle of formalist. The subject matter of the volume returns home as well, recording western North Carolina mountain scenes that evoke the remembered landscapes of a more peaceful and rooted Appalachia as a backdrop. Morgan sometimes invokes nostalgia as mood in reconstructing his native land as a rural retreat, though this may turn attention away from the subregion's pressing socio-economic disparities. However, as the son of a small-farm owner, he is conscious of the struggles of the rural working class in these mountains, an awareness that shows up especially in his early verse. The second part of Morgan's *Topsoil Road* verses us in country things, connecting us to rural labor and knowledge, such as how to sharpen a saw ("Sharpening a Saw"), why a crow string scares crows ("Crow String"), and how to derive the medicinal power of a madstone drawn from a deer's belly ("Madstone"). Often Morgan's small wonders of nature appear primarily as objects of nostalgia for the purity of the natural realm. They become signifiers of a resistant neopastoralism that is typically coupled with rigorous attention to the metapoetic capacity of his poems, although Morgan is not concerned here with exploring the constructedness of nostalgic longing itself. The poems of *Topsoil Road* form a series of narrative vignettes, cloaked in deceptively plain language with foregrounded moments of lyricism. "Signal Fires," for instance, begins with a prose-like opening sentence—

> At Long Rock you still see the holes
> made by fires the Cherokees lit
> there, now pots filled with rain like
> cisterns, where the bonflames roared as
> messages sent mountaintop to
> mountaintop all the way from first
> foothills to Pinnacle on to
> Pisgah, to the Smokies and into
> Tennessee. (2)

—yet concludes with an aesthetic flourish: "the mountains tipped articulate / above the tangled trails and creeks, / across black and multiplying peaks" (2). This interspersing of straightforward passages with punctuated moments of lyrical, overtly metaphoric language is further inflected by Morgan's occasional use of vernacular diction and tone. Many of the short poems add to the list of objects of nostalgia: for the displaced Native American inhabitants of Appalachia ("Attakullakulla Goes to London" and "Signal Fires"); for the compromised ecologies of the American and southern wilderness ("Girdling" and "Wild Peavines"); for regional folkways ("Thrush Doctor," "Fever Wit," and "Sanghoe"); for once natural, now tourist landmarks ("Blowing Rock"), for community ("Squatting"); for kinship ties, especially father-figures ("Care," "Working in the Rain," "Mowing," and "Besom"); for family heirlooms ("Polishing the Silver" and "The Family Bible"); for old topsoil roads ("Topsoil Road"); for the homeplace ("Outbuildings" and "Hearth"); for mountain music ("History's Madrigal," "Tail Music," "Mountain Dulcimer," and "The Grain of Sound"); and for the things of nature, more small than great ("June Bug," "Oxbow Lakes," and "Wind Rider").

"The Blue Hole" contains an account of how restorative nostalgia seeks to stop, temporarily, the flow of time by finding the equivalent of a deep blue pool to hole up in:

> The deepest pool in Green River,
> the Blue Hole under Fish-top Falls,
> never revealed its depths even
> in drought. On brightest days its hue
> stayed dark as thunder, still as
> memory. Once, every year the eels
> appeared here, hundreds of slippery
> whips seething. And cove people took
> them in nets, with hooks and pitchforks,
> took them with dooms of dynamite,
> bushels of glistening spawners that
> had come back to Green River up
> the Broad, up the Pacolet, up
> the Cooper, from the Atlantic
> all the way from the Sargasso Sea
> to trouble waters of this hole
> below the falls where they had hatched
> as elvers and kept the memory
> of the birth waters. The path of
> return's now closed by the dam at
> Lake Adger, dammed by Lake Moultrie
> and Lake Marion, the ancient

long communication broken
between local pool, high ocean. (12)

This is perhaps the most lyrical poem in the book: the eels are metaphorically transformed into an alliterative mass of "slippery / whips seething" and the system of tributaries becomes an "ancient / long communication broken." "The Blue Hole" self-consciously implies the way in which mood nostalgia pools up the fluid movement of the past, trading flux for depth. Memory is figured as a static process, there waiting for you to recover it and thereby yourself, for the deepest pool in the Green River is "still as / memory." In contrast to Charles Wright, who describes memory as a highly shifting, ephemeral force, or Yusef Komunyakaa, who emphasizes the volatile, disintegrating quality of traumatic remembering, "The Blue Hole" invokes memory as a means of recovering the past by stopping time in place. Nature is the model for stability, and we should draw from its steadying power. Yet Morgan also implies that the path of return to a neopastoral vision of the South is now under threat from the potentially damning series of encroaching dams that mar and transform the indigenous ecology. "The Blue Hole" thus opens up some distance from its description of the process of restorative nostalgia, pointing to the creation of artificial lakes that disrupt the timeless flow of the natural world.

"Hearth" and "Outbuildings" evoke nostalgia for the homeplace; however, they offer differing takes on their own repetition of this past convention. "Hearth" seems to be predicated on the commonplace that home is where the hearth is. Even though the old homestead has fallen into disrepair, with only the chimney left standing, it remains still, and always, the houseplace:

> Only the chimney is standing
> at the houseplace in the meadow,
> fieldstone set on fieldstone, flush,
> and scoured by rain and thaw of soot.

> At the houseplace in the meadow
> grass is rising in the fireplace, lush,
> and scoured by rain and thaw of soot.
> Licked by wind it leaps off the hearth,

> grass rising in the fireplace lush,
> and reaches up the chimney's throat;

licked by wind it leaps off the hearth,
kindling in the afternoon sun,

and reaches up the chimney's throat,
bending in the dance of rooted things,
kindling in the afternoon sun.
And bees have found a clover there

bending in the dance of rooted things
where the honey of flames was.
And bees have found a clover there
to sweeten the darkest parlor

where the honey of flames was,
fieldstone set on fieldstone, flush,
to sweeten the darkest parlor.
Only the chimney is standing. (28)

The heavy repetition of the pantoum—the second and fourth lines becoming the first and third lines of the succeeding stanza—reflects an equally fixed stability of place, the structure itself paralleling nostalgia's many returns. There is an overriding sense of rootedness, which connotes a sustained nostalgia for placefulness. It is a ruined site, but all the more beautiful—that is, all the more natural—for its being lost to all but memory: nostalgia's "honey of flames" sweetens even the darkest parlor. The chimney is still left standing at the end, forming a set place for a lasting memory, an Appalachian Tintern Abbey. In "Outbuildings," Morgan presents another view of the pastoral houseplace, but this time the traditional structures of the agrarian past are handled with a rougher touch:

First the woodshed with its overhanging
brim and bin of kindling sticks that burn
a cool incense of seasoning. And then
the outhouse with its intimate shadows
off to one side among the pokeweeds, flower beds.
And the chicken house with its floor of acrid
chalk and dusts that crawl in all directions.
The cloth of wire fence hangs behind the clothesline.

The barn shoulders high above the tackle
and gear of the harness room, above the sweet
herbs and shucks of fodder. Beyond the salty
dark of smokehouse and whispery gloom of springhouse,
the chicken coops and hogpen, the tool shed with its
rust assortments, points and dirty planters,
behind the corncrib and molasses shed,
to the final outpost of the homeplace,
on a poplar at the wood's edge, stares
the birdhouse with its one big eye where
unsettled land touches unsettled land. (9)

This visit to the farm supplies more than a peaceful, easy agrarian vista, probing beyond a nostalgic cartography of the homeplace, which seems to have come uncentered, spread thin into upwards of a dozen countrified constructions, from the woodshed all the way to the birdhouse. The various minor structures viewed on this whirlwind tour of a now outstripped farm redistribute the symbolic weight of Ransom's monumentalist structure in "Old Mansion," scattering the Fugitive ethos into something that begins to look like a *contragrarian* landscape of the poor, rural South. The outbuildings end in wilderness, one of the few places left where "unsettled land touches unsettled land." The homeplace is self-consciously described as a final outpost for rural nostalgia, one that seems about to be overtaken by time's creeping desolation.

Morgan's sense of the two-sided ethos of nostalgia is reiterated in "Atomic Age," which records a sought-for rerooting of collective memory in the rich Appalachian loam:

In yards and medians of interstates,
on grounds of factories and hospitals
in Atlanta, Charlotte, Memphis, Nashville,
see patches of Green River soil. For each
boxwood and sparkling pine, every dogwood
and maple from a nursery here, goes with
its ball of mountain dirt to the new bed.
Every rhododendron must keep its roots
in Blue Ridge loam. And while the loam
is scattered in clots of gunpowder black
all over the South, the topsoil in these
mountain coves gets thinner, pocked as sponges,

fissioned to the suburbs, cities, greasy
savings of centuries of leaf rot, forest mold
nursed by summit fogs and isolation,
sold to decorate the cities of the plain. (17)

If the poem contains elements of nostalgic lament for the loss of root-deep con-
nection to place, it also confronts the thinning of the autochthonous ideal as
a result of increasing (sub)urbanization and Americanization in the catalog of
New South urban centers. Even as the poem longs for something deeper than
the mere surface connections fostered by the contemporary condition, for a
sense of communal and natural relatedness that presses beneath the topsoil,
Morgan appears painfully aware that at times nostalgia can be a form of (home)
sickness, not a cure.

· · ● ● ● ● · ·

The acutely self-reflexive representation of nostalgia in the poetry of Donald
Justice[8] extends Scarbrough's and Morgan's inchoate reckoning of nostalgia as
a means to reflection, stretching the process of memory out to an airy thin-
ness.[9] Generally avoiding a facile acceptance of the restorative capacity of nos-
talgia to create, in the words of "Nostalgia of the Lakefronts" (1987), "the world
we run to from the world" (160), his poetry offers a devastating sense of our
radical disconnection from the past. For Justice, man's misfortune lies not in
his being time bound, as Jean-Paul Sartre suggested, but in being unbound
from time. Even if the psychological cycle of would-be nostalgia continues, pro-
ducing many returns to the scenes of yesterday, there is little in it to comfort
us. Much of Justice's poetic output is properly read as an expression of metanos-
talgia: nostalgia for the process of nostalgia itself. His verse therefore reflects
Stewart's sense of an increasingly abstract version of nostalgic longing:

> Nostalgia is a sadness without an object, a sadness which creates
> a longing that of necessity is inauthentic because it does not take
> part in lived experience. Rather, it remains behind and before
> that experience. Nostalgia, like any form of narrative, is always
> ideological: the past it seeks has never existed except as narrative,
> and hence, always absent, that past continually threatens to repro-
> duce itself as a felt lack. (*On Longing* 23)

Justice extracts the desire for *nostos* into an absorbing, objectless lack, showing
that the deepest ache of *algia* resides in the awareness of the impossibility of

ever living again in the past. The deconstructive ethos of his poems borders on a cultural critique of mode nostalgia and its hollow repetitions of concretized styles. Exploiting formal distance from the past to expose the clichéd nature of overmuch longing for better days, his work points up the fissures in the façade of traditional nostalgia.

A pure poet, Justice makes use of an evocative poetics of abstraction in combination with a singular brand of formalism that involves an adept reworking of venerated forms. His poems create remarkably intricate metrical and rhyme schemes, although these repetitions often come so naturally that the reader can be taken off guard at first and must reread to grasp the larger pattern, as if examining an elaborate mosaic from too close up. As a consequence of his mastery of verse forms, Justice shows a peculiar acumen for pressing out beauty from sadness, a tendency explicitly dramatized in "Sadness" (1995): "Sadness has its own beauty, of course" (24). In its sheer self-referentiality, this line displays a burgeoning sense of nostalgia as mode, the "of course" signaling the transparency of the nostalgic drive to restore beauty to loss. This more critical understanding of nostalgia is evident in the sentiment from "Poem" (1973) that the past "is not sad, really, only empty" (106), which serves as a pointed reminder that, when one strips the veneer of facile romanticization from restorative nostalgia, we are left not with an auratic melancholy, but with an almost unbearable emptiness. Pressing deep within the act of binding together *nostos* and *algia*, only to find the process hollow at its core, Justice's poetry invokes this feeling as a means of structuring the profound nothingness of the past. Even as he elegizes the death of a friend or family member or laments the lost innocence of his childhood, his poems cast a weary eye on redemptively melancholic moods, implicitly acknowledging the absence of "transcendental anchorage" (Frow 125) between a culture and its physical setting; according to his metanostalgic ethos, redemption is a thing of the past. He often recoils as he recalls, calling attention to the shabbiness of his personal past, his memories being typically marked with a sense of unease at his lower-middle-class origins, at his unauratic South.[10]

The self-reflexively titled "Poem" is an exercise in almost pure abstraction and thereby serves as an *ars poetica* for Justice's poetics of metanostalgia. As Justice is a poet's poet, this is a poem's poem. A series of wholly hypothetical conjectures, it nonetheless offers a substantial critique of elegiac nostalgia's tendency to revel in maudlin overtones:

> This poem is not addressed to you.
> You may come into it briefly,

But no one will find you here, no one.
You will have changed before the poem will.

Even while you sit there, unmovable,
You have begun to vanish. And it does not matter.
The poem will go on without you.
It has the spurious glamor of certain voids.

It is not sad, really, only empty.
Once perhaps it was sad, no one knows why.
It prefers to remember nothing.
Nostalgias were peeled from it long ago. (106)

The poem replaces the self-indulgence of melancholic nostalgia with "the spu-rious glamor of certain voids," sadness with metaphysical emptiness. The cli-chéd "glamor" of conventional elegy is exposed as counterfeit sorrow, spurious gloom; the sentimental posturing of Romantic nostalgia, its decadent voids which have become all too certain through poetic overuse, are voided out by Justice's "Poem." As the nostalgic anchorage of the past disappears, however, so does identity, since "no one will find you here, no one" and "Even while you sit there, unmovable, / You have begun to vanish. And it does not matter" (106). Peeling all nostalgias from the past is the equivalent of remembering nothing, thus reflecting the amnesiac state of nostalgia as mode, pointing to the empti-ness of parodic reiteration itself. Sadness at least offers a level of comfort, a stabilizing sense of loss, but emptiness carries a nonsustaining power, for "there is nothing in it to comfort you" (106). Like a poem, life is most pregnant in its pauses: absence, not presence, is the order of experience. What matters is that the poem, like the past, "has been most beautiful in its erasures": "You will forget the poem, but not before / It has forgotten you. And it does not matter. / It has been most beautiful in its erasures" (106).

This sentiment that the past is most aesthetically intact not in sadness but in its absence is reiterated on the level of form as well as content in the po-em's closing stanza, which presents a mirror of formal perfection that reflects the absences left behind by the desiccation of the restorative function:

O bleached mirrors! Oceans of the drowned!
Nor is one silence equal to another.
And it does not matter what you think.
This poem is not addressed to you. (106)

The bathetic "O," the would-be sign of nostalgic indulgence, is emptied of significance. The "O" becomes a zero on the page, the nothing that is there, which forces us to seek value and meaning in something besides a Byronic picking of the unnamed wound that will not heal. Ironically reflecting the clichés of Romantic nostalgia, which have been all smoothed down and rounded out ("Once perhaps it was sad, no one knows why"), the "O" is itself hollowed out into a mere sound effect, aurally connecting the "O" to the flowing repetition that begins "Oceans of the drowned." The mimetic aspect of verse, its capacity to recapture the past, has been bleached out into the rhythmical pulse and counterpulse of the ocean; mimetic sense yields to the negating sublimity of nonmimetic sound. The rhythm is the most telling aspect of the line, flooding the words with a sense of the ineffable power of poetic recurrence. The line demonstrates not only Justice's controlled formalism and his subtlety of feeling, but also his devoted exploration of metanostalgia's double bind: emptying our lives of nostalgia's palliative presence, though a necessary catharsis, leaves us with exactly nothing.

"Poem" is, as the title implies, a representative work in Justice's oeuvre. While his poems are "essentially elegiac," they possess "a wistfulness devoid of sentimentality" because they are

> occasioned in large part by the emptiness, the *horror vacui*, that
> is one of the faces with which the past confronts consciousness.
> This appalling feature is compounded by nostalgia, which is a
> wish not only for a return of past life, but for that life to be rein-
> stated to its rightful position as the center of the poet's life, the
> lack of which spells the impasse before which the poet's career is
> an endless circling. (Rigsbee and Brown 153)

This unveiling of the *horror vacui* at the base of nostalgic remembrance is evident in "Vague Memory from Childhood" (1995), which evokes an impressionistic nostalgia through associative memories of Justice's southern childhood that are engulfed in shadows, blurring into abstraction:

> It was the end of the day—
> Vast far clouds
> In the zenith darkening
> At the end of day.

The voices of my aunts
Sounded through an open window.
Bird-speech cantankerous in a high tree mingled
    With the voices of my aunts.

    I was playing alone,
Caught up in a sort of dream,
With sticks and twigs pretending,
    Playing there alone

    In the dust.
And a lamp came on indoors,
Printing a frail gold geometry
    On the dust.

    Shadows came engulfing
The great charmed sycamore.
It was the end of day.
    Shadows came engulfing. (10)

The poet's memory, in traditional southern fashion, focuses on the family. Instead of offering meaningful interaction, however, the voices of his aunts point up the opposite, stressing the boy's isolation from the family and the poet's later estrangement from his own past. The impressionistic quality of the poem gives the sense that it is a loosely connected list of objects invested with nostalgic attachment: the end of day, the voices of aunts, the bird-speech in the trees, remembering oneself as a child alone at play in the backyard, the lamp that comes on indoors and lights the way into the home, the shadows that collect over the yard, the great charmed sycamore. The poem traffics in metanostalgic remembrance of things past, with an emphasis on the things themselves, which conceal a deeper emptiness: as the material objects pile up, their meaning becomes increasingly ephemeral and abstract until the weight of nostalgia is assumed into "a frail gold geometry / On the dust." The repetition of the lines suggests the weariness of nostalgia's many returns, which are never complete. Through this heavy formal repetition, the poem breathes exhaustion: nostalgia has seen better days, its zenith darkening. "Vague Memory from Childhood" thus provides a pointed vision of nostalgia *for* nostalgia, recalling the impossibility of genuine reconnection with a living past.[11]

"The Miami of Other Days" (1995) is another of Justice's more recent poems that evoke a lyrical metanostalgia for other days, recalling a more traditionally "southern" Miami before it was transformed into an ethnically diverse, international city:

> The city was not yet itself. It had,
> In those days, the simplicity of dawn.
> As for the bonfires up and down the beach,
> They were nostalgias for the lights of cities
> Left behind; and often there would be
> Dancing by firelight to the new white jazz
> Of a Victrola on its towel in the sand. (11)

The lines offer a prelapsarian vision of Miami when it still had "In those days, the simplicity of dawn" before it entered into the American imagination as a multivalent cultural space with distinctive gay, Cuban, and drug subcultures—before the pop image of the city produced by mass culture, from *Miami Vice* to *The Bird Cage* to Will Smith and LeBron James. The figure of the bonfires as nostalgias points up the overriding concern of the poem, as it peels back nostalgias for a time and a place where the overly crowded lights of cities could still be "Left behind." Through this metaphor, Justice reflectively signifies on unreflective nostalgia's means of creating a place of retreat from the increasing urbanization and ethnic hybridity of the New South by constructing this simpler Miami as a holding point. While the Victrola might seem to serve as a simple object of a straight nostalgia, its repetitive, wheeling motion implies something of metanostalgia's circling back around and around the lack at the center of the past.

The poem incorporates several of the commonplaces of southern literature, invoking kinship ("my own people"), community (gathering for news at the old post office) and the oral tradition (news travels by word of mouth), all founded on a stable sense of home: "And crackers down from Georgia (my own people) / Foregathered on the old post office steps, / A sort of club, exchanging news from home" (11). However, Justice colors this down-home scene with a shade of self-deprecating irony. Instead of claiming a distinguished heritage, he admits kinship with "crackers down from Georgia," reversing the tradition of ancestor worship: in place of the venerated "first families of Virginia," Justice gives us his connection to some of the last families of Georgia. The poem's sense of "home" is also balanced by the mention of "the foreign language spoken" amid the downtown shops (11), suggesting the coming transformation of

Miami into an ethnically diverse urban center. He then describes the task of throwaway sidewalk photographers as a much-diminished form of historic preservation: "and there were sidewalk / Photographers with alligator props / Who disappeared a dozen times a day / Under the black hood of their trade—preservers!" (11). With their false alligator props, they are "preservers" of the past, yet they do so not out of piety, but merely to turn a dollar. Under the black hood of their trade, the auratic value of the antiquarian past disappears, and mood nostalgia is flattened out into the depthlessness and instant marketability of nostalgia as mode. Their photographs provide little more than cheap mementos of an ephemeral past, fleeting souvenirs that remind us that a simpleminded nostalgia simply will not last. The kitsch of these sidewalk non-artists trades on the ahistoricity of the past, for their photos squeeze history out of the frame: after terming the sidewalk photographers "preservers," Justice states bluntly, "But there was no history" (12), no larger narrative pattern that imbues these cut-rate and transient snapshots with sustained meaning. The poem's closing lines begin to break the spell of restorative nostalgia that surrounds that "Magic City":

> Nor was the spell that held the city—invisible cloud—
> Ever in those days wholly to be lifted.
> O "Magic City" of my eighth-grade speech!
> Aquarium of the little grounded yacht!
> Bandshell of gardenia moons!
> And Dr. Seward, astronomer, tipping his tall hat
> (Like a magician's) nightly to the stars
> And to little scatterings of applause still circling maybe
> Out there somewhere in the circuits of the lost. (12)

The spell that held the city in those days is the invisible cloud of nostalgia, which has yet to be wholly lifted. The overstated "O 'Magic City'" drips with a minor pathos bordering on bathos, signaled once more by Justice's invocation of the hollow "O," as he again gently punctures his own nostalgic tendencies. The "gardenia moons" painted on the bandshell make a mockery of the worn-out and evasive "moonlight-and-magnolias" brand of nostalgia-laden southern writing. Overmuch devotion to nostalgia's recyclings, Justice warns us, leaves us forever circling "Out there somewhere in the circuits of the lost." In this manner, he implies that his remembered South has already been voided of its spurious glamor, leaving an unshakable nothingness in its wake.

· · · ✦ ✦ ✦ · ·

Akin to Justice, Betty Adcock[12] also describes the process of metanostalgia in her poems, many of which chronicle an absence at the heart of memory. At times, her verse lapses into some of the commonplaces of traditional southern literature, placing a sheen of *nostos* over things like kinship, churchgoing, and the hardscrabble yet artful lives of "the poor-white South," as in "Louisiana Line" (1975), which implies that places can keep the past intact ("The wooden scent of wagons, / the sweat of animals—the places / keep everything—breath of the cotton gin, / black damp floors of the icehouse" [67]), or "Intervale" (2001), her paean to Sacred Harp music:

> In pockets of the poor-white South,
> in Primitive Baptist churches, pure delight
> and grief in equal streams flowed straight
> toward heaven, a preview of the crossing over
> all would make. Workhorses, such churches
> were plain-boarded, offering the simplest
> backless benches to the sore afraid,
> to the lonely and the praiseful to come to sing. (5)

And yet Adcock's nostalgia is rarely unqualified. There is a rough grain to the objects she uses to construct her vision of the past; the pure delight and grief we hear flowing in equal streams in the Sacred Harp chorus is interrupted by buzzing, rippling, roughness, and hard breaks:

> Always one yellowjacket buzzed against
> a rippled windowpane. Always the rough
> grain of the walls held stories
> children could guess at while the old songs broke
> hard as a storm at sea above their heads. (5)

Just as often, Adcock's poetry reflects the *horror vacui* of metanostalgic remembrance.

In a number of her poems, Adcock uses the conceptual terrain of the American South as the specific backdrop for her metanostalgic riffs, but most often region is not a monolithic, foundational entity, but more like a metaphoric green screen for reinventing the past. In "New South" (1995), for instance, we peek behind the curtain of a faux South. Instead of a region of stark belatedness, per traditional visions of southern exceptionalism, we see a space of sheer pastlessness, a suburban subdivision like anywhere, everywhere else:

"This neighborhood is all those natural-seeming / yards that cost so much to keep them seeming / natural" (148). Memories of the dead neither haunt the No South nor anchor it in "realness":

> Sometimes I remember there are no graveyards here,
> no stone angels standing on the dead,
> ready to take to the air but staying.
> Noboby seems to *be* dead. Where are they?
> If they were ever here it isn't mentioned. (148)

This "New South" is a repository of "*nostalgia* tacky as polyester," where we know "the past's not real. And never was, somebody said" (149). Cultural memory becomes almost infinitely malleable, shorn from the illusion of strict reference: "You can hang it up one way (like Williamsburg) / as what you want. Or hang it another way / as what you fear. Either one will change" (149). She then makes a transnational leap to consider the explicitly inauthentic manipulation of Australian Aboriginal art, connecting the U.S. South (the gleaming red-brick and theme-park ethos of "Colonial" Williamsburg) to the global South, a motif that courses through her poems, particularly through images of Southeast Asia and China, the country of origin of her adopted granddaughter: "Once I saw a Native Australian sand painting / reduced to manageable size, made permanent / with glue or canvas so we could take them in" (149). The transcultural crossing continues in the final stanza, in which the speaker feels in transit between Europe and Texas:

> Lately I've not been quite sure
> what ground I'm standing on. As if I'd waked
> in Belgium after starting out for Beaumont—
> and with this hurtful worry, a kind of sickness
> for things changed or missing, things that pass,
> the air around me thick and still. Like glass. (149)

The speaker is moving on unsure ground, migrating somewhere in the in-between from Beaumont to Belgium. The sickness for things changed or missing is of course nostalgia, but there is clear awareness that this stultifies the past, converting the shifting, insubstantial air into a falsely tangible substance: it thickens and stills the frenetic transferal of time. This kind of nostalgic longing is sickening, and wrongly amberizes the changing past—never the thing itself, but a dark and dull reflection of past times.

In "Penumbra" (2001), Adcock recollects her childhood response to the death of her mother when the poet was six years old. Through her aesthetic re-remembering of her mother's funeral day, she converts trauma into a form of nostalgia slanted towards *algia*, toward the pained recognition that the past can never be fully restored. The shadowy, insubstantial quality of metanostalgia is suggested by the very title of the poem: memory lingers in the penumbral space between conscious recollection and subconscious intimation, a kind of psychic Erebus. She begins by detailing an old photograph of a six-year-old girl holding a pet bantam:

> The child in the cracked photograph sits still
> In the rope swing hung from a live oak.
> Her velvet dress brims with a lace frill.
>
> Her pet Bantam is quiet in her lap. (3)

The ABA form plays against Dante's terza rima, a formal hybridization that further echoes the penumbral motif: these remembered things are shades of their former being, existing only in the afterlife of receding memory. Despite the details, the image displays less the mimetic power of memory than its scattering into impressionistic nodes of colors and sounds:

> Black and white, she is hiding
> in every one of my bright beginnings.
> Gold and deep blue and dark-shining
>
> Red the cockerel's feathers, gold the sun
> in that skyblue southern fall, blue
> over the four o'clocks and the drone
>
> of weeping that drains like a shadow from the house
> where someone is gone, is gone, is gone—
> where the child will stay to darken like a bruise. (3-4)

The tone is elegiac, but abstracted, oddly detached, something that slants the poem's atmosphere away from trauma towards nostalgia: the emotional remainders of her mother's loss will darken like a bruise, a painful, deep condition (*algia*), but not an open wound. The repetition of "is gone" speaks to vacant cyclings of the past. In the closing stanza, we switch from third person to first, but the "I" voice is hollowed out, "cold as winter's breath" (3) and colorless. At the same moment, the poem breaks form, departing from the grounding repetitions of the rhyming tercets:

> I am six years old, buried
> in the colorless album.
> My mother is dead.
> I forgive no one. (4)

The mimetic potential of photography, its purported capacity to capture reality by freezing a moment in time, is no longer working, even on a surface level. The past becomes prosaic, a hollow collection of images as flat as they are monochrome.

The abstract process of memory is echoed in "Final Cut" (2001), which also uses old photographs as a means for reinscribing the detached redundancies of metanostaglia. The poem is a series of associative memories brought to mind by a collection of family photos; however, as the title hints, the poem is less about linking together the disparate images/times through a restorative nostalgia than about the temporal and psychic cuts that keep them separate. We piece together two photos, one of the father, and one of the mother:

> The 1940s: my father's hat
> is rakish, cocky, the way men
> wore hats then, though he is sad,
> is lost. I have to find him.
>
> And my mother: a ghostface
> drifting anchorless in the deepened
> dream I'm flailing through at dawn—
> the mother dead now fifty years
> and I'm the child still fishing for the body.
> Not much to go on. (17)

Though the father looks confident, a model of 1940s "rakish" masculinity, he is really an image of incurable lostness, adrift in the past ("he is sad, / is lost"). The speaker sounds far more desperate than sure of finding her father ("I have to find him"): he is unredeemably past, untouchable. The memory of her mother is darker still, but equally intangible, for she is a "ghostface" drifting in an anchorless past for fifty years, her body lost to all but abstract memory.

These metanostalgic shreds leave us with "Not much to go on," not much of a stable rest frame against which to scale our memories. In the photographs, there is a smattering of things, decontextualized objects (e.g., a pony, sling-shots, makeshift dolls, dogs, antique cars, the hat), that loom out from the blank recesses of the pictures, then fade back, the past delinked from the future, no matter the speaker's efforts:

> I work hard to get it right—camera, lights—
> crank up a day in brown with sunspots,
> antique cars coughing into life, dogs
> forlorn, adrift, that hat holding its tilt,
> faces in the fadeout fading back.
> The future is the part I cannot get. (17–18)

The past doesn't last, as its hints of narrative line dissipate into parts without a whole: "And soon enough the whole thing will shut down— / vowel, cadence, image, rhyme— / like an album closing" (18). Metanostalgic memory encodes a virtual past that is partially downloaded and then gets knocked off-line: "Some intelligent machine / is taking itself off-line" (18). Memories are depthless echoes, shadows of shadows, flickering re-creations ("See the shadows vanish / into reconstructed scenery that vanishes" [18]); the past is "blear-eyed, indifferent, perfectly blank" (18). We end with a ceremony of unknowing, alone and unredeemed, an empty performance: "I've been given some sort of award / There's no one here to thank" (18).

The seasons have long been associated in poetry with nostalgia. Adcock evokes seasonal ambience in poems like "December" (2001) and "January" (2001), but the feel of mood nostalgia is, paradoxically, denaturalized. In "January," nature is a palimpsest, a reflection of erased and overwritten reflections: "Dusk and snow this hour / in argument have settled / nothing" (42). The natural world is unsettling in its unsettledness. Set in nothingness, it is doubled over in self-contradiction, a totally deconstructive force:

> Light persists,
> and darkness. If a star
> shines now, that shine is
> swallowed and given back
> doubled, grounded bright. (42)

From the human vantage, nature is full of false fire ("the small fires of birds / at rest lend absences to seeming absence" [42]), our memories like so many *ignes fatui,* illusionary and without warmth, absences layered on absence. Human divisions emaciate in the "dark and light together," which "toll[s] / against the boundary-riven / houses" (42). Just as memory arbitrarily parcels out the overwhelming volume of the past, the land has been divided, in haphazard and changeable ways, into property lines. In its very nothingness, its ahuman opacity, nature exceeds human visions of the past and identity: "Against our lives, / the stunning wholeness of the world" (42). Nothingness is the wholeness of the world, and the re-created sound bites of memory only divulge the truth of nothing: "Truth is, nothing at all is missing" (42).

◦ ◦ ◦ ◉ ◦ ◦ ◦

In permitting a level of distance from restorative nostalgia's placating narratives, Justice and Adcock serve as transitional figures, revealing a South voided of the straightforward rhetoric of monumentalist and romantic nostalgias. Going beyond this deconstructive ethos, Henry Taylor and Dave Smith display a willingness to create new, more open-ended and discontinuous communities of narrative that signifies what Leo Spitzer terms "critical memory," where nostalgia as historical anesthetic transforms into a more resistant aesthetics. Their backward look is a means no longer of merely looking away from the changing of the present, but also serves—and more powerfully—as a way of looking forward, reenvisioning the present by basing it on a new understanding of the codes of the past. Pressing beyond nostalgia as merely "the temporal equivalent of tourism and the search for the picturesque" (Bal, Crewe, and Spitzer xi), Taylor and Smith refuse to blindly accept nostalgia as "an abdication of personal responsibility, a guilt-free homecoming, an ethical and aesthetic failure" (Boym xiv). By contrast, they turn nostalgic longing into a socially vested act, using it as a way to criticize cultural blindspots, not encourage them. Their work treats nostalgia less as a comforting falsification of the past than as a means toward forming a corrective vision of the present, putting forward "an ethical and creative challenge" (Boym viii) to things as they were—and often are. While moving in the direction of a politically engaged aesthetics of confrontation, their poetry is not as stark or vehement in its challenge to traditional southern memory as the stunningly oppositional narratives engendered by the poetics of countermemory discussed in my final chapter. Where Taylor and Smith expose nostalgia as a culturally operative force, the countermemory poets implode the accepted forms of cultural homesickness. However, Taylor's and Smith's invocation of reflective nostalgia marks a significant shift in southern poetics that opens space for the countermemory poets' perceptive mergings of poetic and political acts of resistant memory.

At a surface level, Taylor,[13] a poet who lived nearly all of his life in Virginia in the same town where he was born, might seem to be working the same poetic field that has been already overcultivated, plowing in a rut, as defined by the modes of traditional southern poetry: he is an avowed formalist, he writes narrative poems, he often uses a conversational voice, his poems are connected to place, he often focuses on community and family ties, and he is concerned with nostalgic memory.[14] While he is occasionally prone to drifting off into mood nostalgia, Taylor is typically self-aware concerning his invocation of the past, offering a more clear-sighted view of southern history in general and of the history of southern poetry in particular. Honestly investigating some of the less favorable and limiting aspects of devotion to the past, he is deeply suspicious of the old southern mannerisms, yet he chooses to work within these lines. "Wineberries," a poem from The Flying Change, figures Taylor as one of the current southern poets who are "opening the field" (49), though he does feel some pang of nostalgia for the "something worth keeping" (49) that will be left behind after the clearing is done. Taylor's sense of irony is clear at the start of "Kingston Trio, 1982," which wryly proclaims, "Nostalgia freaks unite" (32). Rather than providing a rallying cry for preservationists, the line parodies the freakishness of overweening dedication to a lost past, in this instance based on nostalgia for a folk band now fallen out of fashion. In moving the poetics of nostalgia in the direction of ironic self-consciousness, The Flying Change reflects a flying change for the history of southern poetry, like a horse transitioning in mid-stride and changing leads, into a more fluid vision of the future. Taylor's verse marks a shift from restorative nostalgia to a more critical stance that takes the blinders off the penchant for mooning over a lost and beautiful past. His critique of how racial turmoil has been whited out of much postwar southern poetry shows how the pastoral ideal may carry within it the germ of its own infection; in Taylor, nostalgia can seem more a chronic disease than a requiem mass for a once-vital South.

The pastoral impulse, portrayed in relatively straightforward terms in poems like "As on a Darkling Plain" and "Projectile Point, Circa 2500 B.C.," is overturned in "Heartburn," one of a series of poems in The Flying Change that offer an antipastoral view of rural experience in the South. The title itself gives a biting rejoinder to the heartwarming bent of nostalgia: too much heartwarming leads to heartburn. Awakened in the night by a literal dose of heartburn, the speaker tries to dispel it by taking a short walk down the driveway and having a look around the property and surrounding Virginia mountainsides, when he is struck by a markedly unnostalgic memory:

> Not far,
> yet as bright as it looms, you remember that right here
> a black cow has been lying dead
> for weeks at the foot of the bank
>
> below the drive, having
> fallen down into the stream
> when a section of the stone culvert caved in,
> and the rock that pins her is bound
> to weigh over a ton, so she'll
> be there, pulsating with maggots, drawing the local
> vermin out of the woods, until
> someday the bones are clean enough
>
> to pick up and ponder. (18–19)

The figure of the decaying cow provides a telling allegory for the cultural work of nostalgia. The material reality of the past, its conflicts, exacerbations, and uncertainties, must rot away before nostalgia can come in to pick up and ponder the time-cleaned bones, now beautified in their abstract detachment from the visceral mess of lived experience. In this case, what is familiar is not comforting:

> It is only farm death,
> the sound and smell you've known all your life.
> Still, you indulge
> for a few moments the notion
> that one day you too might end up
>
> with your head in a creek,
> under a rock, crushed into
> the earth you once found other ways of wishing
> to merge with. (19)

The pastoral ideal of merging in harmony with the landscape is hereby crushed. This motif of antipastoral animal death appears as well in the sonnet "Sick in

Soul and Body Both," in which the speaker ironically merges with a bull, both of them sharing equally antinostalgic sentiments:

> His brain was small
> but he knew one thing: all he wanted to do
> was kill me. Men mean pain. And what I knew
> was, it can work both ways. I wanted to shoot
> that fucker, just to see him jump and fall. (34)

And, more brutally, in "Barbed Wire":

> One summer afternoon when nothing much
> was happening, they were standing around
> a tractor beside the barn while a horse
> in the field poked his head between two strands
> of the barbed-wire fenced to get at the grass
> along the lane, when it happened—something
>
> they passed around the wood stove late at night
> for years, but never could explain—someone
> may have dropped a wrench into the toolbox
> or made a sudden move, or merely thought
> what might happen if the horse got scared, and
> then he did get scared, jumped sideways and ran
>
> down the fence line, leaving chunks of his throat
> skin and hair on every barb for ten feet
> before he pulled free and ran a short way
> into the field, stopped and planted his hoofs
> wide apart like a sawhorse, hung his head
> down as if to watch his blood running out,
>
> almost as if he were about to speak
> to them, who almost thought he could regret
> that he no longer had the strength to stand
> then shuddered to his knees, fell on his side,
> and gave up breathing while the dripping wire
> hummed like a bowstring in the splintered air. (37)

This is one of several poems that offer "a Hardyesque meditation on the violent and brutal realities that lurk just beneath the surface of apparently benign phenomena" (Sharp 63). The "sawhorse" simile becomes grotesquely real, as we witness the animate passing morbidly into the inanimate. The poem exchanges pastoral beauty for animalistic brutality, pointing to the divide between human consciousness of the past, our capacity for nostalgic regret, and the horse's dark parody of "regret." The lines' driving iambic pentameter likewise hums like a bowstring in the splintered air, bleakly plying its strength against the grim and bloody images, and ending abruptly as life ends, leaving an intense silent void. Taylor thus dispels the haze of nostalgic commemoration surrounding the pastoral ideal; he must splinter the air in order to clear it.

In "Landscape with Tractor," Taylor's antipastoral streak returns us to the world of contemporary social reality, exposing southern poetry's tendency to use nostalgia to obscure unsettling racial divisions that persist in the present South. The poem is written in the second person in order to make the reader an active party in the events described and therefore heighten our sense of social responsibility. Though not propagandistic, "Landscape with Tractor" is certainly a political poem. It begins by envisioning what looks to be another peaceful retreat:

> How would it be if you took yourself off
> to a house set well back from a dirt road,
> with, say, three acres of grass bounded
> by road, driveway, and vegetable garden?
>
> Spring and summer you would mow the field,
> not down to lawn, but with a bushhog,
> every six weeks or so, just often enough
> to give grass a chance, and keep weeds down.
>
> And one day—call it August, hot, a storm
> recently past, things green and growing a bit,
> and you're mowing, with half your mind
> on something you'd rather be doing, or did once. (3)

It seems as if we are about to be given over to a nostalgic whim, half-remembering something we would rather be doing, or did once. The poem's commingling of metrical with seasonal repetitions gives a grounding force to the work, promising the constancy of routine in a familiar space: the land and our regular obligations to it hold memory in place. However, this proto-nostalgic sentiment is stopped short:

> Three rounds, and then on the straight
> alongside the road, maybe three swaths in
> from where you are now, you glimpse it. People
> will toss all kinds of crap from their cars.
>
> It's a clothing-store dummy, for God's sake.
> Another two rounds, and you'll have to stop,
> contend with it, at least pull it off to one side.
> You keep going. Two rounds more, then down
>
> off the tractor, and Christ! Not a dummy, a corpse.
> The field tilts, whirls, then steadies as you run.
> Telephone. Sirens. Two local doctors use pitchforks
> to turn the body, some four days dead, and ripening.
>
> And the cause of death no mystery: two bullet holes
> in the breast of a well-dressed black woman
> in perhaps her mid-thirties. They wrap her,
> take her away. You take the rest of the day off. (3)

With this image of a murdered black woman, the field tilts away from nostalgia and toward the disorienting experience of trauma. That the corpse is of "a well-dressed black woman" inverts the typical—and implicitly racist—expectation that a black murder victim would not be respectable, the lack of respectability helping to explain away the inexplicability of violent death: one assumes that the woman was not someone, but no one, and her anonymity makes her in some twisted sense complicit in her own murder. The field is now haunted, a grotesquely embodied site of post-traumatic memory. The formerly comforting redundancies yield to the implacable sight of death's spoiled remnants in the swirling repetitions of bluebottle flies:

> Next day, you go back to the field, having
> to mow over the damp dent in the tall grass
> where bluebottle flies are still swirling,
> but the bushhog disperses them, and all traces.

Weeks pass. You hear at the post office
that no one comes forward to say who she was.
Brought out from the city, they guess, and dumped
like a bag of beer cans. She was someone,

and now is no one, buried or burned
or dissected; but gone. And I ask you
again, how would it be? To go on with your life,
putting gas in the tractor, keeping down thistles,

and seeing, each time you pass that spot,
the form in the grass, the bright yellow skirt,
black shoes, the thing not quite like a face
whose gaze blasted past you at nothing

when the doctors heaved her over? To wonder,
from now on, what dope deal, betrayal,
or innocent refusal, brought her here,
and to know she will stay in that field till you die? (3-4)

As the speaker re-poses the now crushingly rhetorical question "how would it be?" the implied transition moves from what we *would* do (the poetic imagination/will) to what we *should* do (the moral imagination/judgment) in terms of addressing the imbalances of power in the still racially conflicted U.S. South. Like the speaker, we are left groping for answers, inventing narratives to seal up the break caused by this unredeemed figure of death. The poem does not answer its own question, but brings the issue of race into the realm of critical discussion, providing an avenue for examining the historical conditions that have changed the cultural geography of the region and the nation. Taylor's investigation of the nostalgia paradigm brings us to a place where one realizes that "to value sameness or stability is not tantamount to rejecting difference or resisting adjustment" (Ritivoi 10), thereby divulging the ethical value of remembering, its potential to link social others in politically responsive ways.

• ◦ ◉ ◉ ◉ ◦ •

Like Taylor, Dave Smith[15] points up the critical limitations of faith in a fully redemptive nostalgia. Invoking a steadily anti-antiquarian sentiment, Smith refuses to use his memories of the South as wistful mood music that drowns out the real and sustained conflicts of contemporary southern culture. His poetry exposes southerners' sometimes painlessly nostalgic aversion to their own painful history. In her review of *The Wick of Memory* (2000), Helen Vendler views Smith as a poet who connects neatly with the traditional tropes of southern literature. She polls two of her friends from down South about what is distinctive about southern writing, and gets predictable results: one offers "rural life" and the other says "oratory." To this exhausted but unexhaustive list, Vendler adds "the Civil War" and "the question of race" and then proposes Smith as the quintessence of this tradition of southern belles lettres: "All of these can be found in the poetry of Dave Smith, a poet born in Virginia" (44). She suggests that his poems "will do, for the time being, as a source by which a Northerner, long attached to Smith's poetry, can perhaps explain its success in conveying to her a life so different from her own" (44). It is true that Smith "defines himself by region and by history" (44); however, he does so precisely by resisting outmoded definitions of his region and its history, such as the very ones that Vendler's review uncritically replicates. She begins by placing Smith as one of those contemporary white, male poets who is nostalgic for the nostalgia-induced vision of the South as pastoral safe haven. Although Smith acknowledges his attachment to the landscapes of the South,[16] Vendler is closer to the mark when she notes his turn to satire with the publication of *Fate's Kite* (1996): "And the lassitude of middle age is accompanied in *Fate's Kite* by harsh satire of the South—a region no longer, for Smith, a receptacle chiefly for elegiac sorrow or nostalgia" (46). Smith was not suddenly converted to satire, but has integrated ironic strains throughout his career. His nostalgia is aware of what it is shading out from view, always accompanied by a nagging sense of guilt—particularly over the complexities of the South's racial history—and a pointed level of self-parody.

Smith's most substantial critique of the restorative mythos of the southern past occurs in *Gray Soldiers* (1984), a reassessment of the traditional veneration of the Lost Cause and its continuing legacy of defeat, which for many white southerners, including writers, has been raised to an object of nostalgic monumentalism. In "Photograph of a Confederate Soldier Standing on Rocks in the James River at Richmond," Smith makes use of a loose pentameter to describe a photographic memento from the Civil War, a still frame of southern history:

> A light rises,
> falls, floats around the frame, a kind
> of water swirling through generations
> of years, pooling and shining when we look
> at oblique corners, a given-back glimmer of one

come from a thatch of hickory heaving of the home-field
still in his head, this boy turned in the sun's
stunned spilling where the river is
bristly as bayonets rippling, one
hung in light like a leaf above lipping dark,
the hem of his greatcoat outflung. (102)

Not unlike the light that swirls like water through generations, this photograph of a C.S.A. warrior represents the presumed interconnectedness of southern culture, picturing the stabilizing presence of the past in the present and suggesting that white southerners share an inheritance of defeat across the generations. The light is shining with the glow of nostalgia as the remembered home-field remains fixed in the soldier's head, "a given-back glimmer of one / come from a thatch of hickory heaving the home-field / still in his head" (102). The speaker then projects further moments of nostalgic memory onto this figure, though he admits that he may be willfully misreading the scene toward his own ends, eliding potential signs of fear under a dreamy haze of nostalgia:

We think he may dream of days the acorns
shelled down through yellow leafburst,
or mother's hand on him because in pools
the brackish bluegills would not
let him go home on time. Why
do we not think of a throat's thick fear?
Can fear be that shining on his face? (102)

Nostalgia for autumn's beauty, for home, for mother's touch—it is all there, but nothing of fear, since this does not sit well with the traditional southern glorification of the Rebel troop. The opening phrase, "We think," foregrounds the constructedness of this nostalgic overlay of the past. The succeeding lines complete a sequence of metonymic plays on the connotations of "fall," from the fall of Richmond to fall as autumn to a fusion of the two meanings in the pun on "Fall's glory": "Maybe / Fall's glory / that must be in each thread of the sorry homespun / he has taken through a toil of sun somehow / lets loose, leaves him alone" (102). As a result of this symbolic adjacency, the remembered radiance of autumnal glory gives way to the imagined glory of the Lost Cause, to nostalgia for the image of the steadfast Confederate soldier going down in defeat. In the poem's concluding lines, the speaker admits he has imposed an expression of nostalgic longing onto the soldier's "expressionless" face:

Expressionless, he seeks us,
one-eyed, an eyepatch rampant over the left shoulder,
the right eye dark as a wound, and he cannot see
all the light in the world holds us to him,
all we are, the uncreated future,
the image
which begins here as one apprehension
in the nerves of men, the secret
bond we almost know in that
instant we turn and lift ourselves
from the black river-roar and light-swarm. (103)

Nostalgia begins to resemble the memory of trauma in the soldier's rampant eyepatch and his "right eye dark as a wound." He is as blind to the future as we are to the traumatic reality of the past. The secret bond we almost share with this lost Confederate is not the poignant solidarity of defeat, but the apprehension of the abyss of unknowing that haunts our vision of the past, that turns the mimetic powers of the photograph into the confusing and conflicted "black river-roar and light-swarm" of history. Smith suggests that admitting the incomprehensibility of the past is a means to uncreating the future. That is, the dissipation of a stable sense of a common history means that we are more free to create the future on our own terms. This freedom from the past does not come without its cost, since it threatens to push us into the void of postsouthern formlessness. This sentiment is suggested by the doubleness of "apprehension" as both understanding and fear: as we comprehend our failure to create a still life of the past, we also introduce apprehension about our unknown prospects in the uncreated future.

"Caravati's Salvage: Richmond" presents a satirical vision of a broken, disintegrated past, suggesting mood nostalgia's conversion into mode. It describes an antiques dealer in Richmond who traffics in objects ripe to take on the glow of nostalgia's marketable aura:

He's the reaper, the buyer, the keeper of grand houses
gone to pieces, and the choice parts are here.
You want big doors, brass knobs, stained glass?
A hand-carved box? Grandfather clocks, a chandelier?

Maybe those shutters that lined Monument Avenue,
heartwood, the paint age-blistered, kept closed

a decade, some of them, when Lee died? Or you
desire staircase, railing, marble mantels, bellows—

he's stacked it all in heaps high as a pile of guns.
Ask. Caravati keeps. Endless old names, how they lived.
Eighty-three, hair white as nightgowns in the sun,
he'll guide you, touching each piece, a man you'd give

a fortune to, in his foyer, summoned by his bell,
for the secrets you covet. He stands still as delight.
He offers water, a beaded jar, from his old well.
The one his fathers dug. Way down, cold, sweet. (108)

The hexameter lines, replete with heavy-handed spondees and see-saw trochees, seem purposefully clunky, overfull with the pointless accumulation of scrapped items, all the now-devalued detritus of consumer capitalism overspreading the southern cultural landscape. Even the names associated with this heap of broken images ring with nostalgia: the shutters that lined "Monument Avenue" and were closed in homage to Robert E. Lee are made of "heartwood." Yet the past is junked, and the trash heap of cultural souvenirs is kept by a man called Caravati, whose Italian surname replaces the Anglo names of venerated southern history, such as Lee, Jackson, and Davis. The closing image of water from the fathers' well that is, like the ethos of restorative memory, "Way down, cold, sweet," cannot save an Old South that has gone to pieces. In presenting a piecemeal vision of a fragmented antebellum culture, the poem questions the nostalgic underpinnings of the assumption that the Old South represented a more closely integrated society, for it is difficult to imagine all these disparate trinkets ever cohering into anything resembling a whole. Perhaps the lost South was little more than a collection of "Endless old names" that does not match up to the oversimplified three-word explanation of a cohesive community: "how they lived" is too facile a phrase to encompass the jagged-edged mix-and-match of cultural history. This impulse to auction off fractured vestiges of regional memory recalls economic theorist David Harvey's critique of the financial impulse at back of much of the current resurgence of nostalgia: "tradition is now often preserved by being commodified and marketed as such" and the "search for roots ends up at worst being produced and marketed as an image, as a simulacrum or pastiche" that presents "a partially illusory past" in order "to signify something of local identity and perhaps to do it profitably" (*The Condition of Postmodernity* 303). Smith discloses a view of the past as pastiche, of a disintegrating local culture that cannot be pieced back together with the glue of antiquarian nostalgia. Under the sign of Smith's parody, southern nostalgia approaches the level of consumable style, for the past is no longer made to stand "still as delight," but its clarity and coherence disappear into an indistinguishable mess of unhinged signifiers that take on value haphazardly.

In "Night Traffic Near Winchester, Virginia," the poet would seem about to enter into elegiac nostalgia as he leads his family back home after a funeral. The lines are littered with images drawn from the area's Civil War past, leading one to expect a version of neo-Fugitive memorialism of the Lost Cause:

> From Cumberland's funerals, eldest son, I
> lead my survivors south, toward the sea,
> past tall ash, through stunning cidery
> winesaps still bobbing the Blue Ridge,
> the leaf-littered fieldstone walls
> drooping like rebel stragglers away
> from weathered barns, veterans leaning
> quaint as postcards from the dark
> Tomb of the Confederate Dead, never
> Closed, catching the trucks' roar
> at Winchester where my father always
> stopped to eat. (99)

Instead of another melancholic ode to the Confederate dead, we are given the diminishing returns of the gloried past, the petty stragglers of Civil War memory, bits of remembrance thin and clichéd as so many postcards. It is a quaint, not a monumental, history being recalled here. The lines imply that it is about time to close "the dark / Tomb of the Confederate Dead" that has been left open too long by the Lost Causers, now cultural "rebel stragglers." In place of a nostalgic homage to the past, Smith provides an amusement park version of Civil War Virginia, with a stop at Stonewall Jackson's farmhouse:

> Here, we descend
> into the Valley, slow to a stop-and-go,
> crawl through painted brick cottages
> huddled at sidewalks like history,
> heartpine floors sloped so badly
> water runs off before it stains.
> Like the hips of ancestors, each

foundation is cracked and patched,
the windows narrow as eyes, crusty
along the once horse-clotted street.
Tourists find here the cheery, yellow
farmhouse used by Stonewall Jackson
to plot cavalry raids thunderous
as the black Bible he slept with.
It's dark as a mapcase now closed.

I promise the kids we'll stop another time,
long enough to see boots, old orders,
the grim portraits staring at war (99)

The Civil War has become the apotheosis of southern cultural tourism. The picture of a wistfully nostalgic "cheery, yellow" South, Jackson's homestead is part of the new regional sellscape, not so different from "the neon welcome / of blue Sears, Kmart red, streets / steady with taillights like campfires" (100). The construction of a tragically defeated southern past, it seems, is as "dark as a mapcase now closed" (99). In parodying what has happened to the falsely tragic mythos of the Lost Cause, exposing the way it has been commodified as a museum piece for tourists to stop and gawk at, Smith maps out a new direction toward a future evacuated of heavy-hearted nostalgia for the Lost War. In place of a steady, unforgettable history based on a shared legacy of defeat, Smith offers a glimpse into the postsouthern void, "the historical blank / that never stops falling here" (100):

In the cold mountains I'm afraid
at this edge and feel the hand asking
"How far have we come?" I could say
I don't know, the usual evasion,
but over the lights, the dotted road,
I hear an old voice I had thought lost
say *Far, but not far enough yet.*
Ahead, our family will stand awake,
lights on, coffee hot, ready for news. (100–101)

The poem ends on a familiar note of familial vigil, but stripped of melancholic overtones. Even with this emphasis on kinship, there is an overriding awareness that we must first uncreate the past before liberating ourselves to create a divergent future, one that does not long for exacting repetition, but views the past as a form of parting. His poems are acts of critical memory that resist the restorative notion that "the limits of our popular experience have definitively been drawn" and "now look only for a verification of those limits—a recertification of old forms—rather than a challenging of them," almost as if there were "no more stories to tell, no new experiences to share" (Graham 350). Although Smith points us in the right direction, his poetry takes us far, but perhaps not far enough yet. The forms of poetry addressed in the succeeding chapters will take things farther, re-creating the future along compelling new lines. My reading of Charles Wright's verse in chapter 4 will further elucidate poetry as a distinctly historical mode by reconsidering what Vendler has called the "disembodied ethereality" (7) of his poetic landscapes. That chapter moves past the by-now standard interpretations of Wright's work as expressing an ahistorical ethos of nontranscendence to uncover the cultural underpinnings of his poetics of abstraction: namely, how Wright's verse indirectly reflects the historical processes through which the transregional modes of consumer capitalism are assimilated into the contemporary South and, consequently, how the socioeconomic infrastructure of southern culture begins to simulate that of other regions.

CHAPTER 4

Lost Highways and Ethereal Landscapes: Cartographic Memory in the Poetry of Charles Wright

> How shall we hold on, when everything bright falls away?
> How shall we know what calls us
> > when what's past remains what's past
> And unredeemed, the crystal
> And wavering coefficient of what's ahead?
>
> —Charles Wright, "Journal of the Year of the Ox" (1988)

One of the chief concerns of Charles Wright's[1] verse is to determine how to use memory to resist the flattening out of memory itself. It is not simply that one may never recover the vividness of lived experience, but that one may never recover the relevance and depth of memory. Though he is bound to the past, he does not practice a wistful or unreflective nostalgia: in fact, he self-consciously exposes the penchant for nostalgia in "Nostalgia" (SHS). In Wright's doggedly nonnarrative verse, which contrasts sharply with the strong narrative impulse in southern poetry exemplified most vividly by Robert Penn Warren and James Dickey, the accepted faith in the representational power of the storyline yields to acts of remembrance that are drained not only of their mimetic commensurability but also of their narrative coherence. In his work, impressionism punctures subject matter to such an extent that typically there is, by the poet's own admission, "No trace of a story line" ("The Southern Cross," SC/WTT 42).[2] His nonnarrative technique reinforces his inscription of nothingness as a force that "truly is imperiling and against it there may be little that can be done" (Jarman, "The Trace of a Story Line" 102), allowing us no easy escape clause, just a sense of nothing deepening to nothingness, an all-absorbing *via negativa*. Wright's poems are, in his own words, not godly but "God-haunted,"[3] for his invocation of ecclesiastical language and rhythms sifts the traces of godliness in a time of godlessness. His psalmic repetitions simultaneously summon and undo the vestiges of religiosity, an aspiritual reenactment of the theological concept of *kenosis* or emptying out of consciousness in preparation for accepting divine inspiration. (One might note, however, that although Wright himself denies the possibility of transcendence, he paradoxically continues to seek it; he still seems to feel the need of some imperishable bliss.)[4] With regard to the marriage of memory to place, we are almost as likely to find Wright imaginatively wandering in Italy, California, or Montana as in the U.S. South. Even when his poems are set below the Mason-Dixon, there is often as much a sense of placelessness as there is of place in his abstract and repetitive, peopleless landscapes.

The sense of undying abstraction in Wright's poetry is interrelated with his concept of the negative sublime, which he invoked in a 1989 interview:

> It's interesting that, when you think about Keats and the "negative capability" of submerging your own personality or voice for the voice of the character, he says that there's only one person who can't do this and that's Wordsworth because of the "egotistical sublime." When he walks through a field of daffodils, he can pull it off; everyone else had better work with "negative capability." Surely there's been some fusion now after almost two hundred years of the Romantic movement. Maybe it's an egotistical necessity or a negative sublime—maybe I write out of a negative sublime. ("'Metaphysics of the Quotidian'" 35)

Per Wright's description, the negative sublime entails a double negation. There is in the first instance the Keatsian idea of negating the self through the investiture of poetic voice. In Wright's verse, however, negative capability acts in conjunction with a deeper form of negation: the arational stillness that resides at the center of poetic art, the sublime nothingness that inhabits the rhythmic reflow of language as it breaks over a veiled form. I set forth in my introduction the argument that rhythm is a defining feature of a pragmatic definition of poetry, a theoretical position that has been elaborated in the past decade by scholars like Derek Attridge, Simon Jarvis, Marjorie Perloff, and Jonathan Culler. In highlighting sound, rhythm evokes the nonlogical aspect of language, stressing—literally, physically through the enunciation of accented syllables—the material quality of sounded words over their conscious, communicative meanings. The aural dimension of rhythm is meaningless in itself, yet it calls for the reader to make sense of its indefinable freeplay of sound over sense, to recode rhythm's inassimilable, unnameable force into meaningful contexts. Often we do this by "translating" a poem's rhythmic form through recourse to its specific content, its ideas and images, which in turn gesture toward trenchant social and cultural contexts for further understanding the poem's potential meanings. The form of negative sublimity produced in Wright's poems is intertwined with the aural matter of his rhythmic structures. The sublime power of form is "at the center of everything" in Wright's verse: "Like the stone inside a rock, / the stillness of form is the center of everything, / Inalterable, always at ease" (ZJ/WTT 155). The sum total of negating the self through negative capability and through the sublime, at least partially, conditionally, creates something substantial. What that created something is, I argue, is the overwhelming effect of poetic form, as the force of poetic rhythm unsettles conventional forms of knowledge, showing these to be based ultimately on nothing(ness), and this is a potentially freeing operation.

While Wright's poetry is written predominantly in free verse, his poems display exceptional rhythmical variation and force, particularly in the psalmic cadences of his iambic and anapestic recurrences and the almost tautological use of repeated words and phrases that put the same sound in the same bare place (e.g., "The búsh in fláme is the búsh in fláme, / Ímageless héart, imageless ábsence betwéen the héarts" [CH/NB 46]). Although he claims he is "conscious of stress only to try not to make it regular," Wright is highly self-aware about his metrical choices:

> I count the syllables of every line I write, and I tend to work in
> lines from, say, three to nineteen syllables. Mostly they're an odd
> number for some reason. . . . I'm listening to syllables; I'm listen-
> ing to the sound and to what used to be known as quantitative
> meters, which we cannot write in, because the English language
> will not accept them; *but* the idea of them—the weight, the dur-
> ation, the length, the syllable, is very important in my line.
> ("Metaphysics of the Quotidian" 33)

In part through the ghost of (quantitative) meter, his lines accumulate energy as they move across and jut down the page, and the rhythm wells up within the pauses.[5] He has rightly suggested that his poems, like Ezra Pound's, move "syntactically": as electrical impulses are transferred across synapses in the human brain, so poetic energy is transferred across the breaks in the orderly progress of the poem, emblematized by the sharp cuts and expansive spacing created by his split lineation. This seems an apt metaphor for allegorizing the sublime force of rhythmic energy in his poems, which exude a vatic quality through the hypnotic power of cadenced repetition. In doing so, he provides "a new translation of Longinus on the sublime" ("Autumn's Sidereal, November's a Ball and Chain," APP/NB 164), a new form of sublimity that is responsive to contemporary processes of cultural transmission. The negative sublime is hinged between a longing after transcendence and the recognition of nontranscendence, where the sublime is no longer transformative, but leads the way to an arational nothingness, a Nietzschean primal unity. On a metaphysical level, we are chasing "The lapis lazuli dragonflies / of postbelief, rising and falling near" ("Polaroids," SHS 35), believing in nothing but the broken icons of Wallace Stevens's supreme fiction. We are literally beyond belief; as Bonnie Costello puts it succinctly, "There is no God, and Wright is his prophet" ("Charles Wright's *Via Negativa*" 334). In negating the language of transcendence, Wright's evocation of the negative sublime paradoxically calls forth the need for a new kind of language: as poetic form betrays formlessness, so formlessness, in its turn, betrays form, and shape both occludes yet demands shapelessness. As the purest form of representation, rhythmic structure is the "Noteless measureless music," the form beneath musical and poetical forms that creates an "imageless iconography" and induces a feeling of "Endless effortless nothingness" ("Lives of the Saints," BZ/NB 104). If poetic rhythm is an echo of sublimity, a form of the sublime born not of transcendence, but of its powerful and inexorable negation, then the imageless sound effects of the poem become the resounding echo of an echo.

Wright's invocation of the negative sublime is locked in tension with his exercise of cartographic memory: his reflection and critique of the overaccumulation of the past through his poetic mappings of remembered landscapes. The negative sublime of poetic form negates momentarily the excess of fleeting memories, as the pure physical sensation of rhythm, meaningless in and of itself, holds the power to override momentarily overmuch remembrance. As figures of memory, Wright's poetic cartographies—his imaginative retracings of past places—suggest that our apprehension of the past is spread thin through the excess accumulation of ephemeral and disembedded details, disjointed moments that resist the cohesive force of narrative form. Put briefly, we remember too much, and too little of it lasts.[6] Wright's poetics reflects an amnesiac culture where the past is swallowed up in its very overabundance; his poetic maps of remembered landscapes construe a world where memory seems to exceed—perhaps even precede—experience. In *Simulacra and Simulation*, Baudrillard identifies conceptual cartography as a form of simulation, one that plays on "the cartographer's mad project of the ideal coextensitivity of map and territory" (632), which exploits the map's presumed status as a perspicuous and authoritative representation of physical reality. Baudrillard elaborates the notion of the cartographic precession of reality, where "it is no longer a question of either maps or territories," for "something has disappeared: the sovereign difference, between one and the other, that constituted the charm of abstraction" (632). The cartographic impulse in Wright's verse is consonant with Pierre Nora's argument that in the throes of the "postindustrial" information age, there is "an increasingly rapid slippage of the present into a historical past that is gone for good, a general perception that anything and everything may disappear" (7), as the contemporary subject is no longer certain what moments to value, what events to commit to memory: "We speak so much of memory because there is so little of it left" (7). Under the sign of cartographic memory, Charles Wright lip-syncs the void ("Blaise Pascal Lip-syncs the Void," CH/NB). For Wright, landscape is a necessary, but not sufficient condition of memory: one remembers in spatial terms, though ultimately these reimagined spaces come to seem every bit as abstract as the invisible movement of time. Suspended between the purely imaged and the vestiges of the real, his conceptual cartographies plot psychological time over space, yet are aware of what slips through the grid, of the absences between remembered points in time.

Although his poems empty themselves of the sense of objective historical reflection, his cartographic memories are far from being vacuous. In fact, by their gathering of depthless moments, they are overwrought with meanings, while no single, overarching meaning survives this surplus of significations. The remembered scapes that float into and out of Wright's poems at a moment's notice are symptomatic of an age of nonfiltered memory on sensory overload and point up the condensed lifetime of memories, the evanescence of poetic contemplations in the contemporary era. The ephemera of the past—minus guiding narratives—clip our attention span as we move on to the next image, the new new thing. Memory is being continually restructured, endlessly consumed. At a time when the metanarrative of a seamless southern culture no longer holds sway, Wright is witness to the potential dispersal of locality into an increasingly federalized South under the pressures of urban-industrialization and the assimilation of traditional signs of regional distinctiveness into networks of national and transnational exchange. Where other poets attempt to alleviate the loss of deep-set cultural memory by reverting to a time when memory seemed more grounded in the land and tradition of the South, Wright's verse is more deeply informed by the translocations of contemporary history, offering a simulacrum vision of an age of simulacra. His dramatization of the flux of simulated memories can be linked to the historical conditions of the current South, his aesthetic program indirectly shadowing the spread of consumer capitalism into the region after World War II. The question his poetry frames in all but words is "whether a (post)southern literary (-critical) turn away from sociospatial / reality into nonreferential narrative [here, poetic] play merely mimics (and not parodically, but as pastiche) capitalist reification" (Bone 45–46). The immateriality of Wright's landscapes is not a matter of pure aesthetics. His abstract topographies reflect larger philosophical transitions (the turn toward a space-conscious historicism) as well as political-socioeconomic shifts (the borderlessness of the contemporary South). In using the landscape as a metonymy for memory, Wright foregrounds the spatial dimension in simulating the process of remembrance, paralleling the recent theoretical argument that space is as significant as time in shaping history, espoused by proponents such as Michael Foucault and Edward Soja. Wright's work reflects how the contemporary geographic imagination entails an "enhanced preoccupation with the faculty of remembrance" (Brian Jarvis 190), even as these cartographies obscure evidence of past moments by showing the way that a "landscape surfaces over their histories" (37).

The remainder of this chapter analyzes Wright's disembodied geographies to determine which social tensions get shaded away and which are brought into relief by his simulated models. This attempt to unearth a sense of historical embeddedness in Wright's poetic topographies will take more particular shape through two specific, culturally dense sites of cartographic memory in his work: 1) *his lost highways:* Wright's memories of driving along the old roadways of east Tennessee, western North Carolina, and southwest Virginia; and 2) *his ethereal landscapes:* his remembered geographies of southern places that appear even more abstract and repetitive than his lost highwayscapes.[7] This arrangement follows the basic chronology of Wright's verse. The lost highway poems appear most frequently in his work of the 1980s, especially *The Southern Cross* and *The Other Side of the River,* while his ethereal landscapes fill his volumes of the 1990s, particularly *Chickamauga, Black Zodiac,* and *Appalachia.* On a thematic level, his memories of southern roadscapes are more directly related to regional history, to the South as an actual, referential space, whereas his ethereal topographies are connected to the cultural formations of the South at a further remove from history. His 1980s poems place a good deal of emphasis on memories in motion, on the shifting powers of remembering—a mobility of mind best seen in his poetic cartographies of lost highways. His 1990s poems tend toward vignettes of physical stasis as we observe set landscapes, yet these still foster a rich range of meditative energy: even if the poet has settled down in body, he is nevertheless dynamic in mind. His poetic forms remain highly spatialized, pointing up his concern with how remembrance takes place in space as well as time.

In tracing Wright's memories of the South's buried backroads, one takes to heart the assertion that "Such names as Ford, Chrysler, Olds, Willis, Nash, Shakespeare, Reo, Studebaker, and Dodge had more long-range economic meaning for the South than all the Civil War generals combined. The established way of life in the South was shaken to its very foundation by this new Yankee machine" (Clark 127). Wright's cartographic memories record the changing shape—physical and conceptual—of the southern landscape; in the terms of "Sprung Narratives" (1995),

> The valley has been filled in
> > with abandoned structures
> New roads that have been bypassed
> By newer roads
> > glint in the last sun and disappear.
> As twilight sinks in
> Across the landscape,
> > lights come on like the light next door . . .
> (CH/NB 28)

His lost highways indirectly retrace the spread of fordist and flexible capitalist grids into the South, as much of the post–World War II landscape was converted from farmland into profitable roadscape, known as "sellscape." His poems thereby retrench the decline of agrarian culture and the emergence of a more fully Americanized South. Traditional signposts of southern exceptionalism fade in the wake of consumer capitalism while the southern economy shifted toward increasing industrialization and (sub)urbanization in conjunction with the spread of service industries and other related networks of distribution and consumption. Wright's remembered roadscapes register a movement from particularization to standardization, from distinct, bordered places to geographically nonspecific, liminal spaces.

The recurrence of the roadway motif provides a veiled account of southern history, an abridged and refracted version, one that circumvents traditional narrativization. In their repetitive insistence, his cartographies of lost highways map out in an oblique yet culturally significant manner some of the larger patterns of such economic relocations. Even as his poetic spaces seem to disavow explicit historical reference, they ironically leads us—through their very process of abstraction—to distill the deposits of a "real-world" South that appear beneath the gleaming surface of self-reflexivity in Wright's verse. In abstracting out roadways and marking them as essentially replicable, his form of conceptual mapping overtakes all but nominal recourse to literal geography, converting land into scape, place into placelessness. These dematerialized sites of memory seem the antimatter of referential history: their collisions with material history are hidden from view, but it is precisely in such friction that they create space for observing the borderlessness of late capitalism, which entails a compression and disappearance of boundaries in a flood of federal networks of exchange and consumer culture.

Wright's cartographic memories of bypassed southern highways reflect several levels of the literal cartography of the post–World War II South: the Mason-Dixon line is the broadest marker, the state lines represent the next level of demarcation, and then come county lines, city lines, and outlying suburban residential districts. Regional lines and state lines are conditional markers that create identifications, contingent property lines for producing imagined communities. Roadways provide their own coextensive mapping, overlaying the network of state and county lines with a grid that stitches together the region and connects it to the nation's other regions. Wright's lost highways suggest the emergence of automotive culture in the South and parallel the region's shift from the fordist industrial infrastructure of roadways to a flexible economy that focuses on integrating the industrial sector with the "postfordist" service sector by conditioning consumption patterns along highway routes. The purposeful redundancy of these roadscapes standardizes southern distinctiveness, ushering in the cultural stasis and aregionality that historian Richard Current has defined as the "No South." If there is no South, Charles Wright is its prophet.

In re-creating the poet's travels down the old highways of Tennessee, Virginia, and North Carolina, Wright's memories of passed roadways tend to blur together, their boundaries mapped out only approximately. His highway scenes are depopulated spaces (except for the driver-poet himself), and they are as recurrent as they are indistinct. His trips down memory lane take more obsolete routes—the old interstate highways (U.S. 11, U.S. 23, U.S. 52, U.S. 176, etc.)—as opposed to the four-lane divided freeways that crisscrossed the South after Eisenhower's Federal-Aid Highway Act of 1956 (I-81, I-40, I-65, I-10, I-85, I-26, etc.). This new, federally funded interstate network bypassed the previous system, effectively relocalizing the U.S. routes, turning them into backroads for local traffic. As the new grid spread, the old highways became "abandoned structures," lost to all but memory.[8] The construction of a federal interstate freeway system had a particular impact on the South. As fordism had done before, flexible accumulation shifted capital southward along the interstates, which "opened the region for the first time to the rest of the nation" (Preston 7) and flooded the southern roadscape with a proliferation of "filling stations, tourist cabins, endless roadside advertising, autocamps, tin-can tourists, and a variety of automobile-related businesses" (7–8). The highway was one of the primary inroads for national culture to move across the borders of southern history.[9] The geographic outlay of the South was also transformed as the interstate system cut across and against the natural contours of the terrain, providing a concrete and asphalt reconstruction that leveled slopes, tunneled through mountains, and straightened curves, altering the natural lay of the land. In doing so, the roadways embodied the more sinister implications of Henry Ford's claim that we shall turn out to be masters rather than servants of nature. Moreover, the ostensible freedom of movement promised by the propagation of automotive culture in the South was itself something of an illusion. The automobile literally embodies a degree of self-generated ("auto-") mobility, yet the speed, direction, and duration of travel is still controlled in more subtle ways. The economic impetus of the postwar federal interstate network is to move automobile consumers from one site of consumption to the next along the roadway grid, creating an implicit mode of predicting and stimulating consumer desires: via the mythos of automobility and the corresponding physical infrastructure of the interstate system, drivers are interpolated as consumers.

As the grid conditions the movements, desires, and experiences of its users, it also conditions their memories, which is, of course, Wright's main territory of exploration. His cartographic reconstructions of lost highways imply that the interstates' function as a way of organizing consumption is also a means of structuring memory because the highways form a basis for creating a sense of shared cultural memory. Interconnected with conditioning motorists' consumptive desires is the ephermality of memories generated in passing by streaming sites of memory that fade into indistinction as one races down the highway. From behind the windshield, landscapes appear abstract and repetitive, and the process of cartographic memory is considerably sped up: traveling down the highway, one receives only the fleeting impressions of metonymic adjacencies forged between remembered spaces. Automotive travel is an insistently visual, detached mode of perception, creating the sense of a hurrying eye that has difficulty retaining the cartographies it charts instantaneously, moment by shifting moment.[10] The roadscape-as-simulacrum means that attempts to remember the passing scenery, to place highway landscapes in memory, will be marked by an episodic brokenness, a recurrent depthlessness. This is indeed familiar terrain for Wright. In his poetic remappings of forgotten highways, the amnesia-like quality of automobility compresses the landscape of the South, clouding distinctions between cartographically demarcated southern states as well as between different regions. His cartographic memories of the older interstate roadways superseded by the post-Eisenhower system reflect the subcultures produced and bypassed by the federalist highway grid. Empty veins crisscrossing the southern landscape and dividing it up into roadscape, the lost highways are part of the architecture of fordism that has now become an architecture of absence.[11] These relocalized circulation networks subsist primarily in the world of memory, as objects of nostalgia or, in Wright's case, of abstract repetition and reconstruction. As far from welcoming these cultural transitions as he is from heeding Andrew Lytle's call in *I'll Take My Stand* to rebuff the advance of highway culture as part of the forces of industrialism threatening the integrity of the rural South, Wright does not care to repeat the Agrarian nostalgia for a preindustrial world, but also does not embrace the forces of late capitalism—he is their prophet, not their proponent.

"Lonesome Pine Special" (OSR/WTT) is his most concentrated exploration of lost highways as an expression of the cartographic impulse in setting forth a haphazard sequence of redundant roadscapes, mapped out from memory, where repetition does not reinforce identification, but disseminates it. Wright describes a network of overlapping grids, from dirt roads to state roads to the old interstate highways, moving from local to state to federal levels of roadways and paralleling the South's conversion from discrete locale to an increasingly transregional space. These roadscapes are continually restructured into a stream of disconnected memories that fades the terrain into non sequitur simulacra, fragmentary cartographies that bear tacit witness to how deeply national automotive culture has overrun the U.S. South. That Wright charts his travels through liminal spaces, as defined by the cartographic overlay of state boundaries, marks the dissonance between the overlapping grids of the highways and of state lines. The repeated images of liminality reflected in this recurrent transit between states suggest the blurring of clear demarcations of regional identity conditioned by the map. Even on the level of lineation, Wright chooses a recreational pace down a sprawling backroad (writing in looser, extenuated lines) rather than the streamlined path of the interstate (shorter, more condensed lines); as he explained, "With longer lines, say, you don't go on the Interstate, you take the blue highway. You see more, you dawdle, but you're going to the same place" (quoted in Suarez, Stanford, and Verner 47).

The poem begins with a highway that follows the slope of the land, though it leads Wright, per usual, into a liminal space some distance "Outside of Barbourville":

> There's a curve in the road, and a slow curve in the land,
> Outside of Barbourville, Kentucky, on U.S. 25E,
> I've always liked
>   each time I've passed it,
> Bottomland, river against a ridge to the west,
> A few farmhouses on each side of the road, some mailboxes
> Next to a dirt lane that leads off through the fields.
> Each time I'd think
>   How pleasant it must be to live here.
>
> (OSR/WTT 67)

This roadside vista seems to reroot us in a pastoral vision of the rich bottom-land of southern memory. The image of the fertile land with its surrounding river, ridges, and "A few farmhouses on each side of the road, some mailboxes / Next to a dirt lane that leads off through the fields" recalls a simpler, quieter place before the advent of the interstate and its attendant sellscape. But the pastoral ideal is quickly ironized as Wright exposes his nostalgic sentiments, which reemerge whenever he passes by. Though we should not discount the aesthetic pleasure the poet takes in this vision of place—after all, we should not regard as illusionary the idea that there was *ever* any peaceful place or time in the South—his nostalgia here rings somewhat hollow because it describes, in rather cliché terms ("How pleasant it must be to live here"), a social space and way of life the speaker has experienced only in the abstract. This gap between the purely conceptual and the experiential makes his memory of the place seem a passing simulation of what agrarian life would have been, or should have been, but perhaps never was. Never precisely anywhere, he finds himself in un-marked space, moving past ephemeral roadscapes that repeatedly slip through the cartographic net. The poet glimpses another highway, another fleeting, yet insistent memory, this time along a commonly trafficked route for road trips from Tennessee to Virginia:

> In Kingsport, when I was growing up,
> Everyone seemed to go to Big Stone Gap, Virginia, up U.S. 23,
> All the time
>   Everyone had an uncle or aunt there,

Or played golf, or traded cars.
They were always going up there
                              to get married, or get liquor,
Or to get what was owed them
By someone they'd been in the service with. (OSR/WTT 67)

That everyone makes this same trek all the time suggests something of the repetitive patterning of movements along the interstate, a circuit of travel that once again collapses state boundaries. As everyone makes the same recreational trip to experience a variety of services (play golf, trade cars, get married, get liquor, and so on), the highway indeed directs the flow of automotive consumers back and forth along the grid by making movements repetitious, predictable. Although it does allow for some sense of personal automobility, this flexibility of schedule and course is subsumed by a larger sense that as the highway controls movements, it conditions memories. Though there is a commonality of experience in this vision of a repetitive road trip down a now-bypassed highway, a history shared with everyone all the time, there is also a feeling that memory has been homogenized by these overdriven routes. The reasons for going are interchangeable, creating a series of ephemeral economic exchanges, short-lived deals. Whether one gets married or gets liquor (or both), hunts up lost kin or lost money, plays golf or trades cars, matters little. The common denominator is the highway's power to link sites of consumption, to facilitate standard transactions.

After a brief excursion to the West to trace a literary cartography of Pound's and Hemingway's Idaho neighborhoods along state highway 75 ("It was all so American" [OSR/WTT 68], these literary homeplaces awash with nostalgic tourism), Wright is southbound again, this time rolling down U.S. 52 from Virginia toward the North Carolina line:[12]

Another landscape I liked
Was south of Wytheville, Virginia, on U.S. 52
Just short of the Carolina line,
                              a steel bridge over the New River,
Pasture on both sides of the road and woods on the easy slopes,
Big shrubs and trees lining the riverbanks like fur,
The road and the river both
Angling back toward the Iron Mountains,
The valley bulging out to the east
                              in a graceful swirl,

The dead chestnut trees like grey candles
Wherever the woods began . . .

What is it about a known landscape
                                        that tends to undo us,
That shuffles and picks us out
For terminal demarcation, the way a field of lupine
Seen in profusion deep in the timber
Suddenly seems to rise like a lavender ground fog
At noon?
            What is it inside the imagination that keeps surprising us
At odd moments
                    when something is given back
We didn't know we had had
In solitude, spontaneously, and with great joy? (OSR/WTT 69)

That the sequencing of these disconnected roadscapes is metonymic, a func-
tion of random desire, is suggested by the opening phrase, "Another landscape
I liked." This passage presents a double image of liminality, as Wright crosses
a steel bridge "Just short of the Carolina line." As usual, he is neither here nor
there, floating between state lines, hovering over the water that both connects
and divides the two sides of the landscape. The hint of pastoralism ("Pasture on
both sides of the road and woods on the easy slopes") is quickly assumed into
the abstract space of an indistinct roadscape known through a literal version
of cartographic memory: through repeated patterns of travel, the shift of the
road and land become naturalized, remembered as by habit. The valley bulges
out and drops, just as the line itself bulges out, drops, and gracefully swirls
around. However, this "known" landscape is hauntingly departicularized, of-
fering an almost tautological form of knowledge that is paralleled by the rhyth-
mic movement of the poem. The lines draw on an implicit relation between
the unnamable power of their own rhythmic structures and the unanswerable
nature of Wright's rhetorical questions, a connection reinforced through the
emptying reiteration of "What is it": the rhythmic recurrence of the lines, their
timely flow and break, undoes us, replicating the way in which the memory of
a known landscape equally undoes us. Our conceptual remappings of a land-
scape that can be known only insofar as it remains unknown, insofar as we are
undone by our remembrance of it, pick us out for "terminal demarcation." To
know is to undo, to demarcate is to terminate, to map is to reify experience
and memory into a freeze frame of the shifting, racing roadscape. The surprise

of haphazard memory in these unfiltered glimpses of the past reproduces fleeting moments "when something is given back / We didn't know we had had." These passing minor epiphanies that undo knowledge and narrative outstrip any cohesive mapping of the past, just as the lines' rhythm exceeds the images that translate, always incompletely, its telling power.

Driving on a lost highway between North and South Carolina—everyone takes I-26 down the Saluda Grade now—Wright provides one of his most distinct and detailed roadscapes. The land seems to take tangible shape, as kudzu spreads over oak trees and pine trees, climbing a hundred feet over the rock and hard clay. The distances in this landscape, for once, are measurable; for once, the roadscape stays "still enough long enough" for us to get a clear look:

> In the world of dirt, each tactile thing
>   repeats the untouchable
> In its own way, and in its own time.
> Just short of Tryon, North Carolina, on U.S. 176,
> Going south down the old Saluda Grade,
>   kudzu has grown up
> And over the tops of miles of oak trees and pine trees,
> A wall of vines a hundred feet high, or used to be,
> Into South Carolina,
> That would have gone for a hundred more with the right scaffolding,
> Rising out of the rock and hard clay in thin, prickly ropes
> To snake and thread in daily measurable distances
> Over anything still enough long enough,
>   and working its way
> Out of the darkness and overhand of its own coils
> To break again and again
> Into the sunlight, worthless and everywhere,
>   breathing, breathing,
> Looking for leverage and a place to climb. (OSR/WTT 70)

Even as he presents a materialized geography, he is already in process of disavowing it. The world of dirt, of physical reality, "repeats the untouchable / In its own way, and in its own time." We are moved yet again from the tangible to the abstract. There is a correlation between the worldly and the ethereal, but it does not guarantee transcendence, merely continuous variation on a design that is repeated in different ways at different times, an endless patterning of sameness-in-difference. The lines themselves break again and again, not staying still enough long enough, thereby suggesting the relation between the physical sensation of the rhythm breaking off and down the jutting lineation and the ideas expressed through the poem's form. The image of kudzu overgrowing everything further suggests the pattern of overaccumulating memories, "worthless and everywhere," always "Looking for leverage and a place to climb," something made clear in the succeeding stanza:

> It's true, I think, as Kenkō says in his *Idleness,*
> That all beauty depends upon disappearance,
> The bitten edges of things,
> > the gradual sliding away
> Into tissue and memory,
> > the uncertainty
> And dazzling impermanence of days we beg our meanings from,
> And their frayed loveliness. (OSR/WTT 71)

Memory is figured as a translation from the material ("The bitten edges of things") into the immaterial ("the gradual sliding away into tissue and memory"), an equally fitting description of Wright's poetics of the negative sublime, which inscribe a heightened sense of poetry's translation of the visceral experience of rhythm to the abstract figures of the content. By some metaphysical alchemy, things are transubstantiated into tissue, which in turn generates memory—body somehow produces soul. Memory is a volatile and ephemeral thing, for "all beauty depends upon disappearance," on "the uncertainty / And dazzling impermanence of days we beg our meanings from, / And their frayed loveliness." Wright values that which is in process of vanishing, another precise description of his reconstructions of simulated memory.

Finally, tired of trekking down the old interstates, the poet wants to escape the confines of the cartographic grid altogether, to find some space unmarked by the (post)industrial highway:

> The road in is always longer than the road out,
> Even if it's the same road.
> I think I'd like to find one
> > impassable by machine,
> A logging road from the early part of the century,
> Overgrown and barely detectable.
> I'd like it to be in North Carolina,
> > in Henderson County

Between Mount Pinnacle and Mount Anne,
An old spur off the main track
The wagons and trucks hauled out on.
Blackberry brambles, and wild raspberry and poison ivy
Everywhere; grown trees between the faint ruts;
Deadfall and windfall and velvety sassafras fans
On both sides . . .
            It dips downhill and I follow it.
    It dips down and it disappears and I follow it. (OSR/WTT 73–74)

His fantasy of escaping the highway grid for an overgrown logging road leads him, paradoxically, around a circular route. In the early part of the century, logging companies built roads precisely to clear space for improving transport systems in order to welcome in more industry and commerce. Wright thus quotes the southern edition of the American history of "civilization advancing under the ax of deforestation" (Tichi 3). In the road's "faint ruts" are the vestiges of a disappeared, overlapped economic grid that first promised the industrial expansion of a New South. Perhaps this is better than the increased commercialization and standardization of the No South, but it seems a difference in degree, not necessarily in kind. In its totality—if one can ever think of a Wright poem as a total thing—"Lonesome Pine Special" reads like lyrical scraps torn from a WPA guidebook, mapping out old rural routes as flickering sites of memory.[13] The poem inverts the WPA guides' typical mode of historical transmission. Instead of offering "carefully demarcated travelers the opportunity to read themselves into a historically and culturally dense landscape in terms that are coherent, informed, and contained" (Bold 12), Wright's anti-guidebook charts repeated, yet momentary immersions into hurrying roadscapes drained of explicit history, leaving only the faint ruts of the past for examination. In doing so, Wright conducts a circuitous anthropology of the contemporary South's driving behaviors, which uncovers pieces of the history buried in his simulated geographies.

Like "Lonesome Pine Special," "Lost Bodies" (OSR/WTT) provides a loosely related series of disappearing roadscapes that forms a noncausal chain of re-created travels. Yet "Lost Bodies" repopulates Wright's peopleless landcapes, giving us back the bodies lost from his poetic cartographies. In fact, "Lost Bodies" supplies the image of a body that is in excess of any effort to relate its meaning. Just opposite the rhetoric of transcendent spirituality—the cross with the message "GET RIGHT WITH GOD / JESUS IS COMING SOON" that Wright "passed each day of [his] life / In Kingsport going to town" (OSR/WTT 59)—is a spectacle that shocks the abstract into the abject, confronting spirit with body. It is a sight that distinguishes this repetitive roadscape by its stunning embodiment, an image like nothing else in Wright's poetic canon:

> The cross was opposite Fleenor's Cabins below the hill
> On U.S. 11W.
> Harold Shipley told me, when I was twelve,
> > he'd seen a woman undressed
>
> In the back seat of a Buick, between two men,
> > > her cunt shaved clean,
> In front of the motel office.
> They gave him a dollar, he said, to stick his finger up there.
>
> What can you say to that?
> > everything Jesus promised
>
> (My five senses waiting apart in their grey hoods,
> Touching their beads,
> > licking the ashes that stained their lips)
>
> And someone to tell it to. (OSR/WTT 59-60)

The figure of a woman undressed between two men with "her cunt shaved clean" delineates a grotesquely embodied space that countermands Wright's leitmotif of etherealized landscapes. Here is an unforgettable moment, one memory that is not likely to get lost in the shuffle of overaccumulating flux as it nearly splits his senses apart by its abjectness; for the twelve-year-old Wright, this becomes a displaced primal scene. The religious metaphor of the monkish five senses in grey hoods, ascetic ashes on their lips, is out of sequence with the overwhelming physicality presented by the woman, the movement of the rhythm stripping bare our sensory pleasure in its staggered flow, as the lines themselves seem to be both waiting apart, yet touching, spilling into one another across the breaks. Since this spectacle implodes the effort to narrativize ("What can you say to that?"), we are left to piece together the rest of the story, knowing that no narrative can match this excessively physical reality, knowing that there is nothing we can say to that.

Presumably, this is the truncated story of a rural prostitute outside a cheap motel by the highway's wayside. It presents a repulsive image of female sexuality, a reviling moment of Sartrean nausea. The fact that she is in the back seat of a

Buick inverts—one might say perverts—the clichéd image of love-drunk teenagers making out in the back seat of a car, a staple of 1950s Americana. In "Lost Bodies," we are forced to confront a stark physicality, blunt misogyny on sale for a dollar. The woman is herself a lost body, with no identity and no value except that which consumerism's amoral fluidity assigns her, for her subjectivity is voided as she becomes a token exchange in the traffic in women. Further, the woman's degradation is embedded in the contradictory complexities of automotive culture. Surrounding this spectacle are images associated with southern lost highways, implicitly recording the desiccation of the old system, the disappearance of service industry outposts that sprang up along the pre-1956 grid, which fell by the wayside, quite literally, after the construction of the new network. Instead of being an emblem of freedom, the Buick is one of confinement, of a woman being pressed into service, we assume, against her will. She is herself an ephemeral service, providing a short-lived spectacle, a roadside attraction, the main draw along this stretch of U.S. 11W.

Once part of a viable sellscape, Fleenor's Cabins is now dead space, bypassed as the circuit of interstate commerce takes another route:

> Nobody takes that road now.
>   The tourist cabins are gone,
> And Harold, and Rose Dials
> Who lived in a tarpaper shack just off the highway,
> Nailed hard to the mountainside.
>   And the two men and the Buick too,
> Long gone down the Interstate
> And the satellites that have taken us all from town.
>
> Only the cross is still there, sunk deeper into the red clay
> Than anyone could have set it.
>
> And that luminous, nameless body whose flesh takes on
> The mottoes we live by . . . (OSR/WTT 61)

That "the tourist cabins are gone" because "Nobody takes that road now" shows how this area has been terminally detoured off the map. Here, Wright gives us less an anthropology of current driving behaviors than an archeology of past habits. The tourist cabins have been replaced by standardized, "modernized" motels, and in the wake of the new superhighways, the old patterns of consumption have been literally displaced: they are "Long gone down the

Interstate." The poem concludes with another image of how automotive culture is reshaping the land:

> Letting the dirt take over. This is as far as it goes,
> Where deer browse the understory and jays
>
> > leap through the trees,
>
> Where chainsaws
> Whittle away at the darkness, and diesel rigs
> Carry our deaths all night through the endless rain. (WTT 62)

The soil is no longer seen as sacrosanct—it is only "dirt"—and it can only take us so far. However, Wright seems also suspicious of a future where land clearance strips the environment in order to make new space for the built environment and highwayscape. "Lost Bodies" leaves us in the balance: we can neither repeat the agrarian past, nor embrace the destructive effects of a future in which "chainsaws whittle away at the darkness, and diesel rigs / Carry our deaths all night through the endless rain." The highway culture, it seems, may be the symbolic death of us all, as local identification appears in process of losing its traditional gravitas.

"A Journal of the Year of the Ox" sprawls out forty pages' worth of memories, yet begins with the disclaimer "Each year I remember less" (ZJ/WTT 150), thus succinctly reiterating Wright's ethos of overaccumulation. It covers a great deal of territory, moving from the South's version of ancient history (the dispossession of sacred Cherokee burial grounds on the Long Island of the Holston River) to one of its current incarnations as semi-urban-industrial region. Among its several poetic cartographies is Wright's memory of his fiftieth birthday, spent, predictably enough, on the road:

> —On my fiftieth birthday I awoke
> In a Holiday Inn just east of Winchester, Virginia,
> The companionable summer rain
>
> > stitching the countryside
>
> Like bagworms inside its slick cocoon:
> The memory of tomorrow is yesterday's story line:
> I ate breakfast and headed south,
>
> > the Shenandoah
>
> Zigzagging in its small faith
> Under the Lee Highway and Interstate 81,

First on my left side, then on my right,
Sluggish and underfed,
                    the absences in the heart
Silent as sparrows in the spinning rain (ZJ/WTT 178)

The starting point of this remembered roadscape is yet another site of transi-
tion, "a Holiday Inn just east of Wincester, Virginia" (178), that reinforces the
lack of destination in Wright's poetic mappings: there is no endpoint to his
road trips, all are marked destination unknown. This endlessness is reflected
in the image of the Holiday Inn, a liminal point catering to a continual stream
of driver-consumers, of passers-through. There is something unhomelike about
a motel, especially one that has been so explicitly corporatized.[14] This version
of cartographic memory takes us south along the highway system, which passes
over the natural network of rivers (the Shenandoah River zigzags under the in-
terstates, as the lineation zigzags across the page), just as the roadways have long
surpassed the rivers as methods of transportation. Wright's poetic map plots
us "Under the Lee Highway and Interstate 81." The reference to I-81 is the first
and only specific mention of the new superinterstate grid in all of his poetic
cartographies; it is the only highway that is not yet lost, that remains a major
commercial thoroughfare. The conjunction of two roadways reveals how the
older, regionally unique sections of lost highways—the Lee Highway (i.e., U.S.
11) is named, of course, for the epitome of the Lost Cause, General Robert E.
Lee—have been superseded by the new and improved interstate network.[15] This
cartographic overlap of the Lee Highway and I-81 suggests how deeply southern
culture has crossed over into transregionality. The resultant standardization
of goods and services has the effect of standardizing experience and memory,
individual and collective, as southern heritage no longer appears to take the
blue highways, but disappears down the Interstate.

Wright makes a detour by retracing the vestiges of his family history
in Virginia when he returns to the homeplaces and gravestones of ancestors
whose lives were once rooted to the Virginia "red clay": "Yesterday all of us went
/ to all of the places all of them left from" (ZJ/WTT 178). Yet as they dispersed
to different areas, they lost this kinship to place and they vanished "into the
undergrowth / Of different lives" (ZJ/WTT 178). In this road trip to reclaim
something of that faded family connectedness, Wright finds that memory shifts
along the highway route, as the passing sequence of repetitive roadscapes elides
this initial longing for placefulness and makes the past weightless. The same
river, and the same hard-rock landscape are in process of perpetually shifting
to past behind him:

And now it's my turn, same river, same hard-rock landscape
Shifting to past behind me.
                              What makes us leave what we love best?
What is it inside that keeps erasing itself
When we need it most,
That sends us into uncertainty for its own sake
And holds us flush there
                              until we begin to love it
And have to begin again?
What is it within our own lives we decline to live
Whenever we find it,
                              making our days unendurable,
And nights almost visionless?
I still don't know yet, but I do it.

In my fiftieth year, with a bad back and a worried mind,
Going down the Lee Highway,
                              the farms and villages
Rising like fog behind me,
Between the dream and the disappearance the abiding earth
Affords us each for an instant.
                              However we choose to use it
We use it and then it's gone:
Like the glint of the Shenandoah
                              at Castleman's Ferry,
Like license plates on cars we follow and then pass by,
Like what we hold and let go,
Like this country we've all come down,
                              and where it's led us,
Like what we forgot to say, each time we forget it. (ZJ/WTT 178-79)

These lines represent what is perhaps Wright's most eloquent description of the translocations of the southern past. The farms and villages of an older South are continuously "rising like fog" behind him as he speeds past. There is a haze of unreality surrounding these agrarian vistas, which dissolve into the distance almost as soon as they arise. In its very overaccumulation of such specular scenes, the past "keeps erasing itself." It is no longer sustaining but disposable—we use it and then it is gone—for, like "license plates on cars we follow and then pass by," regional identity is viewed as a construct. License plates mass-produce a superficial sense of place, dividing driver-citizens according to arbitrary state identifications and thereby giving a false sense of home in an increasingly homeless age; they associate drivers with a particular state, even as the highway grid facilitates the bypassing of state lines. Just as Wright's poetic cartographies seem to exceed the territory, memory precedes the past, constantly revising it according to a vision of the future: "The memory of tomorrow is yesterday's story line."

"'54 Chevy" (SHS), one of only a few later poems that center on automobility, also figures the southern roadscape as a site of simulated memory. The very title evokes a sense of a bypassed automotive culture, since the '54 Chevy is now either scrap metal or rusting away. Indeed, it seems that the amnesiac quality of automobility has rusted out the power of memory-as-landscape, the unendable force of the rhythm reiterating the circling motion of the repeated participles ("círcling and círcling, hóping") that describe the heart's endless searching for a place to land:

> Sam's Gap, the Tennessee side,
> Kiss-your-ass curve and white house on the poor field's aneurysm,
> A handful of Alzheimered apple trees across the highway,
> South Mountain back to the right,
>
> Delicate short grasses, bird flocks in the trees, pasture
> And cupped orchard
> > > green against the unendable blue
> Of North Carolina sky just over the hill.
> > > > And the heart,
> That legless bird, circling and circling, hoping for anywhere to land.
> (SHS 67)

Far from being held sacred, rural culture is killed off in "the poor field's aneurysm"; the field is lost to memory, Alzheimered by the highway's flow, its acceleration of space. The intersection of poetic cartography and an automotive poetics is suggested in the proffered directions, "South mountain back to the right," as if we are riding shotgun, looking out at the same blurring tableau through the same windshield. There is a literal driving feel to the poem. That automobility can induce a symbolic form of amnesia, personal and collective, which is, in fact, a perfect simulation of the process of simulated memory, is made clear in the poem's closing lines:

> A moment that should have lasted forever and forever
> Long over—
>
>> it came and went before I knew it existed.
>
> I think I know what it means,
> But every time I start to explain it, I forget the words. (SHS 67)

What should have lasted forever and forever is swallowed up in the ever-receding roadscape: driving Alzheimers memories. In this way, Wright's ephemeral roadways take us forever around blind curves. To invoke the closing image from "Appalachian Lullaby" (SHS),

> The darkness is mine,
> Time, slow liquid, like a black highway in front of me
> Somewhere, no headlights, somewhere. (SHS 41)

Memory is a car with no headlights, lost on a darkened highway that seems in process of liquefying at each turn. Each moment, each specular glimpse of roadscape comes into focus momentarily and then dissolves. There is no real end to our journey: we may be forever passing somewhere and somewhere, but we are headed nowhere. Cartographic memory is constantly in motion, endlessly realigning itself in the darkness. Time is a lost highway.

In addition to his reconstructions of the South's lost highways, Wright's poetic cartographies also disseminate memories across recurrent yet fleeting images of the land itself, past places still there, but only partially and momentarily. In these ethereal landscapes, remembered meaning is not condensed on a particular site, but scattered across the evanescent space of reimagined southern geographies. Memory can never be fully placed, but constitutes a sequence of almost infinitely substitutive fragments. The particularities of a remembered landscape become nearly irrelevant: one scenic backdrop will do as well as any other, for the past is incommunicable precisely in its imprecision, its abstract and unlasting specularity. These poetic geographies produce a series of disjunct tableaux without lasting coherence, impressionistic flashpoints that resist absorption into linear causality. Like his lost highways, though seemingly at a further distance from material history, Wright's ethereal landscapes are liminal spaces, and they bear only the faintest trace of a story line. His dismantling of place as a foundation of identity is perhaps most succinctly expressed in the title of "All Landscape Is Abstract, and Tends to Repeat Itself" (APP/NB), which implies that regional identification is a contingent and conflicted process. On the one hand, in abstracting—literally, "uprooting"—the land, the cartographic impulse resists the effort to essentialize southern culture by grounding it quite literally in the soil; on the other hand, cartographic memory provides a means for superimposing a rather serene and ostensibly apolitical simulation of the South on top of an often tortuous "real" southern culture. In this sense, Wright's poetic cartographies depoliticize the southern landscape and all its weight of mythological self-sustenance, abstracting its codes of collective identity and its particular cultural legacy into a conceptual mapping, apparently disembedded from the contradictory forces of history and therefore taking us away from more worldly conflicts. Wiped blank of entrenched regional associations, the South exists nowhere if not on the page, as his blanched-out southern landscapes, archives hollow and transparent as Stevens's famous jar, traffic in ideas about the thing, not the thing itself.[16] On one level then, Wright's ethereal cartographies depict the South as a place beyond "geographical monumentality" (Brian Jarvis 1), a nexus of placelessness overrun by "the rising hegemony of standardised, undifferentiated spaces, areas depleted of history, drained of the possibility for relations, identity, narrative and significant social action" (190).

However, upon deeper examination, Wright's regions of memory do include some traces of historical reference. In particular, the cultural ethos underlying these sites is consistent with the socioeconomic implications of what David Harvey defines as contemporary "time-space compression" and the "spatial fix": late capitalism's paramount concern with undoing and remarking spatial boundaries that are most advantageous for creating market disequilibria since "the inner contradictions of capitalism are expressed through the restless formation and re-formation of geographical landscapes. This is the tune to which the historical geography of capitalism must dance without cease" ("The Geopolitics of Capitalism" 150). Seen in this light, Wright's poetic cartographies record the borderlessness of consumer capitalism by dissolving the geopolitical boundaries of the southern landscape, constructing a territory always in process of accumulating new memories, new meanings. His South is an amorphous space of unfixed value and values. Wright envisions a region that no longer reflects its mythology, that has been Americanized into the circuitry of postwar culture, where place has become almost endlessly malleable.[17]

Wright's ethereal landscaping of the South in his later poetry is evident in the very titles of two of his volumes from the 1990s, which suggest a creative sleight-of-hand: *Chickamauga* and *Appalachia* seem to have nothing to do with their historical namesakes. The titles evoke well-known southern places that outstrip their condensed historic meaning. He invokes these names purposefully in vain, avoiding any mention of Chickamauga as a well-known Confederate battleground (Wright's great-grandfather, wearing gray, was wounded during the Battle of Chickamauga), and thereby offering a subtle, yet effective critique of continuing devotion to the legacy of the Lost Cause. In disappearing the remnants of C.S.A. history, he ironizes the southern proclivity for ancestor worship and Civil War monumentalism, for his simulation of Chickamauga is a dehistoricized cartography, emptied of the prenarrated space left behind by former overlays of history: contemporary Georgia, Civil War history, and the Native American past have all disappeared from Wright's model. By erasing the hard-boiled Confederate past from his ethereal spaces, he draws his own battlelines, expertly undoing the clichés of white southern memory. His Appalachia also seems to be drained of reference to the actual subregion since almost none of its history of economic deprivation survives in his poems. His hyperreal cartographies push open a vacuum that becomes a creative space through its power to replicate and critique the way that Appalachia has conventionally been seen as a "timeless blank" (Cunningham 44).[18] Wright brilliantly fills in this blank with a blank. Even when his poems seem to be talking about a specific subregion of the South, they go on to show that this is not what we typically talk about when we talk about the South.[19]

The idea of a past too irrevocable, too ephemeral to be embodied in an aestheticized vision of the landscape is registered in "All Landscape Is Abstract, and Tends to Repeat Itself," which figures the past-as-landscape as the dull pang of a localized and nonfatal poison after the initial sting of lived experience:

> Over the Blue Ridge, the whisperer starts to whisper in tongues.
>
> Remembered landscapes are left in me
> The way a bee leaves its sting,
> hopelessly, passion-placed,
> Untranslatable language.
> Non-mystical, insoluble in blood, they act as an opposite
> To the absolute, whose words are a solitude, and set to music.
>
> All forms of landscape are autobiographical. (APP/NB 158)

The original passion that has placed the memory is hopelessly deferred into the "Untranslatable language" of the past that offers no promise of transcendence (it is "Non-mystical") nor meaningful, lasting attachment, no blood ties to the land (it is "insoluble in blood"). These landscapes hold no sense of a Platonic idealism or absolute reality lurking on the other side of the mountains, but constitute simulacra, for "they act as an opposite / To the absolute." The phrase, "the Blue Ridge," serves here as it does throughout Wright's poetry as a recurrent and abstract metonymy not just for a particular subregion of the South but also for the arbitrary and constructed nature of regional definitions in general. On a formal level, the poem is "God-haunted," evoking as it does vatic repetitions and ecclesiastical cadences ("Óver the Blúe Rídge, the whísperer stárts to whísper in tóngues"), but these rhythmic structures seem to carry only a patina of spirituality, not root-deep belief. Wright uses these religious forms ironically—they are less godly than God-haunted, and therefore offer no transcendental engagement with the absolute. This form of remembering by remapping the landscapes of the past takes a personal turn; for Wright, it seems that indeed "All forms of landscape are autobiographical," but always in abstentia, devoid of individual identifying details.

"Tennessee Line" (CH/NB) connotes a landscape defined according to the cartographic model of state lines. By virtue of the territorial demarcations of the official map, "Tennessee" is constructed as an imagined community, and Wright wonders where and if he fits in. The poem is a way of asking how much regional affiliation counts in putting together a sense of personal and collective identity, how deeply the music of the surrounding country wells up in you. Insofar as you take the boy out of east Tennessee, to what degree is the remembered landscape of the Tennessee line left in him, the way a bee leaves its sting? Beginning by mapping out a clouded, empty space, another dematerialized vista ("Afternoon overcast the color of water / smoothed by clouds / That whiten where they enter the near end of the sky" [CH/NB 16]), the poem then invokes Wright's memories of his time in California when he was thinking back on his memories of his time spent within the Tennessee line, offering us a layering of second- and third-order acts of remembering, the memory of a memory of a memory:

> In 1958, in Monterey, California,
> I wrote a journal of over one hundred pages
> About the Tennessee line,
> About my imagined unhappiness,
>   and how the sun set like a coffin
> Into the grey Pacific.
> How common it all was.
>   How uncommon I pictured myself.
> (CH/NB 16)

He composes "a journal of over one hundred pages / About the Tennessee line"—literally, the boundary lines of the state of Tennessee and, figuratively, the timeline of his life until he left his native terrain, the cut-off line of his southern history. Now that he has moved into another state, has crossed the California line, he asks himself why and what it matters that he grew up in Tennessee. The standard fable of the southern writer maintains that those born and raised below the Mason-Dixon must perforce write out of this tradition, out of their deep and abiding connection to the autochthonous ideal. Wright wonders if it's that simple. He mimics the southern aura of imagined unhappiness and defeat, not yet aware in 1958 of how clichéd, "How common it all was." From his latter-day perspective circa 1995, he recognizes what he did not recognize in Monterey: that it is all too common to claim regional heritage as the backdrop for one's serious writing. In 1958, he feels he should feel something for his region of origin, but fails in his effort to manufacture a deep-set southern consciousness. But this is an inspired and inspiring failure since through it he finds that the Tennessee line is too arbitrary and abstract a boundary, both as a state line and as the symbolic line of passage between his early life in the South and his later life in the West. The poem is a shifting of the burden of southern history, as the poet writes himself out of the sometimes constraining tradition of southern letters.

In 1995, looking back and writing over his memories of 1957 as well as his memories of his Tennessee youth, Wright reveals a revisionist strain. Despite his professed hope for prescience, what we get is re-remembrance:

> *Memento scrivi*, skull-like and word-drunk,
>
>   one hundred fourteen pages
> Of inarticulate self-pity
> Looking at landscape and my moral place within it,
> The slurry of words inexorable and dark,
> The ethical high ground inexorable and dark
> I droned from
>   hoping for prescience and a shibboleth . . .
> (CH/NB 16–17)

He is not revising the past at the moment of writing (*momento scrivi*), but rather at the moment of remembering writing (*memento scrivi*), thus writing the memory of writing, producing a simulated memory at an additional remove from past reality by adding a further degree of separation from the illusion of referentiality. His past southern identity is depicted as a "slurry of words inexorable and dark," unavoidable and insistent, yet muddled. He drones on for "one hundred fourteen pages," hoping to find the right catchword for admission into the southern community of rhetoric, but the shibboleth never comes to him: the dialect of the tribe is already too purified, and so all that remains is either an empty repetition of the authorized codes, or parody of the same. His journal records his disappointed effort to manufacture a vital, even if critical, identification with a region that has become a dead territory to him. The poem thus marks the residual artifacts of regionalism in a time when regional identification, to reinvoke Kreyling's metaphor, is no longer running on involuntary muscles but has become a willed habit. That southernness is a function of experiential adjacencies, not a deep-structure commitment, is revisited as we return to a further ethereal image of the poet's native terrain:

> Summer hovers in flame around me.
> The overcast breaks like a bone above the Blue Ridge.
> A loneliness west of solitude
> Splinters into the landscape
> > uncomforting as Braille. (CH/NB 17)

This splintered, abstracted southern cartography—replicated as the line itself splinters, breaking like a bone into the deeper solitude at the center of the poem's shifting rhythmic flux—shows the interchangeability of Wright's analogies for the landscape, what Vendler calls his "ostentatious substitutiveness" ("Charles Wright" 16). It is not essential that the summer hover in flame or that the overcast break like a bone: other images could substitute as well and the poem remain intact. The heightened replaceability of his landscapes points to the influence of an increasingly abstract culture where signs substitute freely for one another and boundaries of regionality are openly crossed. Likewise, in Wright, the pliant spaces of memory form permeable, translocatable outlines. This substitutive range is evident in the reinvocation of "the Blue Ridge." Instead of providing a grounding reference, the term evokes the very ethereality of such subregional distinctions, for like the unknown quantity of the Tennessee line, the Blue Ridge marks a departicularized space. Even as the landscape is thrown into the turmoil of a bone-splintering storm, there is something utterly removed, untouched, and untouchable about it. And this is "uncomforting as Braille." The landscape is compared to a sign system at a further distance from lived experience of place, for Braille, like a map, represents another conceptual model at a double distance from the semblance of the real.

The image suggests that one cannot read back from landscape to experience, from region to identity, even if this may leave us disconnected, uncomforted, and blind to our own identities.

"Via Negativa" (SHS) is the *summa theologiae* of Wright's ethereal cartographies of a contemporary South stripped of all but the residue of traditional metanarratives. Once more exercising his trademark psalmic language and rhythms, the poem's *via negativa* has less to do with the state of transcendent nothingness sought after by Eastern mysticism than with the negative sublime's temporary release from the strictures of meaning. The consciousness-draining motion of the poem's rhythm, like the landscape Wright describes, vacuums us out, seeming to hold us on an invisible flame. The opening lines describe a nothingness induced by entering another site of liminality "just this side" of the Virginia-Tennessee line:

> In Southwest Virginia, just this side of Abingdon,
> The mountains begin to shoulder up,
> The dogwoods go red and leaf-darkened,
> And leftover roadside wildflowers neon among the greens—
> Early October, and Appalachia dyes her hair.
> What is it about the southern mountains
> that vacuums me out,
> That seems to hold me on an invisible flame until I rise up and veer
> Weightless and unrepentant?
> The great valley pours into Tennessee, the ridges like epaulets
> To the north, landscape in pinks-and-greens
> off to the south.
>
> (SHS 62)

The landscape is personified—"Appalachia dyes her hair"—but, once again, eerily depopulated. We are given the ghost of Appalachia in a conceptual map that reflects nothing of the political and socioeconomic realities of this section of the South. Like the abstract colors of a map, the landscape runs "in pinks-and-greens / off to the south." Although it seems that the natural terrain overflows the cartographic grid, it is converted into the symbolic coloration of a map: the "great valley" becomes little more than shadings of pinks-and-greens and the ridges become merely decorative, like epaulets. The landscape-as-memory is vacuous space: "What is it about the southern mountains / that vacuums me out / That seems to hold me on an invisible flame until I rise up and veer / Weightless and unrepentant?" This autoreferential Appalachia empties the poet out of memory, positing memory as itself a vacuum. His identity becomes "weightless" through the overaccumulated burden of ephemeral moments, and he remains "unrepentant," unwilling to give himself over to a belief in the transcendental quality of nature.

In fact, nature is just another word for "the blind structure of matter" ("The Secret of Poetry" SHS 24). It goes on with or without us:

> How pretty to think that gods abound,
>   and everything stays forgotten,
> That words are dust, and everyone's lip that uttered them is dust,
> Our line of discomfort inalterable, sun-struck,
> From not-ness into not-ness,
> Our prayers—like raiment, like char scraps—rising without us
> Into an everlasting,
>   which goes on without us,
> Blue into blue into blue—
> Our prayers, like wet-wrung pieces of glass,
> Surf-spun, unedged and indestructible and shining,
> Our lives a scratch on the sky,
>   painless, beyond recall. (SHS 62–63)

The vatic recurrences of words and rhythms ("dust," "not-ness," "Our prayers," "blue") move, not from nothingness into enlightenment, but "From not-ness into not-ness," an experience of nonbeing color-schemed as a negative blue, a feint that erases the distinctiveness of topological variations and cartographic demarcations: the pinks-and-greens dissolve into a primal unity of "Blue into blue into blue." The ennui of nonremembrance is foregrounded in this anesthetized vision of history: "Our lives a scratch on the sky, / painless beyond recall." Contra Komunyakaa, the deadness of the past is figured as a scratch, not a wound, simulating the deadening angst of being "beyond recall." For Wright, the sense of unease lies in its very painlessness, the past so insubstantial that no one will remember to forget it. Indeed, the poet can only remember that he can never remember, as he reinvents his memories of California from his latter-day vantage point in Charlottesville:

> I never remember going out at night, full moon,
> Stalking the yard in California the way I do here,
> First frost
>   starting to sort its crystals out, moon shadows

Tepid and underslung on the lawn.
I don't remember—although I should—the emptiness
That cold brings, and stillness brings.
I never remember remembering the odd way
Evergreens have in night light
                                   of looming and floating,
The way the spirit, leaving your mouth, looms too and floats
In front of you like breath,
                    leading the way as it disappears in the darkness.
(SHS 63)

In figuring the suburban yardscape as an ethereal space where frost and "tepid
and underslung" moon shadows coalesce halfheartedly on the lawn and where
evergreens seem to come uprooted, "looming and floating" in the spectral
"night light," Wright suggests the substitutiveness of suburbanite memory. As
he puts it in "The Southern Cross," "Everyone's life is the same life / if you
live long enough " (SC/WTT 48). His confession that he does not remember,
although he "should," gives an ethical imperative to memory, the way we try
to weave our past lives into a moral pattern, an intelligent design. The para-
doxical statement, "I never remember remembering," sets forth an exercise in
self-reflexivity, defining memory as a second order desire ("I wish I could re-
member to remember") that marks the past as a precious, yet incommunicable
commodity. As often is the case in Wright's work, we find ourselves in process
of remembering remembering.

This seemingly irreconcilable paradox unveils the labyrinthine com-
plexities of memory as the apotheosis of introspection, the mind at its most
intricately and intensively self-conscious. For Wright, memory is a course of
continual foregrounding and backsliding, of simultaneous acts of remember-
ing and not remembering: as one memory develops into focus, others recede.
The impulse to remember never bottoms out, since there is no end to the
unfiltered, discontinuous ebb and flow of memory's simulations of the past,
an egress and regress echoed in the recurrence of "Each year" and the overac-
cumulating rhythms of the lines that overflow and recede across and down the
blank space of the page:

Bottomless water, heart's glass.
Each year the autumn comes that was not supposed to be
Back in the garden without language,
Each year, dead leaves like words

<pre>
                              falling about our shoulders,
        Each year, same words, same flash and gold guise.
        So be it. The Angel of the Serpent That Never Arrives
        Never arrives, the gates stay shut
                              under a shine and a timelessness.
        On Locust Avenue the fall's fire
        Collapses across the lawn,
        The trees bear up their ruin,
                    and everything nudges our lives toward the coming ash.
        (SHS 64)
</pre>

Simulated memory is "Bottomless water, heart's glass." Its self-reflexive surfaces prevent us from gauging its full depth; however, even though we can never reach the bottom of the past's profundity, its weight of influence on the present, we know enough to know that the accumulated presence of the past is there, irrevocably at bottom of all present constructions of the self. As nature continues to cycle into autumn after autumn, landscape and memory tend toward a stoic dissolution: "The trees bear up their ruin, / and everything nudges our lives toward the coming ash." Thus "Via Negativa" maps out the discontinuity of the past from the collective to the individual, from open landscape into closed yardscape. The weightless and unrepentant excessiveness of memory creates an eschatological desire without end. As much he wants his remembered moments to cohere into a redemptive narrative, his past lives to progress toward some apocalyptic moment of wholeness, this cohesiveness, personal and cultural, never arrives.

Wright's ethereal landscapes are defined by what is lost to the contours of cartographic memory. Under overlay after overlay of ephemeral remembrance, they appear stripped of their material histories. Yet this cartographic erasure of historical reference ironically creates a new form of transmitting the past in a time of increasing critical attention to the spatialization of memory, where landscape is another culturally implicated semiotic space. Wright's poetic cartographies disengage the southern penchant for concrete particularity, the South's long-standing fear of abstractions. His form of cartographic memory rematerializes history, however, by replicating the increasing abstraction and shifting values of the No South, mapping out a vision of the nation's most historically dense region at the presumed end of its history. "Sprung Narratives" reiterates his understanding of cultural memory as simulated, short-lived, as the past falls away "Into the black hole of history":

Seeing the past so
                    diminishes it and us too,
Both of us crowding the ghost ramp
And path along the strawberry patch and peanut field,
Down through the hemlocks and apple trees
Behind the house,
                    into the black hole of history. (CH/NB 28)

On a surface level, Wright's poetic maps lead nowhere, save into a black hole of history; on a more complicated level, what appear to be introscapes (emblems of the shifting process of personal memory) double as culturally informed *inter-scapes* (figures of the transformative ethos of collective memory from regional to transregional forms). In the words of "Chickamauga,"

The gill net of history will pluck us soon enough
From the cold waters of self-contentment we drift in
One by one
            into its suffocating light and air. (CH/NB 33)

The self-contentment of sheer abstractionism, of disembodied, ahistorical roadscapes and landscapes, gets caught up in the "gill net of history," circu-itously revealing aspects of the nationalization of the South in the spread of highway culture and the accompanying fluctuations of consumer capitalism. After teaching himself how to know all the emblems that coalesce to form the traditional underpinnings of southern identity, Wright's evocation of carto-graphic memory exposes the South's potential status as merely "an emblem among emblems."[20] Ultimately, Wright offers primarily a negative critique, pro-viding no particular answer for what to believe in in an age of postbelief, save the negative sublimity of poetry itself.

In the following chapter on the poetry of Yusef Komunyakaa—one of Wright's former students in creative writing at the University of California at Irvine—we move from a simulated version of region to a haunted one, shifting from simulacrum to trauma, from the abstract to the abject. While Wright reveals an ethereally disembodied South, Komunyakaa presents a grotesquely embodied southern landscape, a place of terrifying excess. Yet both writers' verse offers means to reassess southern history, with Wright's work recording the culturally transformative force of late capitalism, and Komunyakaa focus-ing his critique on racism and class prejudice.

CHAPTER 5

Ghostwriting the Claims of the Dead:
Traumatic Memory in Yusef Komunyakaa's Verse

> I've been kicking around the phrase, "neo-fugitives" inside my head.
> What I mean by that is that there tends to be a fugitive sentiment
> which can be compared to John Crowe Ransom and Allen Tate.
> The creed states that basically the poet shouldn't get social or politi-
> cal. That he or she would do better to stick with the impressionistic
> and ethereal to the extent that true feeling evaporates off the page.
> That's much safer, and too often it insures a poet's empty endurance
> and superficial reverence in the literary world.
>
> —Yusef Komunyakaa, "'Lines of Tempered Steel':
> An Interview with Yusef Komunyakaa" (1990)

This chapter brings into relief a shift away from what Yusef Komunyakaa[1] terms a "neo-Fugitive" aesthetics of apolitical detachment to a literature of confrontation, marking a turn to a poetics that engages fully with a region put to the fires of race- and class-based conflicts. Komunyakaa's work opposes "a poetry of the moment, a poetry of evasion" since he believes "poetry has always been political, long before poets had to deal with the page and white space" (Gotera, "Lines of Tempered Steel" 225).[2] His poems correct the historically evasive nostalgia that colors traditional southern culture, replacing wistfulness with shock. In the national imaginary, the South, through much of its past, has been synonymous with racial trauma: as Houston Baker and Dana Nelson, among others, have argued, it is in large part the region's status as a site of volatile social conflict that has imbued southern culture with a grim sustaining power in the national consciousness. Komunyakaa's verse converts Dixie's "cotton fields" into the "ghost fields" of southern memory ("Family Tree" [1984]), raising the specter of racial turmoil and substandard economic conditions afflicting much of the black South. Komunyakaa expands his critique of southern culture to include an indictment of U.S. cultural metanarratives through his Vietnam poems. These works represent not only how southern racism troubles the black soldier's experience overseas, but also the ways in which the ghosts of Vietnam continue to unsettle collective memory back home in the United States.

To elaborate further my broader argument concerning the historicity of poetic forms, this chapter establishes an interrelation between the sublime power of poetic rhythm—the aural effects and paralinguistic resonances of which are not fully recuperable in the strictures of communicative sense—and the historical force of trauma in Komunyakaa's verse. This idea is given a further turn of the screw when connected with his aurally concentrated form of free verse. I suggest that lyric poetry registers trauma in a manner distinct from prose: namely, that poetic rhythm, through its pattern of formal repression and return, can approximate the nature of the traumatic experience. This always takes place at a remove, since rhythm itself is not traumatizing, but provides an apt vehicle for representing the unrepresentable quality of trauma. Komunyakaa creates figures of traumatic memory by fusing these with the arational and therefore inassimilable, repetitive force of poetic rhythm, which serves in his verse as a persistent nonverbal analogy for the inarticulateness of traumatic history. His poems about trauma experienced both as an African American growing up in rural Louisiana and as a U.S. soldier in Vietnam represent a poetics of trauma based in two of the most compelling sites for reassessing the value of lyric poetry as a historical form. The unconscious, non-logical aspect of rhythm in his work presents a knowing double bind. On the one hand, it coincides neatly with the traumatic subject matter of many of his poems of the American South and Vietnam, thus merging form and content and marking trauma as a crucial lens for understanding much of his poetry.[3] On the other hand, the play of poetic rhythm aestheticizes the traumatic moments being described: in exposing to view the process through which violent memories are made pleasurable, Komunyakaa's use of rhythm becomes a vehicle for challenging the pathos-laden quality of the current conceptualization of trauma.

Komunyakaa's poetics of trauma engender an account not merely of trauma as a subject of poetry, but of poetry as a specialized means of recording trauma, thereby moving beyond a rhetorical formulation of trauma and into a poetical theorization by focusing on what typically distinguishes poetry from prose: the physical experience of rhythm. My reading of Komunyakaa's poetry is symptomatic—if in ways at once universal and specific—of how poetry can help both to reassess the definition of trauma and, more specifically, to engage with the culturally located traumatic episodes of southern lynch law and Vietnam combat.[4] His poetic representations of traumatic memory not only challenge the linearity of traditional historiography, but also unveil poetry as an especially appropriate vehicle for commenting on a past that cannot be fully recovered by narrative means. In addition to images of violent fissure, the post-traumatic quality of Komunyakaa's poetry takes place at the zero level of form, with an understanding of rhythm as an inassimilable repetitive force.[5] Like traumatic recurrences, rhythmical poetry is founded on repetitions that carry no inherent valence, for "sound, like poetry 'itself,' can never be completely recuperated as ideas, as content, as narrative, as extralexical meaning" (Bernstein, *Close Listening* 21). In both cases, the returns are literally embodied and can be translated into narrative structures only incompletely.

Trauma is this condition of unknowing in extremis: what we should know because we lived through it, witnessed it with our own eyes, is precisely what is unknown and perhaps unknowable to us, and the repetitions only serve to exacerbate this irreconcilable gap: the pain of never knowing is most deeply impressed on us through trauma. The traumatic content of many of Komunyakaa's poems about Vietnam and the South elucidates a context for interpreting rhythm's resistance to meaning, signaling traumatic repetition as the primary and most intensive elaboration of the rhythm's inexhaustible power. His traumatic poetics thus contradicts Theodor Adorno's famous aphorism that "after Auschwitz, it is no longer possible to write poems" (362), instead demonstrating the productive capacity of writing poetry as a particularly commensurate method for confronting trauma.[6] Komunyakaa's broken, yet insistent rhythmic repetitions and splintered storylines convert the traditional introspection and lyricism of this genre into a form of terrifying beauty, illustrating that trauma often can be effectively expressed through poetic form.

Per current theoretical explanations, trauma is inflicted when ruptures in consciousness become inassimilable as a consequence of the untimely arrival of danger. The traumatic moment is marked by an internal divergence, a profound belatedness that means the event is only known insofar as it is not registered in consciousness. Such unexpected divergences in the subject's experience of chronological sequence assault the individual's sense of a cohesive personality and agency. For the trauma survivor, representation and reenactment do not necessarily lead to release or resolution; instead, the traumatic moment is in danger of being recycled in language beyond hope of narrative catharsis. Though repetition is necessary to imbue the event with a degree of valence, to impose some semblance of control around the dislocated moment, the sufferer is never in full command of the effects of his narrative. Trauma theory holds that those who cannot remember the past are condemned literally, viscerally, to repeat it, without the illusion of narrative mastery and cathartic working-through. The traumatic event is beyond the sufferer's ability to distort, symbolize, or sublimate it in meaningful terms and thereby operates as pure syntax without semantic understanding. The time is out of joint: patients undergoing recyclings of traumatic moments endure a parallel reality, as they suffer a precise reenactment of the event that, because literal, has no meaning. Trauma can lead to ellipsis or omission of crucial details from the past as well as paraleptical or dissociative doubling of one's memory into a deviating "sideline" reality.[7] Such chronological doubling creates an uncanny experience of two realities inhabiting the same space, as the traumatic moment recurs psychologically in the present. For the trauma survivor, the past is never dead, it isn't even past.[8]

Traumatic ruptures can occur on cultural as well as individual levels, encompassing broad historical events, such as the Holocaust, Vietnam, and more recently, 9/11, as well as deep-seated social contradictions, such as racism and child abuse.[9] Trauma can serve as a means of trying to explain the effects of ideology-shattering events on collective identity. It can also serve as an enabling fiction for obscuring more insidious political motives, an instrumental use of trauma that shows up in the treatment of the Vietnam veteran as he is repackaged from complicit war criminal to estranged outcast to rehabilitated hero. The broad-scale vision of the contemporary age as a post-traumatic world of teleological dead ends is reflected in Komunyakaa's poems against the all too real trauma of the South and Vietnam, his memories as a black southerner living under Jim Crow and his experiences of combat terror as a soldier during the Vietnam War. His verse explores connections between the pervasive threat of lynching in the U.S. South and the pressures of combat in Vietnam, where African American soldiers who were denied full citizenship at home were enlisted to fight a war to determine the freedoms of the North and South Vietnamese.[10] The intersections of Vietnam with racially divided Louisiana imbue Komunyakaa's poetry with more than regional significance, shifting his work to a transnational level, moving from the South to Vietnam and back again.

What has often been described as Komunyakaa's surrealistic technique—his process of "serendipitous yoking," which creates "a fiercely imagined and stylized world of charged, almost vortexlike, imagery and sensation" (Gotera, *Radical Visions* 307)—functions like a photographic double exposure, where two conflicting realities become superimposed. His terse, two- to three-beat lines are imbued with a frenetic energy through breakneck tonal shifts that commingle vernacular phrasings with images of the surreal. In contrast to the spatialized "visual" rhythms of current concrete and nonlinear poetries, Komunyakaa practices a type of free verse that is still very much bound to aural repetitions. The rhythmical density and unbalanced auditory turns of his verse put words and meaning out of sync, as his rhythms present a broken sequence. The irruptive, start-and-stop pull of his poems—their uneven, halting drive and severely enjambed lineation—suggests the insistence of traumatic recurrence and rupture, especially when contiguous with traumatic subject matter. His lopsided rhythms and truncated lines make poetic sound seem palpable, unavoidable, producing highly resistant material, while his splintered lyrics disrupt seamless narrativization.

In general terms, "Blue Light Lounge Sutra for the Performance Poets at Harold Park Hotel" (1989) serves as an *ars poetica* for Komunyakaa's traumatic vision. Invoking an amalgamation of jazz and poetry, the poem allegorizes a traumatic relation to a nontranscendable past in describing the absorbing repetitions of poetic-musical rhythms, explicitly demarcating the interpenetrations of rhythmic and traumatic recyclings, the sublime and the abject. Both the sublime and the abject involve an awareness of the excess of physical reality and entail returns that threaten to disintegrate the psyche through their inassimilable materiality. According to theorists like Lyotard and Aviram, the contemporary version of the sublime denotes a physical experience of an irreducible reality outside the self that exceeds linguistic registers, while the abject constitutes violent revulsion at "find[ing] the impossible within" (Kristeva 5). "Blue Light Lounge Sutra" uses interweaving figures of jazz and trauma to record a history of serial displacements that parallels his own familial and ethnic past, from the Caribbean to the U.S. South, effecting a transregional exchange on the level of form. The rhythms of jazz described and felt in the poem give expression to a cultural inheritance of dislocations and forced integrations, to the historical trauma of diasporic scattering.[11] The opening lines of the poem announce this inarticulate, yet implacable need:

> the need gotta be
> so deep words can't
> answer simple questions
> all night long notes
> stumble off the tongue
> & color the air indigo

> so deep fragments of gut
> & flesh cling to the song (252)

The monosyllabic base in conjunction with predominantly two- to three-beat lines creates a series of percussive accents, hammering the words to the page. There is an extensive use of assonance to produce rhythmical effects through aural tie-ins, such as the concentration of "e" and "o" sounds, which accentuate sound as pure sensation. The repetitions intertwine the abstract and abject, the airy and the bodily, as the rhythms "color the air indigo," yet are set so deeply that "fragments of gut / & flesh cling to the song." This persistent drive cannot be readily transcended, for "the need gotta be / so deep you can't / just wiggle your hips / & rise up out of it" (253). The traumatic relation extends to the heavens, where, in place of an ordered universe, there is "cháos in the cós-mos / módern mán in the pépperpót" (253), a highly alliterative phrasing that dovetails a vision of chaotic vacuity on a universal scale with the ineffability of rhythmic impulse. Evoking the intractable deadness of the past, the speaker asserts that "the need gotta be / so deep you can vomit up ghosts / & not feel broken" (253), an image that captures the interrelation of jazz and trauma. These lines inscribe a central motion in Komunyakaa's poetry: the effort to sublimate the past into an illusion of mastery is countered by the undertow of abjection that pulls back the very things that have been repressed or rejected. The expulsion of ghosts through the momentary release of jazz/poetic form permits selfhood to keep its artful illusion of remaining intact, enabling one to not feel broken. Yet the traumatic return of repressed material, history's sense of hauntedness and insufficiency, turns the movement of Komunyakaa's verse from egress to regress, and the fabric of subjective autonomy tears under the weight of the unassimilated past. The closing lines provide a view of rhythm as a form of unintegrated yet ineradicable "pre-memory":

> into it into it so deep
> rhythm is pre-memory
> the need gotta be basic
> animal need to see
> & know the terror
> we are made of honey (253)

A poetics of trauma mixes metaphors, fusing terror and honey, decimating the traditional sensibility that art can sugar over the wounds of the past. The indescribable power of rhythm, translated here through the socioculturally weighted form of jazz, provides an apt figure for trauma's incommensurability. In its inassimilable aspect, trauma is beyond memory, and in a similar vein, "rhythm is pre-memory"—its sound patternings are deeply affective, instinctual ("animal need"), lingering beyond strict conscious articulation. Komunyakaa's haunted vision problematizes the reparative function of art that seeks to mediate loss by re-creating a present that is not broken by the ghosts of the past. In his poetry, the exorcism is never complete. His broken rhythms effect a liberation, albeit momentary, which presses out a physically bound sublimity from a thematics of abjection and psychic disintegration, drawing beauty from terror. At the same time, his poetry remains committed to the pained responsibility of addressing the traumatic situation of the past.

Komunyakaa is perhaps most famous for poems filtering trauma through the memory of Vietnam published in *Toys in a Field* (1986), *Dien Cai Dau* (1988), and *Thieves of Paradise* (1998). The killing fields of Southeast Asia, however, share space with the South in his poetry. As the poet himself has noted, "like the word made flesh, the South has been woven through my bones. . . . Coming of age there, I was fully aware of both the natural beauty and the social terror surrounding me. The challenge became to acknowledge and resist this terror" ("More Than a State of Mind" 163).[12] His southern poems included in volumes such as *Copacetic* (1984), *I Apologize for the Eyes in My Head* (1986), and *Magic City* (1992) depict rural Louisiana as a third-world state hidden within U.S. national boundaries, where the pressures of poverty and racial victimage place African Americans in a condition that Orlando Patterson has described as social death: to make southern blacks live in fear of actual death by deprivation and violence is to hollow out their existence of social value, to mark them as socially dead.[13] Komunyakaa's poetry confronts the bloodstained history of the South—its particular legacy of chattel slavery, spectacle lynching, the Ku Klux Klan, white resistance to the civil rights movement, and the bureaucratized violence of the prison system.[14] His verse reflects the South's function as the nation's shadow of racist ideology, exposing southern culture as a primary site of race and class conflict, differing in degree, if not in kind, from other regions. His significance as a national poet is enhanced precisely because of his importance as a southern poet, as the entanglements of southern history reveal deeply set political and social tensions disrupting America at large. In his poetry, the South becomes "an emblem of America writ locally" (Baker, *Turning South Again* 97).

The pervasive dread of social death is coded by Komunyakaa into southern landscapes of fear, abject spaces that rupture a stabilizing sense of place-bound identity, which was never fully accessible to a black southerner born into rural, working class Bogalusa in the late 1940s.[15] In "Landscape for the Disappeared" (1986), he locates the ghostly remains of African American southerners in a vision of the Louisiana landscape that is haunted by the present absence of "the has-been men / & women" who emerge from peat bogs and "come back to us almost healed" (172–73). His darkly surreal landscape of broken bodies with "faces / waterlogged into their own / pure expression, unanswerable / questions on their lips" (173) provides no space for mourning: his dead have already been disappeared. Far from being a nostalgic preserve, the landscape is a figure of memory so scarred by racial trauma that it can not be fully healed through narrative repetition. Nothing out of nothing comes: "Say it again—we are / spared nothing" (173). Forced to live under the conditions of social death in life, the disappeared black underclass is kept inarticulate in literal death: "We call back the ones / we've never known, with stories / more ours than theirs" (173). The eerie returns of the unhealed dead allegorize the function of the poem's rhythm as an absorbing nothingness that is full of physical reality. Read within the context of this grotesquely other Louisiana, the concentrated heavy stresses—in some lines nearly every syllable is accented—suggest rhythm's status as an unrecuperable force.

"Family Tree" subverts the white southern tradition of ancestor worship by detailing the broken heritage of a black family tree blasted apart by racialized trauma, which ranges from slavery to the lynch mob to the institutional prejudice of the prison system. For a black family surviving Jim Crow, the shift from family tree to lynching tree is more than linguistic, showing that, unlike their white counterparts, African American southerners have had little access to a grounding sense of coherent southernness. The interspersion of tightly controlled lines lends an overlay of deadpan restraint to the speaker's protest, though ultimately the form does not absorb, but heightens the driving sense of outrage:

> When my father speaks
> of hanging trees
> I know
> all the old prophets
> tied down in the electric chair. (97)

Prison has become a new version of slavery, the electric chair substituting for the whipping post. Komunyakaa exposes the power dynamics behind a prison system that is doubly biased against the working class and African Americans, suggesting that moving the procedure indoors and giving it legal sanction does not erase the resemblance between official executions and lynchings. The aura of humaneness projected around executions is an enabling fiction that permits a diffusion of the state's powers of surveillance and discipline, which fall particularly heavily on those already marginalized by race and class.[16] That this disciplinary strategy is exercised against lower-class southern black men outside the confines of the legal system is evident in the father's remembrance of the "hanging trees" which have become perversely naturalized into the landscape. The shift from "cotton fields" to "ghost fields" in the final lines reveals a deeply imprinted traumatic relation between the conditions of slavery and the poverty as well as racial brutality that is the double inheritance of the descendents of slavery's victims. The ghosts of slavery are literally reborn in the broken figures of the socially dead:

> We've seen shadows
> like workhorses
> limp across ghost fields
> & heard the rifle crack.
> Blackbirds
> blood flowered
> in the heart
> of the southern sun.
> Brass tambourines,
> octave of pain
> clear as blood on a silent mirror.
> Someone close to us
> dragged away in dawnlight
> here in these iron years. (98)

The southern landscape is stained by the blood of blacks who count as mere "shadows," an underclass of "workhorses" for white interests. Nature itself suffers a traumatic wound as blackbirds become "blood flowered / in the heart / of the southern sun." Komunyakaa's ambivalence over the poetic process of aestheticizing trauma is suggested by this metaphor—when blood becomes flower, trauma is in danger of being sugared over by pathos. His probing into the dangerous space in which haunting is made beautiful is further evident in the poem's closing image, which effects a poetic synesthesia, where sound evokes vision, as the "octave of pain" is translated into the visual register, becoming "clear as blood on a silent mirror." This image reflects a movement from the piercing, kinetic force of sound to the still life of the silent mirror, a figure of empty mimesis that threatens to permit the traumatic image to die away. By placing us between the dead reflection of a silent mirror and the shooting pain of sound and blood, the echo of the rifle crack and the octave of pain, Komunyakaa challenges us to be mindful of the real political aftershocks of racial trauma, to hear the dead's cry as a living protest. The poem's recourse to an appalling, penetrating sound—underscored by the lines' recurrent spondees (e.g., "wórkhórses," "ghóst fíelds," "Bláckbírds," and "blóod flówered" and tight plosives (the hard repetitions of "b," "d," and "k" sounds)—points up the inter-connection of rhythm and the traumatic operation of memory. The final image of "Family Tree" therefore thematizes "the tension between sound and logic" that "reflects the physical resistance in the medium of poetry" (Bernstein, *Close Listening* 21) through a terrifying resounding of the abject, one that emphati-cally echoes the region's history as a space of racial trauma.

Komunyakaa displays an acute historical consciousness in several of his poems set in Bogalusa, a paper-mill town some seventy miles distant from New Orleans near the Mississippi border that has amassed its share of racial inci-dents. His poems often intersperse well-known events, such as a Deacons for Defense and Justice rally and the arrival of freedom marchers, with instances drawn from the area's veiled history. "How I See Things" (1986) describes a reflective return to a Bogalusa taut with racial conflict as northern freedom marchers square off against southern racist nightriders:

> I hear you were
> sprawled on the cover of *Newsweek*
> with freedom marchers, those years
> when blood tinted the photographs,
> when fire leaped into the trees.
>
> Negatives of nightriders
> develop in the brain.
> The Strawberry Festival Queen
> waves her silk handkerchief,
> executing a fancy high kick
>
> flashback through the heart,
> Pickups with plastic Jesuses
> on dashboards head for hoedowns.

> Men run twelve miles into wet cypress
> swinging bellropes. Ignis fatuus can't be blamed
>
> for the charred Johnson grass.
> Have we earned the right
> to forget, forgive
> ropes for holding
> to moonstruck branches? (142)

We are again exposed to the brutally eerie terrain of rural Louisiana, where leaves are turned blood red and bear the strange fruit of lynched black bodies: "Men run twelve miles into wet cypress / swinging bellropes. Ignis fatuus can't be blamed / for the charred Johnson grass." The freedom marchers go home to New York, while the victims of racial violence must remain in a perilous Louisiana and endure the backlash of the nightriders' revenge, acts of retribution from the men behind the windshields of "Pickups with plastic Jesuses / on dashboards":

> You're home in New York.
> I'm back here in Bogalusa
> with one foot in pinewood.
> The mockingbird's blue note
> sounds to me like *please,*
>
> *please.* A beaten song
> threaded through the skull
> by cross hairs.
> Black hands still turn blood red
> working the strawberry fields. (143)

The freedom marchers' experience of the South is safely mediated relative to that of southern blacks, a fact made evident by the media-produced image of the conflict in the blood-tinted photographs and articles of *Newsweek*. By contrast, those who endure racial oppression are neither free nor at home in Bogalusa, where traumatic memories threaten to "flashback through the heart" endlessly. "Knights of the White Camellia & Deacons of Defense" (1992) reflects another publicized segment of Bogalusa's history, recording a militant black counterrally spurred on by the Deacons for Defense and Justice, the armed civil rights group that was founded in Jonesboro, Louisiana, in 1964, and voices a call to

overt political resistance and even necessary violence, as the landscape itself
again blooms with threat:

> Next day, in the hard light,
> In a show of force,
> Dark roses outbloomed
> Camellias, a radiance
> Not borrowed from the gleam
> Of gun barrels. Sons
> & daughters of sharecroppers
> Who made sawmills
> & cotton fields hum for generations,
> Encircled the slow-footed
> Marchers like an ebony shield.
> Bullhorns blared, German
> Shepherds whined on choke chains,
> & swaggering clubs throttled spring.
> Resistance startled crepe myrtle
> & magnolia, while a clandestine
> Perfume diluted the tear gas. (303)

The deep racial unrest of the scene is signaled by images of sensory overload—
underscored by the rhythm's eerie thrum—that inundate the tense confron-
tation, evoking a menagerie of sights ("hard light," "radiance," and "gleam"),
sounds ("hum," "blared," and "whined"), and smells (the scent of "Dark roses"
and "Camellias," "clandestine perfume," and "tear gas").

"History Lessons" (1992) reclaims the unwritten histories of specific
lynchings that have been deleted from the official public account. The first
two memories involve unnamed victims, their very anonymity exposing the
pervasiveness of white mob violence as well as the terrifying arbitrariness with
which lynch law was applied: if a "legitimate" culprit could not be found, al-
most any young black man would do as substitute. Accompanied by his mother,
the speaker revisits a scene of violence that has taken place, pointedly, on the
local courthouse lawn, the supposed site of protection under law.[17] His vision is
haunted by what he could not see:

> No, I couldn't see the piece of blond rope.
> I stepped closer to her, to where we were almost
> In each other's arms, & then spotted the flayed

Tassel of wind-whipped hemp knotted around a limb
Like a hank of hair, a weather-whitened bloom
In hungry light. That was where they prodded him
Up into the flatbed of a pickup. (283)

It is only in the concluding stanza with the mention of Emmett Till that the sanctioned historical record intersects with the speaker's blood-felt history lessons:

When I stepped out on the back porch
The pick-up man from Bogalusa Dry Cleaners
Leaned against his van, with an armload
Of her Sunday dresses, telling her
Emmett Till had begged for it
With his damn wolf whistle.
She was looking at the lye-scoured floor,
White as his face. The hot words
Swarmed out of my mouth like African bees
& my fists were cocked,
Hammers in the air. He popped
The clutch when he turned the corner,
As she pulled me into her arms
& whispered, Son, you ain't gonna live long. (283–84)

The poem closes with a moment of resistance, although, given the weight of history against him, it is not altogether certain how effective his defiance will prove—his fists, after all, are only "Hammers in the air" and his hot words may swarm back to sting him. His mother provides him with a final message that, like many versions of southern black history at this time, is as much warning as lesson: "Son, you ain't gonna live long." Nevertheless, the poem does reveal some chance for disrupting the standard flow of history, providing its own hot words that swarm the reader's psyche and offer resistant undercurrents against the larger stream of white southern memory. The poem presents a microcosm for the ethical burdens taken up by Komunyakaa's art, betraying a clear recognition that the ghosts haunting the speaker's experience are not singular but shared, and the effort to exorcise such specters must be a communal one.

The post-traumatic force of Komunyakaa's rhythmic returns equally gives form to the traumatogenic history of the Vietnam War as he invokes a traumatic poetics to explore how American racism has been exported to Southeast

Asia on two interrelated levels: 1) the violently enforced racist codes of the U.S. South were still in place for African American servicemen in Vietnam, and 2) as a global form of manifest destiny, the war was an extension of American chauvinism and our willful misreading of the political and ethnic nuances of Vietnamese history and culture. His poetry invokes the traumatically delineated boundaries of the South at the same time that it points to violent recurrences in a transnational context by probing a Southeast Asian cultural landscape also burdened with traumatic memory, both for American soldiers and for the native Vietnamese. Komunyakaa exploits the powers of the uncanny in an effort to record the radical alienation of southern blacks as well as Vietnam soldiers and veterans, subjects connected by their traumatic disconnectedness through the pressures of racism and combat. In the words of "Monsoon Season" (1986), his poetry is an exercise in "unburying the dead" (132), an attempt to point the way to surviving—if not fully surmounting—trauma, for "to be a survivor is to be bound to the dead" (Tal 120).[18] *Dien Cai Dau*, a phrase meaning "crazy" in Vietnamese,[19] records the trauma—personal, regional, national, and international—of the Vietnam era. The characters in these poems seem forever "nailed to the moment" of trauma ("Ia Drang Valley" 366), searching for the right language to bridge the tautological repetitions of conflicted memory. As they move among surreal landscapes, they are caught in continual expectation of the Freudian uncanny in its most literal sense as the internally divergent experience of an "unhomelike" (*unheimlich*) feeling, a moment of extreme psychic displacement. The open field of the Vietnamese terrain produces a discontinuous feed of traumatic memories, particularly for the African American soldier in Vietnam, who suffers a doubled sense of self-estrangement. In the words of "Jungle Surrender," Komunyakaa carries us to the unhomely space "between / central Georgia & Tay Ninh Province" (217). Transferring his critique to the combat zones of Vietnam further exposes the continuing contradictions of social death as African American GIs are exploited for American political and military gain—a condition made all the more painful for southern blacks who endured lynch law only to be exposed to further racism and trauma overseas.[20] Struggling with "the uneasiness of the soldier of color sent to battle other people of color" (Salas 82), Komunyakaa's poems share an awareness of the incapacity of the U.S. national narrative of progress to integrate the political and military failure of Vietnam: the redemptive mythos of manifest destiny has withered in its attempted transplantation to Southeast Asian soil.

Komunyakaa's traumatic poetics thus takes us beyond the South and establishes Vietnam as a further, intersecting space of historical trauma.[21] The conjunction between the South and Southeast Asia is dramatized in repressed memories of racial turmoil that return to haunt African American soldiers in Vietnam, such as in "Hanoi Hannah" (whose eerily disembodied voice invokes Ray Charles and Tina Turner and coos to black servicemen, "You're dead as King today in Memphis" [198]), "Re-Creating the Scene" (which connects the racial chauvinism that permits the rape and probable murder of a Vietnamese woman by U.S. soldiers to the image of a Confederate flag flapping from an Army jeep's antenna), "One-Legged Stool" (in which a black POW resolves to survive, although survival means that he will return to the threat of violence back "home" in the South), "Camouflaging the Chimera" (where soldiers put on an ironic form of blackface: "We painted our faces & rifles / with mud from a riverbank" [191]), and "Communiqué" (which describes a U.S.O. show with an all-white cast of performers—save Lola Falana who "looks awful white" [211]—that reminds black soldiers of their roots in the racially splintered South: "We want our hearts wrung out like rags & ground down / to Georgia dust" [211]). Against sentimental tales that posit Vietnam battlefields as real-life melting pots where interracial bonding occurs under the pressures of combat, Komunyakaa's poems record the frustrations of a black GI who confronts continued segregation on account of white soldiers. The figure of cross-racial bonding is a momentary illusion, for, as the black speaker of "Tu Do Street" remarks, "We have played Judas where / only machine-gun fire brings us / together" (210); off the battlefield, he is met with blunt racism, as "Music divides the evening" between black and white and he returns in memory to Bogalusa with its "White Only / signs & Hank Snow" (209). "Report from the Skull's Diorama" further darkens the racial politics of the war effort, describing five black GIs who died on night patrol, their bodies "left below / to blend in with the charred / landscape" (224). The scene of trauma is enfolded into a highly aestheticized vision as bright red and yellow propaganda leaflets dropped by the Viet Cong remind black soldiers that "VC *didn't kill* / *Dr. Martin Luther King*" (224). Here again, aesthetics pull against politics, art against message, as "Psychological / warfare colors the napalmed hill / gold-yellow" (224). In his role as ghostwriter, Komunyakaa tells us that dead men "have lost their tongues" with "silence etched into their skin" (224), refusing to sublimate their loss into an honorific dealing in the politically expedient rhetoric of sacrifice, which is founded on a belief in cause. For these African American soldiers, the cause, in a real sense, may already be lost.

Continuing—perhaps even intensifying—his concern with landscape as vehicle of memory, Komunyakaa's Vietnam presents raw spaces of fear for the invading forces who, despite supposedly superior technology and training, appear strangely unarmed against the foreignness of this unknown and seemingly unknowable terrain. "Monsoon Season" casts the speaker as a debt collector for the lost, seeking to bury the dead for good. But the bodies return, literally rejected by the landscape itself:

> A river shines in the jungle's
> wet leaves. The rain's finally
> let up but whenever wind shakes
> the foliage it starts to fall.
> The monsoon uncovers troubled
> seasons we tried to forget.
> Dead men slip through bad weather,
> stamping their muddy boots to wake us,
> their curses coming easier.
> There's a bend in everything,
> in elephant grass & flame trees,
> raindrops pelting the sand-bagged
> bunker like a muted gong.
> White phosphorus washed from the air,
> wind sways with violent myrtle,
> beating it naked. Soaked to the bone,
> jungle rot brings us down to earth.
> We sit in our hooches
> with too much time,
> where grounded choppers
> can't fly out the wounded.
> Somewhere nearby a frog
> begs a snake.
> I try counting droplets,
> stars that aren't in the sky.
> My poncho feels like a body bag.
> I lose count. Red leaves
> whirl by, the monsoon
> unburying the dead. (131–32)

Subjected to another landscape of fear, the speaker attempts to put some semblance of order back into the viscerally unsettled world by "counting droplets / stars that aren't in the sky," yet his efforts are ultimately meaningless. As Tuan notes, the "forces for chaos being omnipresent, human attempts to control them are also are omnipresent" (6). Under such conditions, human resistance, though perhaps omnipresent, is often bootless; it makes no difference that he loses count. The speaker is brought down to earth, to the level of primal existence. Nature has come undone: there's a bend in everything, the wind beats the trees naked, and the stars have been blacked out by a monsoon that unburies the dead. Only the nonliving can thrive in such a brutally uncanny landscape, as "Dead men slip through bad weather, / stamping their muddy boots to wake us, / their curses coming easier." In a war where survival is all, the speaker counts himself among the dead, for his "poncho feels like a body bag."

Komunyakaa's landscapes of fear are set against the falsely cohesive mappings of Vietnam provided by the U.S. Army, bringing into relief the insufficiency of maps in dissecting a place flooded with the shock of violent injury and death. The gap between cartographies and the land they simulate is often fatal. The American military's attempt to reterritorialize Vietnam according to its own models is literalized in topological maps that segment the landscape into manageable units. The potentially traumatic discrepancy between cartographic representations and the enemy territory of Southeast Asia is evident in "Le Xuan, Beautiful Spring" (1986), in which "High-ranking officers let their eyes / travel over silk as they push pins / into maps under a dead-looking sky" (132). The deadness of the sky exceeds the power of the maps to contain it; the smoothness of the silk is at odds with the roughness of the land. In "A Greenness Taller Than Gods" (1988), we are again shown a haunted vision of the jungle that overrides cartographic control:

> When we stop,
> a green snake starts again
> through deep branches.
> Spiders mend webs we marched into.
> Monkeys jabber in flame trees,
> dancing on the limbs to make
> fire-colored petals fall. Torch birds
> burn through the dark-green day.
> The lieutenant puts on sunglasses
> & points to an X circled
> on his map. When will we learn
> to move like trees move?
> The point man raises his hand *Wait!*
> We've just crossed paths with VC,
> branches left quivering.
> The lieutenant's right hand says what to do.

> We walk into a clearing that blinds.
> We move like a platoon of silhouettes
> balancing sledge hammers on our heads,
> unaware our shadows have untied
> from us, wandered off
> & gotten lost. (196–97)

The landscape is teeming with snakes, spiders, jabbering monkeys, flame trees with fire-colored petals, and torch birds. This fearful excess cannot be pressed onto the surface of the officer's map, for "landscapes of fear are not permanent states of mind tied to invariant segments of tangible reality; no atemporal schema can neatly encompass them" (Tuan 8). The speaker poses a plaintive question for all U.S. soldiers struggling against the terror-threaded Vietnamese geography: "When will we learn / to move like trees move?" Unlike the VC, the American soldiers are never fully camouflaged, but are continually exposed to and by the hostile landscape. The lieutenant's right hand points the way to another traumatic scene of soldiers' death. Indeed, untying from their own bodies in the contested space of a bleakly disconnected topography, the soldiers become "a platoon of silhouettes," their disembodiment shadowing the insubstantiality of the officer's one-dimensional map.

Komunyakaa is highly self-conscious about how his poetic representations of combat trauma potentially can drain away the particularity of traumatogenic moments, especially the repeated figures of the unexpected and therefore unassimilated deaths of fellow soldiers. He is concerned with committing "a betrayal precisely in the act of telling, in the very transmission of an understanding that erases the specificity of death" (Caruth 27). The problem of representing a moment that is ontologically beyond representation is thematized directly in "We Never Know" (1988):

> He danced with tall grass
> for a moment, like he was swaying
> with a woman. Our gun barrels
> glowed white-hot.
> When I got to him,
> a blue halo
> of flies had already claimed him.
> I pulled the crumbled photograph
> from his fingers.
> There's no other way

to say this: I fell in love.
The morning cleared again,
except for a distant mortar
& somewhere choppers taking off.
I slid the wallet into his pocket
& turned him over, so he wouldn't be
kissing the ground. (207)

The "blue halo of flies" functions as a self-reflexive trope for the process of narrativizing a traumatic event—a figure of something surrounding but not touching, just as Komunyakaa's poetic reconstructions of such fissures can only surround, but never touch the moment of injury. The repetitive circling of the flies suggests the recycling of the episode, which does not necessarily lead to cathartic progression and resolution. Moreover, the pattern of the flies over the dead body foregrounds the interrelation between rhythmic and traumatic recurrences. The stark iambic-trochaic shift in "a blúe hálo" and the rough enjambment that breaks the line point up the insistent force of emphatic rhythm. The flies' halo signifies a post-traumatic form of metrical repetition that is hollow at its core from the vantage of rational observation. The dead man's momentary dance with the tall grass of a fatally estranging landscape denotes poetic meter's dance within the interstices of rationalized language. Rhythm's negating structure, its capacity to make nothing happen, parallels the traumatic recalcitrance of the past—how, despite its returns, its claims on the present can never be totally restored. In light of the poem's traumatic subject, its sound points to a post-traumatic conceptualization of memory, allegorizing an awareness of the past as a repetitious and yet indescribable process. The mimetic power of art folds, like the soldier's "crumbled photograph." Komunyakaa's poetics of trauma at once disables meaning (through paralinguistic power of rhythm that shadows the inassimilable repetitions of trauma) and enables it (spurring us, through the rhythm's nonverbal presence, to translate its possible meanings). His poetry nails us to an irrevocable moment while at the same time driving us to invent compensatory narratives to account for the holes that trauma leaves in memory. His taking of range in subjectively correlating traumatic emotions and symbolic codifications exposes how trauma threatens to break conventional narratives of the past; there are undoubtedly other ways to say this, nearly infinite means to describe this event, but none will fully capture the experience. The arbitrary, yet motivated nature of symbolic correlation, of metaphors that surround but never touch, of witnesses who see but never comprehend, emblematizes the capacity of rhythm to hollow rationality out of past order, creating a riveting nothingness that is intricately patterned, thereby paralleling the poem's traumatic failure to make the wounds of history speak plainly. And yet it still holds the desire to connect with the other, embodying a traumatically and historically impacted instance of poetry's intersubjective capacity to sustain and transform "the threshold between individual and social existence," the way in which "metered language, language that retains and projects the force of individual sense experience and yet reaches toward intersubjective meaning," devotes itself to "the unending Orphic task of drawing the figure of the other—the figure of the beloved who reciprocally can recognize one's own figure—out of the darkness" (Stewart 2). Just as the American G.I. "falls in love" with the fallen enemy soldier, the poem itself attempts to establish some grounds of reciprocity between the speaking witness and the reader.

Komunyakaa's poetry demonstrates that traumatic memories of Vietnam continue to resurface after the combat survivors return to native soil, creating a series of eerie unhomecomings that reveal the interpenetrations of traumatic recurrences across cultural boundaries. These poems show that the traumatic past can often only return as content—albeit always incompletely—through the fractured narratives and implacable rhythmic reiterations of his poetics. The most startling moment of racial threat in *Dien Cai Dau* occurs in "*Bui Doi*, Dust of Life," which suggests how deeply Vietnam and the American South shadow one another, encoding the southern cultural landscape as a region of almost equally horrific violence to that endured by combatants in Vietnam. When an Amerasian child comes to the South seeking his soldier-father, the father mimics a posture of paternal tenderness: "Come here, son, let's see / if they castrated you" (230). The spectacular brutality of lynch law is invoked in the image of castration, evoking the terror of organized violence against blacks in the South that ironically repeats the organized violence the U.S. military brought to Vietnam. The sins of the father are visited on the son, as the father, transformed now from culprit to victim, in distressingly subdued terms, tells his son to join the club. Just as Komunyakaa shows the black soldier's experience in Vietnam to be marked by codes of racial segregation, he suggests that the South, in its turn, is similarly disturbed by the undying memories of the war.

"Ia Drang Valley" (1998) likewise shows the returned veteran still nailed to the moment of trauma. In playing dead, the trauma sufferer attempts to overcome the moment of shock that forces him to search nightly for a subjective correlative to bridge his past. He is pulled back by memory's repeat action, self-medicating his psyche with broken narratives that confront but do not surmount:

To sleep here, I play dead.
My mind takes me over the Pacific
to my best friend's wife nude
on their bed. I lean over
& kiss her. Sometimes the spleen
decides what it takes to bridge
another night. The picture
dissolves into gray as I fight,
cussing the jumpcut that pulls me back
to the man in a white tunic,
where I'm shoved against the wall
with the rest of the hostages.
The church spire hides
under dusk in the background,
& my outflung arms shadow bodies
in the dirt. I close my eyes
but Goya's *Third of May* holds
steady, growing sharper. I stand
before the bright rifles,
nailed to the moment. (365–66)

The jump cut that relocates the veteran in traumatically lost time represents Komunyakaa's use of filmic technique, making a parallel cut from sex to death, love to war. The further shift from a cinematic metaphor to the closing glimpse of Goya's painting suggests a movement from kinesis to stasis, from a form of art that moves in time to one that is nailed to a single moment. In doing so, "Ia Drang Valley" replicates the very movement of trauma from kinetic response— the effort to assimilate and understand the traumatic event with compensatory narratives in hope of displacing the trauma—to a static relation to the traumato-genic situation, pulling us back to the disordered time of shock. This transfer reflects a traumatic poetics' double edge, its rhythmic repetitions expressing a visceral kinetic power but also bringing articulate meaning to a dead stop. The lines are marked by a recurrence of double accents, a haphazard, yet insistent sequence of a primary stress followed immediately by a secondary stress (e.g., "sléep hére," "pláy déad," "júmpcút," "óutflúng." The monosyllabic base fore-grounds the uneven meter, a jump-cut rhythm that does not hold steady, but varies between being outflung and nailed down. The kinetic and emphatic re-currence of double beats in Komunyakaa's jagged free verse makes the rhythm palpable, creating a style more suggestive of traumatic repetition and rupture in its uneven and unexpected returns. The undying force of rhythm parallels the abject undeadness of the traumatic past, producing a distinct form of playing dead that underscores rhythm's post-traumatic play within the dead spaces of language and memory. The form and content grimly play off one another through the image of the faceless firing squad of Napoleon's invading army that shoots resisting Spanish citizens in Goya's *Third of May, 1808*, an image that puts Komunyakaa temporarily in the position of the invaded, not the invader, which is the role he may represent as a U.S. soldier in Vietnam but not what he is as a southern black.

The final poem in *Dien Cai Dau* recounts a black soldier's visit to the Vietnam Veterans Memorial.[22] "Facing It" shifts Komunyakaa's critique to an explicitly transnational level, as continuing racial divisions between blacks and whites in the South and in America at large mirror the racial chauvinism that led the United States to intervene in Southeast Asia. As the American military, like Napoleon's faceless soldiers in Goya's painting, has brought further suffering to the Vietnamese people through the war, now the traumatic legacy of defeat in Vietnam is set at the center of American cultural memory, embodying another post-traumatic unhomecoming. Throughout the volume, Komunyakaa has exposed the vulnerabilities and cruelties of all sides in the Vietnam conflict; he ends with a radically ambiguous account of survivors who are never merely invaders and never merely victims. "Facing It" suggests the ironic monumentalism of the Wall as both a reflection and critique of trauma's paradoxical power to engender pathos on a collective scale, even as the poem immediately announces the persistence of racial divisions for the African American vet at "home":

> My black face fades,
> Hiding inside the black granite.
> I said I wouldn't
> dammit: No tears.
> I'm stone. I'm flesh.
>
> . . . .
>
>   I turn
> this way—the stone lets me go.
> I turn that way—I'm inside
> the Vietnam Veterans Memorial
> again, depending on the light
> to make a difference.
> I go down the 58,022 names,

half-expecting to find
my own in letters like smoke.
I touch the name Andrew Johnson;
I see the booby trap's white flash.
Names shimmer on a woman's blouse
but when she walks away
the names stay on the wall.
. . . .
A white vet's image floats
closer to me, then his pale eyes
look through mine. I'm a window.
He's lost his right arm
inside the stone. In the black mirror
a woman's trying to erase names:
No, she's brushing a boy's hair (234–35)

The black veteran's reflections on the Wall literalize the concept of traumato-genic history as a phantom pain in the figure of the white vet's lost arm, a wound which may or may not exist, leaving us suspended between mimesis and simulation, mirror and window, trying to see through the self-reflexive power of the stone's "black mirror." The Wall offers no narrative, just names arranged by temporal proximity of their deaths, offering a stark allegory of the nonrecuperable nature of traumatic memory. The names invoke a literal reenactment of the soldiers' deaths, as the speaker touches the name Andrew Johnson[23]—a pointed allusion to Lincoln's successor who failed to heal regional wounds following the Civil War that reasserts Komunyakaa's concern with the ways regional and national identifications collide—and experiences a flashback to the moment of injury. Yet the mood of the poem seems at times as much cathartic as traumatic. Can the proper light, the right kind of cultural per-spective, ameliorate the initial trauma of the war and lessen the splintering blast of the "booby trap's white flash"? The poem raises the further issue of whether Vietnam has become for some a prenarrated cultural space, the sub-ject of a marketable form of collective memory generated by mass media—TV, films, documentaries, novels, and music—what Marita Sturken has termed "the Vietnam War nostalgia industry" (75) of the 1980s.[24]

   Throughout his Vietnam poetry, Komunyakaa avoids the clichéd rheto-ric of personal and national healing, or else points up its very overtransparency. "Facing It" continues this critique by revealing the potential for the Wall to be converted too readily from a place of mourning for the veteran into a site of cultural tourism for those less deeply connected to the traumatic aftereffects of the conflict. If the trauma reflected in "Facing It" is made to seem illusionistic from the viewpoint of those not directly affected by tragic memories of the war (thematized in the illusion of the white vet's lost arm—perhaps a phantom phantom pain), then the contrary mode of emotional detachment seems equally so. The woman brushing the boy's hair may really be only erasing names—a cheap pasting over of the psychic wounds of the war. This gesture may be less a sign of her maternal connectedness than of her sheer disconnectedness from the Wall and the violent past it reflects as through a glass darkly. The poem therefore admits detachment as one of the range of meanings produced by the war and the Wall, as the woman and her son may represent not mourners, but simply tourists on a visit to the National Mall. The idea that the Vietnam Veterans Memorial reflects for some little more than a tourist stop or else is translated too easily into a reassuring form of cultural pathos and healing is set against the poem's painstaking description of the shared, yet inarticulate trauma of the two veterans, black and white, who remain inextricably bound to the dead. The depiction of the two survivors struggling to confront the Wall reveals the intersubjective power of poetry to make us see, at least momentarily, from the vantage of the other, however difficult this exchange may be. In this interchange of perspectives reflected in the dark surface of the memorial, the poem may contain an allusion to *12 Million Black Voices* (1941), in which Richard Wright urges: "Look at us and know us and you will know yourselves, for *we* are *you*, looking back at you from the dark mirror of our lives" (146). The truncated lines, telling enjambments, and concentrated stresses condition our experience of the poem's rhythms, causing us to share, for the time being, the language of the black veteran. We literally conspire (from the Latin meaning "to breathe together") with the rhythm of his words and are made to see the past through his eyes: our eyes look through his, and the speaker indeed becomes "a window" for us. The Wall, like the war itself, raises more questions than it answers, as does Komunyakaa's closing poem, which provides only an ironic sense of closure for *Dien Cai Dau*, leaving us unsure of precisely what we are left to face. The poem suggests that government-sponsored memorials are meant to exorcise as much as commemorate the dead, and the balm of public pathos may not cleanse the wounds of the individual soldier or of the nation.

Thieves of Paradise denotes a further transnational shift by reexamining the war from outside the frame of American collective memory. These poems return to the geopolitical territory of Southeast Asia, asking us to consider "Vietnam" not merely as a name for the American war and its effects on the

U.S. military and homefront, but as a people and a culture unto itself.[25] In "Buried Light," the trauma of the war threatens to irrupt once more, as the dead past literally resurfaces, embodied in the fragmented bodies that emerge in a modern Vietnamese rice paddy:

> Mud rises, arcing across the sun. Some monolithic god has fallen
> to his knees. Dead stars shower down. It was there waiting more
> than twenty years, some demonic egg speared by the plowshare.
> Mangled legs and arms dance in the muddy water till a silence
> rolls over the paddie like a mountain of white gauze. (401)

There is confusion between the mutilated bodies of the past and the present. The uncovered land mine unearths a land still entrenched in the war, a nation that cannot so easily turn swords into plowshares. Vietnamese history is still traumatized: the silence that "rolls over the paddie like a mountain of white gauze" provides a figure of the possibility of healing (medical gauze wrapping up the wounds of the nation) counterbalanced by the impossibility of healing (the white gauze as a death shroud, where the future of Vietnam is bound to its violent past). The poem darkly works back against the flood of global capitalism into Southeast Asia, recalling the existence of an agrarian-based Vietnamese culture altered by U.S. political, economic, and military interference. The prose-like structure maintains Komunyakaa's distinctive two- to three-beat, stress-heavy pattern, with its insistent double accents and trochaic starts, yet this base is submerged within the extended lineation. The buried rhythm emerges, producing another post-traumatic dance of death that ends in ineffable silence, underscored by the repetition of "l" sounds that (dis)connects mangled legs with the rolling silence. Through the inexhaustible force of its rhythm, "Buried Light" exposes a vision of history that is no longer progressive, but recursive and digressive, a vision of history that has no end. The poem serves as a haunting repetition of the earlier "Landscape for the Disappeared," producing one further connection between Vietnam and the South, one more in the sequence of uncanny returns that remind us how history is marked by the loss at the center of commemorative rituals. It is this embedded sense of loss—paralleled by the abject returns of the lines' embedded meter—that persists despite narrative distortions that attempt to bury the deadness of the past. In this way, "Buried Light" fulfills the cycle of Komunyakaa's traumatic poetics.

The geographic and historical particularity of Komunyakaa's traumatic subjects in conjunction with his attention to the nonrecuperable, repetitive quality of rhythm provides a critique not only of southern and American racism but also of the definition of trauma itself. Overriding essentialist definitions of place-bound identity by exposing the overlapping identifications engendered by arbitrary yet powerful regional histories, his verse reveals how the conflicts of southern culture were exported to Vietnam, and how the international politics of Southeast Asia have overshadowed the inner turmoil of the U.S. South. His poetics of trauma demonstrates why these transcultural connections are so powerful, specifically through his poems' disruption of narrative continuity and the compulsion to repeat. His poetry merges the excessive materiality of rhythmic repetition with the inassimilable quality of traumatic recurrence, thereby exposing the facile psychiatric and political rhetoric of healing. And yet his poetics also offers a sustained challenge to standard-issue trauma theory by demonstrating a productive responsibility to the past without merely reiterating the dying words of such trite narratives of personal and cultural redemption. His poems remain to bring the buried into the light, manifesting a need to make trauma meaningful for the survivors and for others through poetry's intersubjective potential. In doing so, his verse both records and challenges, reflects and refracts, the political and philosophical limitations of the current theorization of trauma. His poetics invokes a pointed sense of history, but refuses, in post-traumatic fashion, to assimilate accepted tropes of historiography. Instead, the uncanny returns most forcefully through the recalcitrant repetitions of his poetic form, which provides resistant cultural material by producing one of the most compelling—because traumatically imprinted—instances of what Bernstein defines in A Poetics (1992) as the "non-absorbability" of poetic discourse. By commingling the sublime power of poetic rhythm with the abject force of traumatic memory in the transnational landscapes of Vietnam and the American South, Komunyakaa's poetry forces us to reassess the claims of trauma theory by challenging it as a potential mode of political solipsism. His verse questions the endgame that drops us into a fatalistic cycle of repetition without hope of amelioration—if the past is nontranscendable, resistance is futile. Rejecting such a quietist position, his work shows us that poetry is an acutely historicized form, one that can foster responsible engagement with the traumatic past. His poetics of trauma frees us momentarily by leaving us to unbury the dead.[26]

As Komunyakaa's poems trace an arc from the South to Vietnam and back again, from regional to national to global levels, it becomes evident that pressures from without are increasingly brought to bear on the South and its perceived ideological stagnancy. These transregional, transformative aspects of the contemporary U.S. South are examined closely in the next and concluding chapter, where we see how other current poets invent new narratives of transsouthern identities that do not sever all attachment to the past, but extend the range and diversity of local connections. In their poetry, region becomes a site of multiple identifications as they embrace transitions (political shifts, identity shifts) as well as transmissions (the past is still a vital force, but it is now multidimensional), and take us into the contested space of hybrid allegiances.

CHAPTER 6

Transouthern Hybridities:
The Poetics of Countermemory

Those people, black and white, who care about their particular
South should take heart from a vision in which regional identity is
continuously being replenished even as other forms, older forms,
erode and mutate. Anything that has happened and is happen-
ing in this corner of the country rightfully belongs to the South's
past, whether or not it seems to fit the template of an imagined
Southern culture. There is no essence to be denied, no central
theme to violate, no role in the national drama to be betrayed. The
South is continually coming into being, continually being remade,
continually struggling with its pasts.

—Edward L. Ayers,
"What We Talk about When We Talk about the South" (1996)

Speaking to the complexities of transregionality, the contemporary poet-
ics of countermemory, produced by writers such as Kate Daniels, Judy Jordan,
Rodney Jones, Harryette Mullen, and Natasha Trethewey, reinvents southern-
ness not merely after the desiccation of the mythos of the autochthonous ideal,
but also after the transformation of regional identity with the flows of global
capitalism. Willful fugitives from the Fugitive tradition, these poets gather a
centrifugal (literally "fleeing the center") force for their verse by transferring
the momentous weight of the renascence South into less "certain," yet more dy-
namic energies for the futures of southern culture. In their poetic construction
of various natural and built environments, locality becomes a space of transcul-
turation, "globalism is grounded, even as it transforms that ground" (Peacock
132). While still committed to southern culture, their poetry explores formerly

underrepresented subcultures as loci of entangled forms of cultural memory, expanding and intensifying their identification with the South by interposing this affiliation with politically trenchant issues of race, class, and gender that circulate within but also beyond the traditional bounds of region. Their work replaces faith in place-bound identity with knowledge of the diverse and even conflicting levels of shifting identifications, enabling a reassessment of the value of such contingent—yet compelling—affiliations. Their poems reflect a historical moment in which the traditional definition of the American South in opposition to the rest of the nation "remains part of the landscape, but it is now situated within structures that subsume it" (133). Accordingly, these poets do not seek to dynamite the rails, but rather to reroute southern poetry and culture along new lines that expand tangentially.[1]

And, indeed, they literally invent new lines, new poetic structures through which to develop their views of a pluralistic southernness. Making use of a variety of forms—such as Daniels's extended lineation, Jordan's expansive line breaks and eerie abstractionism, Jones's new narrative technique, Mullen's interspersion of the blues stanza with linguistic freeplay, and Trethewey's ekphrastic poetics and revisionary neoformalism—these writers demonstrate that there is more diversity within current southern poetry than the critical consensus has typically allowed. Their output thereby dismantles the stereotypical equation of "southern" poet with privileged white, and usually male, author. Their poems can be read as acts of countermemory, which invoke "residual or resistant strains that withstand official versions of historical continuity" (Davis and Starn 2).[2] They challenge the constantness of southern identity through the dissociative quality of their poetic countermemories. Against a traditional conception of southern culture as a continuous progression with its own teleological justification, its own set origin and end, these poets reverse this formulaic brand of cultural inheritance, exposing "the errors, the false appraisals, and the faulty calculations" (Foucault 146) that gave birth to this essentializing tradition and enshrouded it in an abiding "naturalness." The poetics of countermemory untells the standard fable of the southern writer, disrupting the purported continuity of this heritage through calibrated misfirings while constructing alternatives to the time-worn story of the South.

These poets maintain the importance of region as a site of difference but place it in conjunction and at times in conflict with other means of differentiating subjectivities. They envision the U.S. South as the geographic basis for a circuit of socioeconomic and political exchanges, an ideological space where regional ties constitute a powerful but not exclusive level of social definition. In reinventing the South as a site of circulating identifications, the poetics of countermemory draws a distinction between *anti-* and *counter-: anti-* is against for the sake of being against—it is dynamiting the rails and reducing the offending tradition to rubble—whereas *counter-* implies a different use of the past, manipulating the momentum of tradition to rechannel it in more liberating and productive ways that are responsive to current sociopolitical dilemmas. In Ayers's terms from this chapter's epigraph, these poets are cultural agents who constantly remake the image of the contemporary South, struggling with the region's pasts in order to bring into being its potential futures. They embrace the heterogeneity of past and present, offering a more inclusive transouthern ethos; against a sense of history as "a form of reconciliation to all the displacements of the past" (Foucault 152), their poems understand southern history as itself a process of displacement in terms of the region's dynamics of racism, antifeminism, and class bias. Their work enacts "the reversal of a relationship of forces, the usurpation of power, the appropriation of a vocabulary turned against those who had once used it" (154). Although they practice poetic forms of countermemory, they do not give way to a Foucaultian fatalism; for them, all resistance is not futile, but works as divergent material that can potentially disrupt and therefore redirect contemporary cultural memory.[3]

* * * * * * *

Of these five poets, Kate Daniels[4] is perhaps most embedded in the history of southern letters, as she reverses past codes from the inside out and exposes the misogyny, class struggle, and racism concealed under the veneer of tradition. Relying on narrative structure, Daniels revises the legacy of defeat attached to the Lost Cause. Her most recent poetry presents an alternate version of the history of the blue-collar South, thus countering the monumentalist nostalgia *of* the Fugitives as well as continuing nostalgia *for* the Fugitives.[5] The poems that make up her fourth collection, titled *A Walk in Victoria's Secret* (2010), offer pointed instances of countermemory, "mutated flowers" that bloom with a chilling beauty in figuring the literal and cultural poverty of growing up in the urban, working-class South. These poems practice a form of counternostalgia, drawing on the Fugitive tradition as a counterweight to swing against in order to create momentum for moving forward. This is especially evident in her motif of modern-day "Confederates," contemporary doppelgängers of the traditional men in gray. These heirs to the Confederate cause have not fared well—they have been pointedly left behind, stuck in a dead past. Daniels thus uses the Lost Cause ideology to foster a critique of class relations in the contemporary South. In recovering the marginalized presence of the white working class in the South, her poems are remarkably concentrated with narrative details, making relatively short pieces read like full-blooded stories. Her style is often proselike, even conversational, although it never loses sight of the driving energy of the underlying rhythms, the way the southern vernacular breaks across her lines.

Daniels's "Porch-Sitting and Southern Poetry" astutely comments on the current state of southern poetry and reflects her counternostalgic perspective. The essay begins with what seem to be purely nostalgic memories of sitting on the porch with family and sharing stories:

> When I recall these years, I see that porch where we sat on warm
> evenings from May to September of each year eating homemade
> ice cream and sometimes singing oldtime Baptist hymns to my
> grandmother's awkward accompaniment on a beat-up guitar. I can
> recall, without any effort at all, her voice, always midpoint in one
> of her long and psychologically fascinating family narratives. She
> was an uneducated person, having only gone through the eighth
> grade, but her language—marked by an endless digressiveness and
> a deep, "country" accent—was the one that first introduced me to
> the possibilities of verbal expression. (62)

This account fits the typical fable of southern writing, incorporating the motifs of place, storytelling, dialect/voice, as well as family and community ties. However, Daniels takes what she sees as good about the South—it is "more value-oriented, less secular, conscientiously holistic in its integration of work, family, and pleasure" (69)—and uses it not to elide but to bring into relief the darker aspects of the southern past, its "specious history of racial discrimination against blacks, political conservatism, and sexism that continues to masquerade as Old South chivalry" (69). Recasting the time-honored objects of southern nostalgia in proletarian counternarratives, Daniels's poetry is not fragmented on a formal level, though it records a series of deeply fragmented lives, the rough edges of which are the submerged snags that disrupt the orderly flow of official history. Their experience is a nonevent on the grand historical stage, but Daniels summons them front and center, imbuing meaning into otherwise devalued existences in verse that is "resolutely antisolipsistic" (70). Working within but against southern tradition, she does not wish to splinter this inheritance, but to redirect its power by forging "a new vision of wholeness that will reflect the changes the twentieth century has brought to bear on the region" (65).

"Autobiography of a White Girl Raised in the South" recounts how the nostalgic remembrances of a white girlhood in 1950s Virginia are shadowed by a counternostalgic awareness of other southerners' lives, the white me asymmetrically doubled by the black not-me:

> In any self-portrait from the '50's, you'd have to see the me
> that was not me: the black girl trudging along the side of the road
> while I whizzed past in my daddy's car. Or the not-me
> girl in the bushes, peeing, while her mama kept watch
> and I relieved myself inside, daintily, in the sparkling facilities
> of the Southside Esso, labeled WHITES ONLY. All those
> water fountains I drank from unthinkingly, the lunch counters
> where I disdained my lunch—she was there on the wooden benches
> Bleached by sun out back of the store, or squatting on a curb
> sipping from a Mason jar of tepid water lugged from home,
> or eating her sandwiches of homemade biscuits and a smear of fat. (7)

The drawn-out lines alternate between six to eight accents, a technique that gives the poem an almost sermon-like resonance, intensifying the prosaic with a concerted attention to heavily cadenced common speech in order to present a darkened portrait of race relations in the segregated South. The ubiquitous "WHITES ONLY" markers are confining for both whites and blacks, though, clearly, the burden falls heavier on the racial "not-me," whose identity has been erased through the forced cultural identification as essentially not white. Daniels presents poignant details that give weight to the abstractions of this conflicted racial history. The pairing of these contrasting realities mirrors the binary structure of racial identification at the time, an arrangement so deeply ingrained that it, like the holy Word, seems to have existed from the very beginning ("From the beginning, then, there were always two: me and not-me" [7]). Looking back, the speaker wishes she had tried harder to escape a parasitical view of the two races stunting one another's growth. In a more open system, race would remain a crucial factor in creating individual and collective values, but would no longer constitute a demeaning level of segregation, de jure and de facto. The poem extols poetry's intersubjective potential to cross socially created identities, yet avoids abstract humanist platitudes by making sure that the ethical role of art is enacted in real social and political terms. She returns to the specifics of personal memory that is also an invested cultural memory, using a "wide palette of color and hue" to fill in the scene, making it real to us, "various and multitudinous, aswarm / with rich textures" (8). However, her fantasy of coming to more open terms with her racial other "beneath the cherry tree, /

where blossoms plopped down in tiny clouds of air and color" (7) fades to the monochrome memory of binary divisions ("Instead, I kept my head down and watched her toes, bare and curled / in the powdery gray-brown dust" [8]), as she is summoned back into the reality of race in the early postwar South:

> Then I hear my granny's much-loved voice,
> calling from the porch, to come away and go inside. She sent away
> the not-me's daddy without a sale, and chastised me throughout
>   our lunch
> for what she called "familiarity." And through the back screen door,
> I saw the not-me girl, walking away behind her daddy, not
> looking back, and I heard his voice, querulous, too, chastising
> her, as well, for something bad, whatever it was we almost did
> but didn't, finally, dare to do. (8)

The projected nostalgia for the two girls reaching across the gulf of race, their "hands reaching out / to fill with blossoms, dumping mine to her and hers to me," is a knowing fabrication that points to the lack of such productive interaction between races. As things were, there is only space for counternostalgia, since "granny's much-loved voice" changes to harsh tones of default racism as she chastises her granddaughter for "familiarity" with her "not-me" double. The southern saving grace of familiarity, of community and family, is perverted by the naturalized codes of an unthinking racism. Daniels's created nostalgia for a racially open South that never was and, perhaps even today, largely still isn't, uses the counterforce of a resisting strain of memory to remind us what we have missed by holding to a strict separation of black and white.

"The Figure Eight" is perhaps the pièce de résistance, in its literal meaning, of A Walk in Victoria's Secret. The poem describes the stalled-out life of the speaker's brother. We see the dead-end experiences of some of those who lived Ransom's famous advice in "Antique Harvesters" for the sons of the South not to forsake the "Proud Lady" of their heritage ("The sons of the fathers shall keep her, worthy of / What these have done in love" [71]). "The Figure Eight" is written primarily in hexameter lines that are weighted with narrative particularities and extend to the very edge of the page. The extenuated lineation seems to pack in each moment of significance, to tell the story as fully as possible, and her technique thus functions as a telling variation of the southern emphasis on sprawling oral histories. Daniels's lines empty out the traditional forms of storytelling in order to fill them back in almost to excess. But "The Figure Eight" makes it clear that her new narrative style will not tell the same old story. Sitting by a public pond, the speaker-poet watches a swan drift over the water's surface, repeating its path in "a calm infinity" (12), forming a pattern that is "closing back on itself / after every turn" (12). The swan's continuous patterning without progression, its doubling-back figure eights, calls to mind a counternostalgic memory of her younger brother, a "fragile image" that breaks across her mind's eye (12). The repetitive rhythms of the swan take her back to a time "before his marriage failed" when he lived in a "rented farmhouse" south of Richmond, which he shared with one or two friends, who were blue-collar "laborers / like him at DuPont Chemical" (12). She provides a jaded vision of this rented homestead that plays against the traditional southern nostalgia for its fallen men in gray:

> In the evenings,
> their gray uniforms dark with sweat, their hair flattened into oily mats
> they squat together on the worn wood steps to smoke
> a few joints and guzzle cheap beers, tossing the empties
> towards the edge of the wood. They ignore the shattering. (12)

They ignore the shattering of their lives into daily rounds of labor at a chemical factory, an ominous symbol of the shadow that industrial capitalism casts over the contemporary South. Their frustration wells up in blunt hatred of blacks and women. After a "few minutes of silence before the alcohol kicks in," its "spidery fingers scrambling gratefully in their guts," they begin "bitching themselves into a state of restlessness" (12). Once "they've finished with the niggers and the god-damned democratic / president," they let their seething mistrust of women have free reign:

> They're onto women now—
> what cunts they are, how all they want is to take you
> for a ride. Pissed at the child support somebody's
> paying, the abortion another one's wife refused to have. (12)

Then they walk down to a decidedly unpastoral meadow, "the place where the old car rests, a junker someone finagled / for $85 and a lid of dope" (12).

One of them hotwires the "once turquoise and sleekly desirable" 1950s Oldsmobile, "or something that / glamorous" (12); the brother gets behind the wheel and, with speakers blaring, starts spinning circles in the mud of the meadow "as if—this time—he might really be going somewhere" (12). His buddies "howl" when "the car stalls out in a deep rut"—the story of his life—but he manages to bring it back to life again, though blue smoke is "breaking / through the back of the engine" (12):

> The car is whining and popping
> with breakage, its back end swinging back and forth, the way
> a wounded dog keeps going, homing for its master. The wheels
> are straining, like that, trying to move forward,
> but he's just going around and around, around
> in the mud stiff ruts, somewhere there in the dark cab,
> his head cloudy, his mind set on nothing but the figure eight
> he's making in the mud, inscribing it deep in the earth
> so when God looks down He'll see the sign for infinity,
> the same shape of the neat path the swan swims
> in the pond at the public gardens where I sit, years away
> several lives distant, a universe removed, my hands
> shaking, my mouth dry, writing down the words of this poem. (12-13)

The vision of a swan that begins the poem is exchanged for the figure eights cut in the mud by the junked Oldsmobile, "whining and popping / with breakage." The poet's delicacy is notably out of place in the counterpastoral meadow slashed with "mud stiff ruts." In the line, "the sáme shápe of the néat páth the swán swíms," sound and sense coincide to suggest the very repetitiveness of the pattern that her brother's life has taken, his mind "set on nothing," his life going nowhere fast, ad infinitum. The line's spondees dovetail neatly with the memorable alliteration of "same shape" as well as "swan swims" and with the monosyllabic repetition of "neat path." On a metapoetic level, Daniels's own line, with its heightened attention to the sound of its own making, reveals the counternostalgic movement of her poetics: her words repeat the neat path of the past, as she self-consciously resists the repetitive formal requirements of the southern poetic tradition. Where her brother's life is too centered, going around and around toward no end, allowing him to accept uncritically a blatant racism and misogyny, the speaker's life is in danger of becoming centerless: though she is now "several lives distant, a universe removed," she seems to have lost almost all connection to a productive sense of the past. The poem ends with a desperate moment of self-reflexivity, the poet overcome by the resurfacing vestiges of counternostalgia, her "hands / shaking, [her] mouth dry, writing down the words of this poem." It is a viscerally moving experience, but it is unclear whether this poetic act can offer any greater sense of redemptive purpose. The poem itself, as Daniels painfully and knowingly implies in closing lines that hold no lasting closure, may represent little more than another kind of empty patterning, going around and around in self-generating circles to infinity.

Perhaps "Rebel Yell," with its striking retake on the venerated subject of the Lost Cause, brings us full circle by counternostalgically reversing direction. Published in *Five Points* in 1999, the poem tears away the bands of glory from the Lost Cause, exposing to view the underlying wounds of a vexed history.[6] She gives us a politically invested portrait of a walking lost cause:

> It's just the way he bites
> his lip—this fair-skinned, fair
> haired Southern boy, splay-footed
> in the automotive aisle of the discount
> store in Marietta, Georgia—that breaks
> my heart. Something I see there
> in his gnawed, raw lips, his battered
> fingers, stained with oil, nails
> broken off below the quick.
> One more boy pivoting
> on the edge of a short, hard life
> still convinced that's not
> his call, he's got it all still
> ahead of him. But he's misled.
> It's in his genes to keep on spinning,
> back and forth, from tenderness to rage,
> car wreck to bankruptcy, trailer to prefab,
> divorce to divorce, a walking body bag of stifled
> affect, the world untranslated, in perpetuity. (49)

The poem ironically invokes a Menckenesque version of eugenics, damning the boy to his genetic destiny of being "poor, white trash" forever, as his life degenerates "from tenderness to rage, / car wreck to bankruptcy, trailer to prefab, / divorce to divorce" (49). But against Mencken's condescending and classist biodeterminism, Daniels shows an awareness that it is the stifling effects of socially and economically deprived conditions that have converged to make him "a walking body bag of stifled / affect." In his unreflectiveness, the world will always remain untranslated, since he cannot transpose his marginalized past into a future that is culturally valued, but will be continually misled into a working-class existence "broken off below the quick" (49). The vision of this member of the socioeconomic walking wounded forms a sustained memory for the speaker:

> I can't stop pondering my unchosen
> brothers, those wild-eyed, jar-headed
> boys, storming their pick-ups
> down the pine-lined highways
> of the South, outrunning the fearsome troopers
> of the state police who, once, were just
> like them—lining the fence of the bloodied pit
> at the Cajun cockfight, or paralyzing
> each other in a game of ball. It kills me, the way
> they'll give it all up for just about anything
> they believe in, whatever roots down
> deep enough inside it has to be avenged
> if hurt. The way you can tease that blood
> right up to the surface, easy
> as pulling a sweater off a sleeping
> infant, the soft, full weight
> that neither helps, nor hinders
> the removal. And, then, it's bared—
> too late to rewrap now. The child's disrobed,
> the wick is struck, the fuse ignited.
> Already, a butcher knife juts from the back
> of the possibly faithless lover. (49–50)

The lines move from tenderness to rage, interspersing a moment of maternal care amid a slew of acts of reckless violence, culminating in the grotesque image of a murdered lover for being "possibly faithless." Her "unchosen brothers" hold fiercely to a contemporary version of W. J. Cash's savage ideal, avenging every hurt. The play on "blood" as unwieldy passion as well as genetic inheritance again summons up stereotypes of "primitive" southerners, though it does so in order to reveal the devastating effects of such infantilization of working-class southern men; the southern-boys-will-be-boys formula, the cliché of their childlike emotionalism, blossoms into an act of brutal misogyny, a butcher knife jutting from the back. One final time, we see resurrected the remnants of the Confederate dead, minus the elegiac tone in vogue from Henry Timrod and Sidney Lanier to Davidson and Tate:

And those boys charging up the hill
at Gettysburg were just like this, I guess,
vocal cords blooming sore blossoms
of mutated flowers, mutilating
their enemies with nothing more
than the sound of their own wild blood. (50)

The underprivileged descendents of underprivileged forebears—those who were the roughshod foot soldiers, not the stately C.S.A. brass on horseback in dress grays and plumed hats—form an oppositional legacy of the war. The cry of the rebel yell curdles the blood in its sheer inarticulateness, as the "mutated flowers" of countermemory leave nostalgic history dumbfounded. The poem finishes with an ironic flourish, a wildly intense reenactment of Pickett's Charge that answers Davidson's pained desire to undo this fatal moment in the history of the Confederacy when he channels the voice of Robert E. Lee after Appomattox in "Lee in the Mountains": "I face what long I saw, before others knew, / When Pickett's men streamed back, and I heard the tangled / Cry of the Wilderness wounded, bloody with doom" (6). Stripped of its grandiose associations with a romanticized and spiritualized Confederacy in Daniels's resetting, this final charge has nothing of glory or heroism in it, just mutilating fear. Once the icons of the Old South have been smashed and the temple razed, the working-class inheritors of the rebel yell are themselves left with "nothing more / than the sound of their own wild blood." The poem thus pointedly violates the Cult of the Lost Cause, not permitting us to "romanticize and spiritualize defeat," instead leaving us with the socioeconomic realities of "a shabby and problematic present" (Polk 39). Through her poetry Daniels tries to reclaim something of value from the economically and culturally deprived lives of her working-class, white characters.

· · · ▪ ▪ ● ● · · ·

Exploiting a line that breaks and drops down the page (in the mode of Charles Wright, one of her mentors at the University of Virginia), Judy Jordan's[7] verse often bathes Carolina farmlands in a mysterious, ethereal light that suggests the region functions as a thoroughly contingent space. Yet she fills in these abstract landscapes with figures of the rural working class, populating her diffuse ghost fields with real-life specters of poor, white farmers: in *Carolina Ghost Woods* (2000), her ghosts are very much of this world. Using sprawling lineation as well as the ecclesiastical undercurrents of her language and rhythms, Jordan depicts eerie landscapes peopled with the residual presence of lives lost to the grind of socially disenfranchised existence and to flashes of terrible, nonregenerative violence. Through her creation of uncanny spaces fleshed out with the bodies of the literally and socially dead, one believes in Jordan's ghosts, such as the apparition of her mother in "Walking the Geese Home":

> When my grandmother went to the door, there, she insists,
>
> > was my mother,
> unchanged by death,
> perhaps brought home by our hopes,
> two years after she'd been lowered into the earth's throat.
>
> My grandmother, astonished to silence,
> simply watched her walk from pie-safe to fireplace,
> studying the shelves of peaches, stewed tomatoes,
> corn like fistfuls of baby teeth
> and finally out the screen door into the new season
>
> > where I,
> my expectations raised by an arrival,
> > wait. (35)

Her verse is evocative and impressionistic, backlit with a restrained mournfulness. Jordan crafts the dark lyricism of her words into rough storylines, backsliding to a revived faith in the power of narrative, if not to transcend the vicissitudes of lived experience, then to better account for these by setting the human and cultural need for narrative alongside the impossibility of its seamless cohesion. She constructs splintered counternarratives of the impoverishment, physical and cultural, of her familial subsection of rural North Carolina. These forgotten spaces of official history are cursed by blunt and inarticulate violence. Self-inflicted brutalities and death seem to be primary expressions available to her characters as members of a displaced subclass pressed to the unseen edges of cultural memory.

Jordan's volume creates heterotopic spaces, eerie and unkempt sites of irreconcilable otherness that draw forth the dissociative effects of countermemory.[8] The opening poem, "Sharecropper's Grave," dedicated to Jordan's grandmother, is a "white trash" revocation of the Fugitives' elegiac veneration of fallen white-columned mansions and weather-worn cemeteries weighted with monumentalist history, focusing instead on the unmarked countermonuments of a sharecropper's graveyard in Depression-era North Carolina, where the corpses of dead children are "scattered around the iron fence," buried in "Small holes, secret graves" with "Not even a scratched stone" (1) to individuate their lives and identities. Infant mortality is an intensive problem, yet the small farm-owning family keeps trying to replace the children who die not just for emotional reasons but also for economic ones: the family needs to produce more hands to aid with the heavy work of sharecropping. The lines, and the disappearing gravesites they represent, record the sharecropper's response to Ransom's dutiful history of the once great, but now decaying mansion and to Tate's melancholic posturing at the Confederate cemetery, which, though decomposing, still serves as a monument to the fallen heroes of the Old South. Jordan uses sharecropping here and throughout *Carolina Ghost Woods* as a form of *contragrarianism*, one that remembers the other agrarians, the farm workers upon whose difficult and at times dangerous labor much of the regional economy was based. "Sharecropper's Grave" counts the holes that official history leaves, an act of countermemory paralleled on a formal level by the poem's harsh and draining sound effects as well as its crushing series of negations. The psychological and economic deprivations that fill these rural laborers' lives is ironically affirmed in the emptying rhythmic fullness of the opening line, "The night is hóot ówls, wind-whístled flúe, bábies búndled in búrlap," which contains telling assonance (hollow *o*s and *u*s) and alliteration (hard *t*s, *w*s, and *b*s) as it presents a gothic catalog of uncanny and unredeemed things. In a dark double entendre, the aural roughness of "babies bundled in burlap" suggests the rough cloth used to warm the tender skin of the living and/or as a makeshift shroud for the dead. The graveyard contains nothing more than a series of stones that are unmarked with memoriousness, erased memorials to the rural underclass. The family do not have the psychic or financial resources to forge a more lasting monument to their dead children, their lives too slight to make a mark.

The living and the dead seem almost indistinguishable in the poem, and these mirroring images serve as a figure for the ghostly process of memory itself, the way the past shadows the present, inalterably different yet inextricably entangled. It is also a trope for the socioeconomic displacement of the sharecroppers, who are marginalized to the extent that they endure a social death-in-life. The poem ends with a poignant examination of how to fit the past into meaningful repetitions, patterns of remembering that diverge from traditional acts of memory. The closing lines focus on the centrality of lost children to this process: "My children who won't hear. / The night full of cries they will never make" (1). Generational memory—or, more significantly, generational loss—is transmitted through a maternal chain, one defined by absence, by the children who will remain forever unborn, a sign of unliving history that nevertheless crowds in on the present. The poem itself is the memorable act, the lasting book of the dead that recounts the felt lack of the past in the present through this deeply impressed vignette of a nonredemptive cemetery. Although it cannot transcend the sordid conditions of an estranging past, countermemory is for her a necessary act, a ritual of exorcism that resurrects the partial bodies of the past in the hope of making them whole again—a self-consciously impossible task.

Jordan's poems reflect the steady erosions of class-based deprivation and the threat of haphazard violence. In "Carolina Ghost Woods," the speaker remembers her father's going into the woods to kill himself and "returning, days later, / not talking, dirt-scuffed and smelling of smoke" (15). The family homestead is literally a haunted house, preserving the post-traumatic remains of slavery in its floorboards stained with the blood of a slave "murdered in 1863 when he tried to escape" (8): "this land of ghosts and amulets, / where the bloodstain on the attic floorboards won't wash up / and locked doors fling themselves open" (15). The landscape, like cultural memory, is bounded by what lingers outside the frame of consciousness, as the dead, shrouded in a "mist of absence," still await: "Those who wait outside the frame / raise me each morning, / constant in their mist of absence" (15). The family farm becomes a heterotopic site, unveiling the unsettling presence of those pushed to the fringes of collective memory. The ghosts of sharecroppers get their say; but, in reflecting the contrary movement of countermemory, it is just out of hearing: "Still I understand the words jostling / just out of hearing better than anything ever said" (16). Their value is articulated most forcefully through the silences that mark their absence from official history.

The "Along an Unseen Edge" section of *Carolina Ghost Woods* contains a series of poems that focus on deaths in the family, revealing the ubiquity of violent death that stuns comprehension once more into silence, as the speaker remembers when her uncle shot and killed his own son ("Through These Halls") and when her "mother tried to shoot my brother / not mattering, the pistol's trigger pulled again / and again, the bullets striking ground / between my brother's feet" ("Hitchhiking into West Virginia" 24). In "Two Hours before Sunrise," the family history of violence repeats itself in a meaningless cycle:

Strange, the brain's leaps. The deli, then my cousin
who taught me to drive a column stick shift
in the rust-blotched Ford behind our grandmother's cabin, gets life.

Over the years things happened I don't understand,
                                        and he kills a roomful of men.

A twist in the chain of neurons
                        and he decapitates them.

Who's to say what curves and u-turns haunted him,
which smudges on that strange map he couldn't follow
so the same night he'd leave the poolhall, that roomful of bodies,
and shoot Johnny Jones,
                        set him on fire
then watch as the flames rose to smoke, rose as the dead do
and like the dead, drifted in the gauze light of the bruised sky, back to me.
As one by one their stories are told
they fold themselves into the sledged dark and ask the same thing,
track the edges of my body, give me a name. (29–30)

The segment ends with a dead end, coming up against the wall of an unspeakable past, what can't be said, what Jordan "still can't say" (30).

"Dream of the End," the volume's final poem, suggests a model of memory that is internally splintered, a contradiction in terms: "A moon like a glass eye, staring and sightless, / memory that grows false, / and bones. Always bones" (58). Memory is both self-conscious and unknowing, staring and sightless, a false construction like a glass eye. Despite its artificial quality, its tendency to grow false, cultural memory nevertheless contains powerful resistant strains that expose authorized structures of collective remembrance. *Carolina Ghost Woods* is an exercise in telling the bare bones of sanctioned historicism, offering a dissociative understanding of the past that grants a limited sense of freedom for the future, which becomes inconsequential, literally out of sequence with the past:

But I sleep and dream of the moon's mule-whiskey drunk,
the anvil shot of the rave falling from night's pockets
and our inconsequentiality
stubbing beside the swollen bodies
dumped into the river with the two-headed fish. (58)

Despite this grotesque allegory of our inconsequentiality, the poem, and the volume as a whole, ends with a call to narrativize the past, repeating but abridging the famous line from the concluding section of *Audubon: A Vision*. Warren's "Tell me a story of deep delight" becomes simply an invocation to "Tell me a story," since delight is no longer the goal of the narrative impulse:

> Tell me a story, the round-headed boy said,
> and I did, by god, in this year of our lord,
> war oncoming from all sides. Why wouldn't I?
>
> In the night of the soul's dance across luminous skulls,
> it's the land that inherits me by the bulked black end. (59)

The contingency of the narrative drive, its ultimate incohesiveness, is announced with the perfectly rhetorical question, "Why wouldn't I?" For Jordan, storytelling's point lies in its apparent pointlessness, in the human need to make meaning for meaning's sake. Countermemory is a darker form of this nonredemptive commemoration, a dance across "luminous skulls" of the past.[9]

· · ◉ ◉ ◉ ◉ · ·

In *Elegy for the Southern Drawl* (1999), Rodney Jones[10] ventriloquizes regional "voice," one of the traditional marks of southern culture, as a form of counterdiscourse, less elegy than parody. The volume records the South's changing of the present, to borrow one of its section titles. Through an avowed contrarianism, his poems almost always move forward by misdirection. In "Natural Selection," for instance, he debunks the pomp and ritual of a high school coach who is a wannabe Bear Bryant, ironizing the Darwinism that is the presumed rule of nature between the goalposts and painted lines. His use of religious imagery is equally iconoclastic, particularly when read in relation to a customary southern context, reversing the sanctified meaning of terms like holy ground ("Holy Ground") or the sacraments ("Sacrament for My Penis") or sainthood ("Doing Laundry," the opening line of which declares "Here finally I have shriven myself and am saint" [101]). "Holy Ground" further reverses emphasis on place-bound identity. The poem starts out looking like an innocent account of the values of placefulness, as the speaker recalls a scenic vignette from his Alabama youth: "One place comes back from my early ranging ground: / A shelf of limestone alive with cedar and cactus, / A sampler of Palestine in North Alabama" (22). However, Jones takes this pastoral momentum and abruptly shifts direction, converting the landscape into a space of counterpastoral memory:

The glinting sewage of blue and brown glass

Made me know that the widow who'd lived below
Had made this unplantable tract a dumping ground.
The rock was pocked and puddle with rainwater
And felt blood-soaked and haunted with prophecy. (22)

The holy ground of the southern pastoral turns into an unhallowed dumping ground, glinting darkly with "sewage of blue and brown glass." The tract was never plantable to begin with, the agrarian ethos falls on unfertile ground, and now is a sad catch-all for modernity's detritus and remnants of built-in obsolescence. The rock, which, in its sheer material thingness, seems to loom out of the pages of the Old Testament, delivers an inarticulate prophecy of modern endlessness. Having stripped away the regional inheritance of pastoralism, Jones's childlike imagination then converts this rough ground into a site of faux primitivism, offering in the poem's closing image a glancing blow at primitivist mythology:

Stripping the bark, I'd find the balance
Of a handhold, then the stock and bolt.
Others may have seen sticks. I saw guns
To shape and stock carefully among the limbs

Of leafless trees. These would stem invasions,
And if the bomb fell, the one like a club,
Dark red and rich with pith, was the torch
That would lead me to shelter in the cave. (22)

Primitivism is mere child's play, a fantasy of regression appropriate to the mind of a child. In reversing the cultural nostalgia for both the pastoral and the primitive, Jones leads us to seek a new form of holy ground, not of transcendence but of cultural transformation.

In "The Assault on the Fields," pastoralism is not merely dangerous in a metaphoric sense. It is literally carcinogenic. Fields that seem to be covered in an idyllic blanket of snow are actually being converted into a chemical wasteland:

It was like snow, if snow could blend with air and hover,
    making, at first,

A rolling boil, mottling the pine thickets behind the fields,
    but then flattening
As it spread above the fenceposts and the whiteface cattle,
    an enormous, luminous tablet,

A shimmering, an efflorescence, through which my father
    rode on his tractor,
Masked like a Martian or a god to create the cloud where
    he kept vanishing;
Though, of course, it was not a cloud or snow, but poison,
    dichlorodiphenyltrichloroethane,

The word like a bramble of black locust on the tongue,
    and, after a while,
It would fill the entire valley, as, one night in spring,
    five years earlier,
A man from Joe Wheeler Electric had touched a switch
    and our houses filled with light. (85)

DDT is described as the ultimate counterpastoral force, a sign of presumed progress that has turned horrifically against the rural South. Even the word itself, *dichlorodiphenyltrichloroethane,* sounds like an alien dialect, the harsh, chemical syllables of science bringing a plague to the fields "like a bramble of black locust on the tongue." Jones does not, however, condemn all things associated with industrial technology: electricity is a positive addition to the countryside. However, the DDT-poisoned fields embody an uncanny space of countermemory—otherworldly in the worst sense (either Martian or godlike)— that is physically as well as psychically hazardous. In a sequence of two lines that mirrors the counterbalancing movement of Jones's chiasmatic sensibility, he invokes an ostensible nostalgia for the homeplace only to invert it just as quickly: "But home place still meant family. Misfortune was a well / of yellowish sulfur water" (85). The poem reeks with counterpastoral vistas that reflect the chemically induced desiccation of the land:

Carp have rotted from the surfaces of ponds, there is no
    stench to it;
It is more of an absence of things barely apprehended,
    of flies, of moths;

> Until one day the hawks who patrolled the air over
>   the chicken coops are gone (87)

And naturally—or rather, unnaturally—the human animal is also endangered. Jones's poisoned fields bring humans down to an animalistic level, ironically through our very overmastery of nature, our ability to manipulate the natural cycle and to create synthetic blends that have the bleak power to unravel our own DNA:

> And when a woman, who was a girl then, finds a lump,
>   what does it have to do
> With the green fields and the white dust boiling
>   and hovering?
> When I think of the name Jenny Flowers, it is that
>   whiteness I think of.
>
> Some bits have fallen to clump against a sheet of tin
>   roofing
> The tornado left folded in the ditch, and she stoops there
>   to gather
> A handful of chalk to mark the grounds for hopscotch. (87–88)

Once more in a countermemorial reversal, we are presented with a dark parody of child's play that grimly inverts the normative structure of a child drawing hopscotch squares by exposing the radical unhealthiness of this seemingly innocent act. Nature is not figured as a particularly benevolent force—the tornado has ripped off a sheet of tin roofing—but human nature doesn't seem to be faring much better, proliferating cancer by polluting our food source.

"Elegy for the Southern Drawl" presents an unelegy for the supposed loss of a distinctive southern voice. In doing so, it provides a metapoetic exploration of the state of current southern poetry. The opening stanza is a litany of the peculiarities of southern expression, encompassing a range of working-class characters associated with the South's stereotypical status as underbelly of the nation "writ large," including a forklift worker, fundamentalist spinsters, and Shoney's customers:

> It is all dying out now in a voice asking,
> "Where you from? How y'all folks doin'?"

On the blank verse of the forklift man,
From way off down there and yonder,
Is draining, thou and thine, from prayers
Of spinsters in the Nazarene Church—
Is dying of knowledge of the world,
But still going, barely, in a grunted "hidey"
In the line at the cash register at Shoney's,
A father telling how he came north
To visit his son, impatience starting up
Its coughs behind him, his *yes'ms* and *no'ms*
An impediment here, Confederate money.
Kid's in my office, slow-talking. I ask,
"Where you from?" He doesn't seem to want
To say, thinks again, then does. "All over." (47)

The southern drawl is an impediment up North, an outworn currency; however, within the context of southern literature, it has proven a valuable commodity, a way for regional writers to differentiate their product by marketing the strangeness of its local accents to a national audience. Through its rhetorical difference, the South appears to be a more authentic, even autochthonous region, and the signs of authenticity are indeed profitable. Jones is aware of this problem: if you kill off the southern drawl, you kill off much of the draw of southern literature. And so he constructs a sleight-of-hand performance that evokes what it is supposed to revoke, that falls in love with the thing it was sent to kill:

The old people in the valley where I was born
Still held to the brogue, elisions, and colortura
Of the Scotch-Irish, and brandished
Like guns the *iffens*, *you'ns*, and *narys*
That linked by the labyrinthine hollers
Of the foothills of the Appalachian Mountains
The remnants of a people whose dominion
Obtained no less from unerring marksmanship
Than their spiteful resolve never to learn
Any tongue as remote as Greek or Latin,
Much less the Cherokee of Sequoya
That still haunted, like mist, the names of rivers.

"And there was May," my great-grandmother would say,
After May Collum's husband had been cut in half
At the sawmill, "lookin' like the hind wheels of destruction." (48)

Even as Jones preaches the South's eulogy, he shows that reports of the demise of the fable of southern exceptionalism have been greatly exaggerated. He records his embarrassment at *talking*—and therefore *being*—southern, for language and identity are intertwined:

All the time I was learning the telling of time,
The names of county seats, and division,
I was blotching red with self-loathing,
And mumbling to mask the raw carcass
Of the mispronounced deep within myself,
Which was only the accent of the dying
Language of my South, which is a defeated country. (49)

If, as Lacan tells us, language is the basis of identity, then "southernness" is a linguistic construction, given to the ambiguities and contrary impulses, the existential uncertainties, of discursive acts. The southern drawl is a means of identification with regional culture, not a root-deep basis of subjectivity. Language and its socially conditioned "mispronunciation," however, do strongly influence the creation of the self, seeming to lie "deep within," when they might be more properly seen as contingencies that have been naturalized by common use. The places he must commit to memory are also linguistic constructs—the county seats are merely names. This point is reiterated by the interconnection and slippage between racial dialects in the South. The southern drawl comes in both black and white, for Jones hears in "The almost *r*-less river talk of merchant planters, / Droned out and of a lazy kinship to the sleek, / Ambidextrous blackspeak of their former slaves" (53). Indeed, language becomes a marker of identification on transnational levels as well. The southernized sentence, "Murtis, this hair's my naiphew Graig—" (54), harbors "Only a hair shallower in the mouth than / The London cockney of a Lebanese immigrant" (54). In a brief turn of phrase, the South and its accent becomes globalized, its hybrid nuances transportable across cultural lines. Moreover, Jones uses the language of the Lost Cause to effect a turnaround ("the accent of the dying / Language of my South, which is a defeated country"), replacing the pathos of a long-past defeat with the contemporary status of the South as an increasingly malleable and transferrable space.

In scouting the limits of what counts as southern nowadays, Jones makes a stop in Nashville, which has become a decidedly international city where country music, it seems, takes on a multiplicity of different countries. Nashville is figured as a music-producing conglomerate, a rhinestone-studded backdrop for mechanically produced yee-haws and faux cowboy-ism, for singers who have gone country only after country has already become cool. These walking parodies of "southernness" seem to be mimicking—as sincerely as possible—what Jones later calls "the exaggerated drawl of country singers / What I took for false emphasis, a pandering / To the cheap seats" (56):

> Some kind of hippie cowboy on the elevator
> Going up in the Music City Days Inn,
> He's apologizing for his pink hardshell
> Guitar case jammed in the closing door,
> Thanks, and he's gone, the only white
> Man I've heard speaking the hoarse,
> Barreled-in English of a native of India.
> Later, in the lobby, more cowboys,
> Chaws in their mouths like extra molars,
> Rhinestone collars, tight black jeans,
> Luminous belt buckles, big fellows,
> Talking Russian. This is Nashville,
> Shrunken world, a hundred twenty miles
> North of home. Anna Karenina,
> Meet Minnie Pearl. At the bar
> Of Tootsie's Orchid Lounge, where
> All the rednecks used to dress like Johnny
> Cash or Patsy Cline when they came
> To be discovered, I stand a welcome toast
> To the new line of wannabes: Yoruba
> Dolly Partons, Cuban Robert Frosts. (52–53)

The invocation of a passing sense of "home" is set against the thoroughly transregional, transnational space of the Music City Days Inn lobby, where "the hoarse, / Barreled-in English of a native of India" commingles with strains of Russian speech. Here, money, not music, is the universal language. If Yoruba Dolly Partons were not shocking enough, there is the final reference to Cuban Robert Frosts. On one level, this surprising cameo by Frost elevates the value of older, less obviously artificial country music by connecting it to one of the most venerated U.S. poets of the twentieth century, who famously schooled his audience in the need of being versed in country things. It also relocates the poem in a metapoetic context, suggesting a twinge of nostalgia for the making of poetry, often a financially unrewarding but aesthetically rich enterprise.

The loose, associative style of the poem's various vignettes satirizes a folksy voice with little new to say, as Jones even incorporates its share of faux Faulknerisms. In aping Faulkner's dialect, Jones chooses form over content, converting Faulkner's Nobel Prize acceptance speech into hollow forms, as the master himself was wont to do about so many other versions of clichéd expression. Faulkner's speech is "Just words" that offer little hope of enduring or prevailing:

> In a recording of Faulkner's speech,
> The words wallow and hover, *endyuah*
> In a line all to itself, *prevaiah* like Isaiah
>
> Salted and drying behind the tongue—
> Just words—no human but the language
> Grinding at the shackle of the quotation.
>
> One way to learn a language might be
> To forget yourself, ape everything you hear.
> Another would be to shut up and listen. (55)

Jones, like so many post-Faulknerian southern writers, has had to serve his apprenticeship to Old Bill, but now grinds at the shackle of Faulkner's influence. He has had to shut up and listen and has learned to speak the language well, fully schooled in the standard codes of "renascence" literature. Like Prospero to Caliban, Faulkner taught Jones language, and his profit on it is he knows how to curse. Learning to curse means turning the language back against itself, twisting it up in a countermemorial manner that, to reinvoke Foucault's terms, functions as "the appropriation of a vocabulary turned against those who had once used it." Jones seeks to mangle the high-minded airs of self-consciously "sophisticated" literature, sharing a parable on the fantasy of diction, on the arbitrary limits imposed by language: as a boy, he "mistook the meaning / Of *sophistication* for *constipation*, / A parable, perhaps, on the fantasy of diction" (56). In the end, Jones acknowledges that dialect offers a shaded, indirect, and incomplete record of a region's cultural history, if we can pick out the meaningful strains:

I feel odd hearing a tape of my own voice
That marks wherever I go, the sound

Of lynchings, the letters of misspellings
Crooked and jumbled to dupe the teacher,
Slow ink, slow fluid of my tribe, meaning

What words mean when they are given
From so many voices, I do not know myself
Who is speaking and who is listening. (57)

Meaning is contextual, audience-based; who is listening is as important to the meaning of an utterance as who is speaking. The contingencies of identifications made in language are self-reflexively proposed in the wry statement, "I do not know myself." Identification is a multi-voiced discourse: being true to oneself is a contradiction in terms. The final stanza offsets an Eliotic narrative of a redemptive, culturally purifying tribalism ("my tribe")—Eliot's desire to purify the dialect of the tribe—with a blunt recognition of the darker aspects of such clannish thinking, made poignant in "the sound / Of lynchings." In evoking a gruesome countermemory of the sound of spectacular violence, Jones *putrefies* the dialect of the white southern tribe.

· · ◦ ◉ ▦ ◉ ◦ · ·

Harryette Mullen[11] is the writer most eccentric to the southern tradition, biographically and poetically. Arguably southern poetry's fullest subscriber to the L=A=N=G=U=A=G=E movement, her poetics departs significantly from the narrative mode. Yet her connections to the region are apparent in images of a vehement southern racism not yet past as well as her manipulation of a blues-based style and black southern dialect. Her verse is imbued with a notably transouthern quality, intermingling different spheres of regional influence, shifting, as Mullen herself has done, from South to Southwest to West.[12] Her poems expose the constraining as well as liberatory possibilities of such transculturation. Mullen's work gives Homi Bhabha's thesis about hybridity a regional demonstration, illustrating his argument that models of identity should admit the existence of "cultural liminality *within the nation*" (148). Such "borderline existences" disrupt the "linear narrative of the nation" (142), and the cultural hybridizations fostered by the interaction of contending ethnic traditions "emphasize the incommensurable elements as the basis of cultural identities" (218). Indeed, her verse fashions a hybridization on a formal level through its invocation of blues meters in conjunction with experimental linguistic play, providing a trenchant example of how poetic form embodies mixed cultural inheritances. In *Muse & Drudge* (1995), she commingles a highly improvisational two- to four-beat grounding rhythm—with heavy echoes of the southern blues stanza—with verbal freeplay to provide a vision of southernness as a portable phenomenon. Her poetry plays on crossovers between highbrow and vernacular discourses, wrenching together high and mass cultures and in the process exploring the way that folk art can be commodified and circulated on a mass scale. Engaging in a highly elusive allusiveness, Mullen supplies a mix-and-match sequence of linguistic snippets, jarring sound bites that are radically recontextualized. Far from being a meaningless jumble of random images, *Muse & Drudge* is carefully arranged. The overall pattern of four-line stanzas with a rhyme scheme that comes and goes signifies off the communal form of the blues stanza, while still engendering a healthy amount of surface-level chaos. Mullen puts the necessary mediating influence of language front and center, making a spectacle of the materiality of words themselves by putting "prescribed mediation / unblush-ingly on display" (2). The start-and-stop syncopation of the rhythm alongside defamiliarizing puns that disrupt the flow of expected meanings (e.g., "there's more to love / where that came from" [14] or "heavy model chevy of yore / old time religion / low down get real down / get right with Godzilla" [14]) and sur-prising enjambments as well as heavy alliteration and assonance (e.g., "muse of the world picks / out stark melodies / her raspy fabric / tickling the ebonies" [17]) call especial attention to the processes of language itself, taking apart the way social categories of value are put together.

Mullen is concerned with matching up the aesthetic and ethical dimen-sions of her verse, asserting the political effect of the volume's interspersion of high and mass cultures, its tonal breaks and turns, its allusive play, and its concern with the shifting nature of identity. Her political critique takes on issues of regional identification, especially as imbedded in entrenched racial inequities. Thadious Davis contends that many African American writers, in-cluding those who were not born in the South, draw on the southern tradition, looking southward "to claim a history, to explain a legacy, and to understand the regionality of the black self" (7). In bluesy lines that incorporate images of the surreal, *Muse & Drudge* investigates the regionality of the *ex*-centric black self through shock poetics, exposing the ways in which race functions in col-lusion and collision with regional allegiances. To invoke the title of Houston Baker's recent book, Mullen's poetry embodies a poetic act of "turning South again"—with a vengeance. She both celebrates and critiques the hybridizations of transouthern culture: the liberating quality of crossing culturally impressed boundaries of identity is tempered by an awareness of the potential for this multiplicity of identifications to be placed in the service of consumer culture.

The "breakneck beauty" (55) of *Muse & Drudge*'s diehard autoreferentiality is apparent from the opening page, which declares tauntingly: "you've had my thrills / a reefer a tub of gin / don't mess with me I'm evil / I'm in your sin" (1). Mullen includes a heavy dose of linguistic performance concerning the volume's heavy dose of linguistic performance, even naming referents by name: "missing referents murking it up / with clear actors lacking" (12). The pun on "missing referents" implies that, though strict referents will be absent from Mullen's verse, we won't miss them, since the intuitive quantum leaps of an arch yet politically pointed self-reflexivity will more than compensate. While there is sometimes a play of art for art's sake ("a picture perfect / twisted her limbs / lovely as a tree / for art's sake" [17]), she realizes that, unless this linguistic open-endedness is responsive to a social context, "bric-a-brac's got no home" (48). So Mullen is and is not writing a kind of "mumbo-jumbo palaver gibber blunder" (57). The ideological payoff is in the challenge to rethink facile solutions to contemporary socioeconomic issues, exposing the unreality of current social realities, especially the insidiously enigmatic figure of racial imbalance. She dares us to impose what can only be provisional interpretations on her starkly ambiguous text—"think you're able to solve / a figure, go ahead and risk it" (70)—yet she does provide some occasional semblances of grounding contexts to point us in the right directions through flickering snippets of narrative. In connecting the unwieldy play of poetic meanings explicitly to current issues of race, region, and gender, Mullen takes us beyond the funhouse of first-wave postmodernism that John Barth built: "houses of Heidelberg / outhouse cracked house / destroyed funhouse lost / and found house of dead dolls" (76).

This extreme freeplay takes on racial and regional dimensions as Mullen describes her desire to "shake it down south": "get a new mouth / don't care what it costs / smell that hot sauce / shake it down south" (8). The lines signify on "down south" as both region and race, invoking the racially plagued terrain of the U.S. South and summoning up the power of the body to resist those social meanings imposed on it. Like Yeats's famous "body swayed to music," though with a distinctly southernized bent, Mullen's gyrating body shaking down south is a figure for rhythm's unconscious flow, for the merging of form and content that erases, for the time being, the litany of social inscriptions that racially encode the body. Throughout *Muse & Drudge*, region is second skin to racial identification, since the sorrow that has bowed her body owns southern origins, as Mullen directly quotes the quintessential Southern Baptist hymn,

"Just as I Am, Without One Plea" (1849): "just as I am I come / knee bent and body bowed / this here's sorrow's home / my body's southern song" (80). Identify with region, Mullen tells us, and experience powerful results, even if taking on this affiliation is a sorrowful process, given black southerners' cultural inheritance of living through racial violence and apartheid. In doubling up the forces of race and region, Mullen is shaking up the Southland, making troubling ruptures for a regional hierarchy based largely on racial politics. She takes us down home, back to the rural South for a rather unidyllic, but invigorating, "ramble in brambles":

> a ramble in brambles
> the blacker more sweeter juicier
> pores sweat into blackberry tangles
> going back native natural country wild briers
>
> country clothes hung on her all and sundry
> bolt of blue have mercy ink perfume
> that snapping turtle pussy
> won't let go until thunder comes (3–4)

The effort at "going back native" among the "natural country wild briers" does not demarcate a root-deep affinity for the South, but shows Mullen to be trying on "country clothes" for size. Her concern with the language of African American spirituals and blues is hinted at with the interjection of a "have mercy" that comes into the line like a "sundry / bolt of blue." In fact, *Muse & Drudge* carries on a particular dialogue with Mississippi bluesman Robert Johnson, sampling his lingo throughout her poem (e.g., "drylongso" from "Come into My Kitchen" and "feets too big" from "They're Red Hot") and channels the voice of a raucous blueswoman, who is "talking shit up blues creek" (55). The blues as a form of signifying against racism is brought into play at times playfully, not without laughter: "pot said kettle's mama must've / burnt them turnip greens / kettle deadpanned not missing a beat / least mine ain't no skillet blonde" (7). Mullen makes it clear that the blues are best when played in the dark, implying that the codes of hybridity should not be used to excuse the stealing of the aesthetic property of black artists disenfranchised by the workings of Jim Crow and its continued legacy of more subtle institutionalized racism. The appropriation of black southern folkways represented by white covers of blues and jazz is specifically called out: "white covers of black material

/ dense fabric that obeys its own logic / shadows pieced together tears and all / unfurling sheets of bluish music" (32). Making money off the labor of black artists is the equivalent of cashing in on "black veins hammered gold" (41).

For Mullen, region is a way of further complicating the already deeply conflicted issue of racial subjectivity, a means for "a major retrospection" (21) that realizes a transouthern multiplicity. She reveals that there is no deep-structure relation between place and race, but these categories still represent compelling metonymic adjacencies as the two spheres of influence edge up against each other, creating overlap and friction: "my skin but not my kin / my race but not my taste / my state and not my fate / my country not my kunk" (10). Just as Mullen's race does not determine her taste and her state does not make her fate, race and region are not destiny, but that doesn't mean they don't count. The social fictions of race and region function as arbitrary but power-fully motivating factors in contemporary formulations of identity, condition-ing in part our material experience of the world. Instead of summoning up these social borders to root identity in a stabilizing relation to place and race, Mullen uses them to debase the cultural currency of singular concepts of racial and regional identity. Her poetry explores "how a border orders disorder" (10), how re-reifying the edges of dominant culture by ironically replicating these in her verse paradoxically produces space for resistance, bringing into focus a dy-namic form of countermemory: "edges sharpened / remove the blur / enhance the image / of dynamic features" (19).

Mullen avoids the fraying of meaning involved in signifying for signify-ing's sake, where all topics can become equally untopical, exploiting an irrever-ent irrelevance to point up pointlessness itself. Mullen puts stones in the pas-sageway of traditional historicism, setting countermemories against sanctioned cultural memory—that is, against "history written with whitening" (45). *Muse & Drudge* is not merely an exercise in "hip hyperbole," but speaks to the racing of history that continues to mark contemporary definitions of the South. In so doing, Mullen drags southern poetry out of the backwoods and makes strong "blackward" progress: "with all that rope they gave us / we pulled a mule out of the mud / dragging backwoods along / in our strong blackward progress" (33). The volume's resistance to facile analysis parallels countermemory's modes of historical resistance, "dark work and hard / though any mule can / knock down the barn / what we do best requires finesse" (49). Mullen's play of poetic rhythms and meanings supplies the finesse required to inspire "the dark work and hard" of knocking down dominant structures of the southern past.

· · ● ● ● · · ·

Natasha Trethewey[13] is a southern poet of mixed racial identity whose work often intertwines the poetic and the photographic in order to challenge hierarchical constructions of race, gender, and class against the changing frame of regional dynamics. Many of the poems included in Trethewey's three published volumes speak to elements of her own history, especially her inheritance of growing up as a biracial child in the Deep South, the daughter of what was in 1966 still an illegal marriage between a white man and a black woman. As Trethewey has commented, "it seemed to me that because I had been born into the state in 1966, when miscegenation was still illegal, I was rendered a kind of psychological exile" (Rowell 1032). Other aspects of her southern upbringing have also played a significant part in her cultural work as a poet, and her personal past reflects some of the broader trends of contemporary southern history, embodying the frictions between blacks and whites, matriarchal and patriarchal lineage, rural and highway cultures.[14] One of Trethewey's major concerns, perhaps her primary thematic commitment to date, centers on a countermemorial practice that Charles Henry Rowell terms her penchant for making "*inscriptive restorations.*" During their interview, Rowell suggested that Trethewey, along with writers like Komunyakaa and Rita Dove, is shifting African American poetry away from "the prescriptive pronouncements of the Black Arts Movement" and towards "the restoration of what is not seen or is forgotten as a result of erasure from local and national memory" (1021), to which Trethewey responded:

> Yes, I think I've been concerned with what I have noticed to be the erasures of history for a very long time. Those stories often left to silence or oblivion, the gaps within the stories that we are told, both in the larger public historical records and in our family histories as well, the stories within families that people don't talk about, the things that are kept hushed. And so I've always been interested in those contentions between public and cultural memory, larger history and private or family memory and stories. And so I do seek to restore or to recover those subjugated narratives. (1021)

In her effort "to create a public record of people who are often excluded from the public record" (1025), Trethewey strives "to restore what's been erased from the landscape and left out of the public record or forgotten" in order "to make poems that will stand as monuments to our overlooked past" (1034). Like Mullen, her creation of poetic countermonuments is interfused with a thorough awareness of the hybrid nature of subjectivity as part of a disrupted and disruptive regional and transregional narratives. She likewise fashions a vision of identity as a mediated process, exchanging a rigid understanding of essentialized being for a potentially liberatory and socially inscribed sense of existential becoming. Her verse captures "that idea of becoming, of constantly making one's self, of striving to move to the next thing, as opposed to a kind of stagnant being" (1024–25). And the definition of southernness is crucial to her construction of dynamic becoming: when I asked her during our interview whether she considers herself a "southern" writer (with its traditional overtones of white male privilege), she responded by suggesting that transculturation should be built into our evolving understanding of southernness:

> I am the quintessential Southern writer! Quintessentially American too! Geography is fate. Of all the kinds of fate swirling around my very being, this place in which I was born and this particular historical moment matter deeply. The story of America has always been a story of miscegenation, of border crossings, of integration of cultures, and again, I embody this in my person. To me, I fit in as the quintessential Southerner. Perhaps even now my role is to establish what has always been Southern, though at other points in history it has been excluded from "Southernness." We just hadn't found the right metaphor yet. Which is to me one of the reasons why *Native Guard* has been successful. People finally saw the American story. I think Mississippians see our story in that American story. I boldly think of myself as that native guardian. Not to mention that my name, Natasha, actually shares the prefix of words like "native" and "national" and "nativity." It's there in my very naming. (Turner, 2010)

As Trethewey invokes, yet passes beyond traditional ideas of southern identity, her verse also manipulates received forms, including sonnets and other verse conventions, but fills these with politically dynamic contents, as a crucible contains the roiling energies of fired metals.

Frequently these twinned concepts of recovering an officially deleted past and the openness of hybrid subjectivity are channeled through an intensive exploration of the practice of photographic art. When asked about the motif of photography in her work, Trethewey replied that she is "especially interested in absence" created by photographic form (Petty 364).[15] Her poetry has been influenced by the photographic theories of Roland Barthes and Susan Sontag.

Both theorists explore the mimetic, enworlded quality of the photograph that lends it an aura of objectivity in tension with its often veiled artifice, which connects the image to a range of sociocultural meanings. What Barthes terms "the photographic paradox"—"the paradox which makes an inert object into a language and which transforms the non-culture of a 'mechanical' art into the most social of institutions" (*The Responsibility of Forms* 20)—has become a center-piece of critical inquiries into the *techne* of photography and underlies much of the dynamics of the photographic motif in Trethewey's poems.[16] If we learn to pay attention to the cultural encoding of what appears to be a transhistorical, uncoded medium, we can infuse our experience of viewing a photograph with an ethical and political motivation, for photographs "are a grammar and, even more importantly, an ethics of seeing" (Sontag, *On Photography* 3). Trethewey investigates the ethical dimensions of photography by extending the range of suppressed hierarchies from gender to ethnic and class imbalances, recording a volatile convergence of these cathected elements.[17]

Bellocq's Ophelia (2002) depicts Ophelia as a "very white-skinned black woman" who, because her veins contain an ounce of black blood, is relegated to second-class citizenship according to the fiercely held racial binarism of the 1910s South. The figure of Ophelia was inspired by a series of photographs produced around 1912 by E. J. Bellocq, who visited the red-light district of the French Quarter in New Orleans in order to find his subjects, taking candid photographs of prostitutes, some of whom appear to be of mixed race.[18] The explanatory note for the volume describes the origin of Trethewey's Ophelia:

> Ophelia is the imagined name of a prostitute photographed circa 1912 by E. J. Bellocq, later collected in the book, *Storyville Portraits*. A very white-skinned black woman—mulatto, quadroon, or octoroon—she would have lived in one of the few "colored" brothels such as Willie Piazza's Basin Street Mansion or Lula White's Mahogany Hall, which, according to the *Blue Book* [the book of advertisements for the New Orleans brothels], was known as the "Octoroon Club." (6)

Trethewey describes her reaction upon seeing Bellocq's photographs in an American studies course at the University of Massachusetts: "They were stunning, they were compelling, they were filled with the 'punctums' that Roland Barthes talks about—those little things within a photograph that often will draw you out of the immediate action of the photograph to contemplate all that is behind it or outside of it" (Rowell 1028). In *Camera Lucida* (1980), Barthes defines the notion of "punctum," which literally means "puncture" or "wound" and reflects our immediate reaction to the photograph, especially the personally wounding detail that evokes a visceral, emotive response between the viewer and the pictured subject: "A photograph's *punctum* is that accident [of photographic detail] which pricks me (but also bruises me, is poignant to me) . . . for *punctum* is also: sting, speck, cut, little hole—and also a cast of the dice" (27). A punctum is usually an inadvertent detail that becomes imprinted on the viewer's memory and leads to a recognition of the constructed nature of the "reality" depicted by the photograph, thus leading us beyond merely the literal subject matter. The punctum establishes an emotional link with the picture and gestures toward the world outside the photographic frame.

Through her depictions of a number of Bellocq's photographs and her accompanying instances of poetic punctums, Trethewey construes photography as at times a nonmimetic, even countermimetic force: for her, the camera *does lie*, eliding as much as it presents within the frame. Her renderings of Bellocq's portraits show that photography, in the very process of presumably "realistic" disclosure, can close down other realities, other vantage points. Trethewey's work demands, however, that we go beyond merely cloaking her verse in the platitudes of the inexpressibility topos. By commingling poetic with photographic modes, *Bellocq's Ophelia* demonstrates that the tears in the fabric of representation—in this case, the aural dimension of poetry in friction with the visual technics of photography—expose tears in the social fabric as well.[19] In fleshing out the veiled history of Ophelia, Trethewey practices a "calculated disarray" (44) that seeks to expand the narrow array of regional emanations of racial and gender identities, disclosing the severity of these socially constructed codes. The spectrum of hybrid identifications is broadened by her concerns with economics as a further band of subjectivity, as the poems are set in a working-class quarter of multiethnic New Orleans, a heightened nexus of creolization on the Gulf Coast, of globalism grounded.

The title poem of *Bellocq's Ophelia* announces the photographic motif by distinguishing it from painting. In contrast to Millais's pre-Raphaelite rendition of a drowned Ophelia among watery flowers that preserves her pristine melancholic beauty, Bellocq's photographic record of Ophelia is a more grittily realistic account. Yet photography can be an equally disingenuous art, also prone to the vicissitudes of a perspectival relativism:

> In Millais's painting, Ophelia dies faceup,
> eyes and mouth open as if caught in the gasp
> of her last word or breath, flowers and reeds

growing out of the pond, floating on the surface
around her. The young woman who posed
lay in a bath for hours, shivering,
catching cold, perhaps imagining fish
tangling in her hair or nibbling a dark mole
raised upon her white skin. Ophelia's final gaze
aims skyward, her palms curling open
as if she's just said, *Take me.* (3)

Trethewey deromanticizes the pre-Raphaelite concern with lyrical subjects of a bygone era. In a poetic reenactment of Barthesian punctum, she muddies the waters by introducing the issue of race through the image of fish "nibbling a dark mole / raised upon [Millais's Ophelia's] white skin." The lines run in a more or less steady iambic pentameter until the closing line of the stanza, which contains only two unaccented syllables in order to make the final spondaic imperative more abrupt and forceful. The accented "*Táke mé*" makes emphatic the volume's concern with gender relations, challenging the cultural equations of males as artists (Millais and Bellocq) and females as objects of art (the two Ophelias). Trethewey thus signifies on her own power as a female artist, who is particularly invested in tracing the collisions of racial and gendered identities within the specific regional currents and countercurrents of the South. Against Millais's lily white Ophelia, Trethewey presents an "other Ophelia":

I think of her when I see Bellocq's photograph—
a woman posed on a wicker divan, her hair
spilling over. Around her, flowers—
on a pillow, on a thick carpet. Even
the ravages of this old photograph
bloom like water lilies across her thigh.
How long did she hold there, this other
Ophelia, nameless inmate in Storyville,
naked, her nipples offered up hard with cold? (3)

This is not a pretty picture: far from being a placidly mimetic form, photography is an art that ravages. The hard enjambment that splits "other" and "Ophelia" emphasizes Trethewey's understanding of her subject as a countermemorial figure of otherness. However, this first glimpse we receive of Bellocq's Ophelia makes her seem utterly passive, a pure object of the male gaze; in fact, the poem then exposes the scopophilic potential of the photograph: "The small mound of her belly, the pale hair / of her pubis—these things—her body / there for the taking" (3). Like her painterly namesake, this Ophelia too appears to be ripe for the taking. However, in the concluding lines, Trethewey reverses field, reading between the lines to reveal a daring woman ready to talk back:

> But in her face, a dare.
> Staring into the camera, she seems to pull
> all the movement from her slender limbs
> and hold it in her heavy-lidded eyes.
> Her body limp as dead Ophelia's,
> her lips poised to open to speak. (3)

In a moment of resistance, she returns the male gaze, which is mechanically reproduced by the distant yet absorbing camera eye. Despite her limp body, she is no longer merely posed, but now *poised*, prepared to speak for herself. Though in a position of abjection, the subject here speaks through her very silence.

While Ophelia is now on the verge of redefining her identity, coming into her *selves* is an arduous process. In "Letters from Storyville," she confesses that she took arsenic tablets in an effort to bleach her skin "white as stone" (20). Still awaiting the approval of a white man to reflect her own identity, she makes a spectacle of her body so it can be fetishized through the camera's power to capture her image and keep it vulnerable to the scopophilic pleasures of an always screened viewer/voyeur. As she poses for one of Bellocq's photographs, she faces the camera, waiting "for the photograph to show me who I am" (20). At this point, Ophelia believes in the power of photography to reproduce a faithful vision of material reality, implying a stable relation between an inner core of essential identity and external processes of representation, a seamless interchange between interiority and exteriority. She later recognizes that identity is not so easily fixed, but can offer only a rough outline of possible identifications. Subjectivity is a trick of the eye that allows us to substitute the signs of the real for the real, to accept the pictorial surface as depth, in photographic art as well as the art of subjectivity. This falling away of socially inscribed meanings into a sense of selfhood as fluid multiplicity begins, appropriately enough, in the shadowlands of nightmare:

> in the dream where I have run, again,
> into the tobacco barn at the back end
> of the plantation. The light I let in startles
> the cockroaches, and they fly from the eaves,

their wings beating toward my face.
The man who comes wears a carnival mask,
and I am the grinning *nigger*
on whose tongue he places a shiny coin.
When I try to speak, more coins fall
from my mouth, and I can't cry out
or say what I want. (23)

The return, "again," to the horror-laced space of the plantation startles the unspeaking speaker into recognition. In the Freudian space of the absurd, yet meaningful dream, Ophelia first becomes aware of her desire to tear off the mask of a kind of blackface minstrelsy, to say what she wants. In doing so, she gives voice to a call for countermemory, a desire to be free of the forms of memory that have been impressed on her psyche: "I want freedom from memory. / I could then be somebody else, born again, / free in the white space of forgetting" (24). The white space of forgetting combines photographic and poetic metaphors for uncreating subjectivity, invoking both the blank surface of the unused photographic plate as well as the open space of the unwritten page. "Memory" here connotes the entanglements of the personal and the collective. As stressed by the distressingly confined alliteration of the phrase "I am the grinning *nigger*," the self is defined in devastating terms as the unblinkingly racialized I. Her effort to unwrite the naturalized codes of memory coincides with her becoming "both model and apprentice" (27), learning the tricks of the trade from Bellocq so that she can seize the means of artistic production. As a poor, part-black woman in the segregated South, Ophelia is excluded from the white, male sphere of commerce. She can only sell herself, something made clear in the poem titled "Bellocq":

I try to pose as I think he would like—shy
at first, then bolder. I'm not so foolish
that I don't know this photograph *we* make
will bear the stamp of his name, not mine. (39)

The pronoun shifts of the final lines tell the story: their composition will be marked as his, not hers. The supposedly open market of democratic capitalism is closed down on the levels of race, gender, and class, especially down South.

Trethewey then describes a spectrum of photographs that envision Ophelia's different postures, her separate disclosures, portraits of resistance. Through these photographic memories, Trethewey creates a counter-history for

Ophelia that frees her, at least temporarily, through the self-reflexive as well as the culturally reflective qualities of photographic/poetic art. In "Portrait #2," one of Bellocq's nude photographs of her, she thinks "how not to be exposed, though naked, how / to wear skin like a garment, seamless" (42). In the segregated South, race was much more than skin-deep, signifying a range of cultural affiliations, marking whites as superior, blacks inferior. But the open space of art—particularly one that maintains piercing traces of the real and therefore keeps us mindful of history—allows Ophelia to imagine that she can change her racial identification as she would her garments. Trethewey's ekphrastic form unstitches the seams that bind together the social fabric, revealing the artificial constructions of identity, a point reiterated when Bellocq reminds her that "*These plates are fragile*" (42). Through the process of photographic art and, by metapoetic extension, of Trethewey's own poetry, Ophelia begins to understand the fragility of self-identification, "how easy it is / to shatter this image of myself, how / a quick scratch carves a scar across my chest" (42). The sonnet titled "Photography" provides a telling site of countermemory, as the binary structure of the racist and antifeminist codes of southern culture are inverted, picturing an alternate reality: "In the negative the whole world reverses, my black dress turned / white, my skin blackened to pitch. *Inside out, /* I said, thinking of what I've tried to hide" (43). The lines develop a photographic negative of things as they are, for the external signifiers of racial difference are turned inside out and shown to be hollow at the core. Ophelia then superimposes her own perspective over the falsely objective viewpoint of the camera lens, drawing attention to the "other things," such as a hidden bruise, afterimage of violence and literal instance of the punctum, that Bellocq's trained eye has missed:

> I look at what he can see through his lens
> and what he cannot—silverfish behind
> the walls, the yellow tint of a faded bruise—
> other things here, what the camera misses (43).

Ophelia's reframing of the signs of otherness that the camera has excluded imbues the photograph with a kind supramimetic quality, a graphic account of what is above and beyond the camera's range.

In "Disclosure," the photographic plate becomes a palimpsest that records the vestigial presence of countermemory even as it is scratched out from the official history:

When Bellocq doesn't like a photograph
he scratches across the plate. But I know
other ways to obscure a face—paint it
with rouge and powder, shades lighter than skin,
don a black velvet mask. I've learned to keep
my face behind the camera, my lens aimed
at a dream of my own making. What power
I find in this transforming what is real—a room
flushed with light, calculated disarray.
Today I tried to capture a redbird
perched on the tall hedge. As my shutter fell,
he lifted in light, a vivid blur above
the clutter just beyond the hedge—garbage,
rats licking the insides of broken eggs. (44)

Ophelia discovers power in the transformative force of photographic art, just
as Trethewey's own manipulation of poetic form also displays a powerful "cal-
culated disarray," using a tight formalism to disarrange the tight spectrum of
identifications made available by a backward-looking southern culture. The
sonnet closes with another disclosure of countermemory, as the idyllic glimpse
of a perched redbird is counterweighed by a decidedly unpastoral scene: pasto-
ral nostalgia becomes little more than "a vivid blur" that gives way to a cultural
space cluttered with social problems, emblematized by "the clutter just beyond
the hedge—garbage, / rats licking the insides of broken eggs." "Spectrum" again
calls attention to the dull palette of racial definition in the South, where a body
is either black or white, one or the other:

No sun, and the city's a dull palette
of gray—weathered ships docked at the quay, rats
dozing in the hull, drizzle slicking dark stones
of the streets. Mornings such as these, I walk
among the weary, their eyes sunken
as if each body, diseased and dying,
would pull itself inside, back to the shining
center. In the cemetery, all the rest,
their resolute bones stacked against the pull
of the Gulf. Here, another world teems—flies
buzzing the meat-stand, cockroaches crisscrossing

the banquette, the curve and flex of larvae
in the cisterns, and mosquitoes skimming
flat water like skaters on a frozen pond. (45)

The poem pictures a world teeming with decay and disarray, yet the confining hierarchy of race relations stays put. This ekphrastic depiction seems consonant with Sontag's notion that "one of the tasks of photography is to disclose, and shape our sense of, the variety of the world. It is not to present ideals. There is no agenda except diversity and interestingness. There are no judgments, which of course is itself a judgment" (*Where the Stress Falls* 250). The fluidity of subjectivity, its multiple formations, is frozen in place, the array of selfhood so strictly conditioned that it is reduced to a dull monochrome state. The agenda of Trethewey's photographic poetics comes into focus. By contrasting the multiplicity (even, or especially, in decay) of the material world with the closely bound meanings permitted it by the received codes of social relations, the poem is a protest against the binary construction of race relations in the South that can only be imagined in terms of black and white. In the concluding lines of "Vignette," the poem that closes *Bellocq's Ophelia*, Trethewey replaces this still frame of racial politics in traditional southern history with a moving countermemory, a form of resistance evident in a final imaginative vignette of this other Ophelia: "Imagine her a moment later—after / the flash, blinded— stepping out / of the frame, wide-eyed, into her life" (48). In this closing shot, Trethewey sounds a call for poetry to step out from behind the self-reflexive frame and into life, a vital acknowledgement of the political dimensions of contemporary southern poetics.[20]

· · ● ● ● · ·

The poetics of countermemory expressed in the work of these five current poets serves as a pointed argument for the continuing, yet changing significance of the regional, not as a nostalgic respite against the forces of globalization, but as a means of holding onto local distinctions in conjunction with an awareness of an increasingly interconnected world. In privileging multiple and heterogeneous imagined communities over a single, unified source of identity, they open up new regions of identification across the physical and conceptual space of the U.S. South, reflecting the transregional affiliations that mark contemporary culture. Daniels, Jordan, Jones, Mullen, and Trethewey recognize implicitly that regional boundaries, though contingent, are powerfully motivated and motivating, and their association with the South further punctuates their critiques of racism, misogyny, as well as economic imbalances and class chauvinism. The countermemory poets' identification with region redoubles the force of their constructions of subjectivity as well as the power of their objections to politics as usual in southern history. While region is still a load-bearing wall, their poems break the façade of traditional southernism, leaving critics the useful work of uncovering what remains of lasting value under the aegis of transouthernism.

In closing, we should return to one of the essential questions of this book and attempt to answer once more, why region? This seems a particularly trenchant issue in discussing poets who self-consciously reveal the workings of a transregional condition. If the poets of countermemory use extraregional issues as the operative terms of their cultural work, why and how does region still count in the equation? If their political engagement is directed against what used to be defined as southern, why should we continue to call this critique of it southern? Why not argue that the critical force of the poems comes not from their southernness, but from the standpoint of the various other affiliations the poetry constructs? Despite Kreyling's argument, invoked in the introduction, that the South is "the richest site yet discovered in the U.S. cultural terrain for the study of and participation in the reinvention of culture" (*Inventing Southern Literature* 182), how do we know that richer sites will not become available? Restraining myself from sweeping predictions of what the long-view future holds for southern literature—indeed, the diverse work of these countermemorial poets suggests that there is no longer a single, cohesive future of southern poetry, but an open-ended sequence of heterogeneous futures—I would underscore the persistence of place as a crucial determinant in the forging of identity and the importance of region as a material site of both continuity and contestation. Even as we move into an era of heightening globalization, of trans-, if not post-nationalisms, the significance of the particular lives on. Identification, if not strict identity, is still founded in large part on local culture. And the South remains an ideologically vexed zone of contact and conflict, a compelling locus of collective identification and memory. Region provides a constructive and crucial means of talking about the actual space in which cultural conflicts are enacted. Subjectivities are formed over space as much as time, within and across "real geographies of social action, real as well as metaphorical territories and spaces of power" (Harvey, *The Condition of Postmodernity* 355); the local is still a main space of political activism, of economic exchanges, of social interaction. In imagining communities and countercommunities, place counts: where we live still conditions how we live, even if not in traditional ways.

For figures of southern distinctiveness, no longer iron-bound to essentialist models of regional identity or to ideas of pure exceptionalism, endure and recur. The politics of place are very much with us, though it is time for a more forceful restructuring of the codes of southern culture; as Peacock asserts, "space and place, together with their visual representations, show how an essentialized oppositional southern identity is altered by global forces that de-essentialize and de-oppositionalize. Spatial redefinition ricochets into modes of making sense, and calls for new frames for making meaning and for framing existence, spatial or otherwise" (133). In an age of proliferating new forms of differentiation, of multiplying identifications, regional borders are still useful to gauge the depth and breadth of transregional associations, however open-ended and even contradictory these might be. As region persists as a significant political, economic, and social category of meaning, it seems that the South will rise again, though never in the same form: the proliferating ends of southern cultural memory will know no end.

Notes

Introduction

1. Larry J. Griffin's countercheck to belief in an inflexible, unitary South is relevant:

> When we talk about "the South," for example, which South, exactly, are we talking about? The glittering Sun-Belt, franchise-laden South of Houston, Atlanta, Nashville, Charlotte, or the rural, small-town and disappearing South of coalminers in eastern Kentucky, sharecroppers in the Mississippi Delta, textile workers in small Carolina towns throughout the Piedmont? In our definitions of southerners, do we include the Chinese in Mississippi and the Cherokee in Georgia? The Cuban Americans in Miami and the forty thousand or so Hispanics in Nashville? The Cambodians in Atlanta and the Vietnamese along the Texas Gulf Coast? (62)

2. In *Southern Writers in the Modern World* (1957), Davidson identifies this "autochthonous" state of social unconsciousness with respect to the shared, yet unspoken assumptions of the Vanderbilt Fugitives in the 1920s:

> Our great good fortune was that we shared pretty much the same assumptions about society, about man, nature, and God. And we were most fortunate in not even having to ask ourselves whether or not we were on common ground in such matters. As yet we did not know that we were lucky in being able to assume that we had common assumptions. We did much thinking, but there were some important matters that we did not have to think about. It was a blessed sort of ignorance, and I believe it marked us as definitely Southern. It was, in fact, a condition of being Southern-born. In the South of those days

there was a great deal that could be taken for granted. There were many questions that did not need to be asked, and some of these were large metaphysical questions. (6)

3. In *The Narrative Forms of Southern Community*, Romine describes the interplay in southern life of two categories of communal self-definition: community produced by rhetoric and community produced by narrative. While the community produced by narrative is more self-conscious about its artificial status and allows for internal divisions, in the community produced by rhetoric, repetition suppresses discordant meanings and stabilizes a distinctively "southern" theatre of social transactions, thereby concretizing restrictive representations of history (or "heritage") as well as individual and racial identity.

4. In *History and Memory in the Two Souths* (1999), Deborah Cohn offers a succinct account of the emergence of the Fugitive-Agrarian ethos:

> during the late 1920s and 1930s, the Agrarians reconciled their own modernism (which had placed some of the writers in the literary vanguard even as it led them to eliminate all references to the South from their work) with a developing southernism by apotheosizing their heritage, elevating it to the status of myth and ideal. . . . Thus they promoted the image of the plantation as a bastion of the South, of civilized values characterized by order, stability, and immunity to the ravages of time, and as a space that set the region apart from the North's materialism and commercialism (24).

Perhaps one should balance this critique by mentioning how prophetic the Fugitives/ Agrarians were in predicting the practical dangers of unbridled industrialism, an ecological concern that has come increasingly into the public eye with the emergence of environmental conservation as a major political issue. Some readers might also object that compiling the Fugitives and Agrarians into a single movement conceals real differences between the two groups. Though distinct in some of their aims and even in their members, the Fugitives and the Agrarians are deeply connected. In the long view, it seems reasonable to take them at times as if they were separate but interrelated manifestations of the same basic movement.

5. Michael Kreyling's *Inventing Southern Literature* (1998) argues that, following the Fugitives themselves, Louis D. Rubin and those southern literary critics whom his work has closely influenced tend to believe in an essentialist South, for "Rubin sees historical continuity as nonproblematical, seamless, untroubled by 'forgetting,' and immune from vexing questions of gender, sexuality, race, and class. What is southern literature will always be recognizable by a formula as constant as the thing itself, for the South and its history are 'facts' and 'entities' that remain intact in and impervious to literary representation" (xi).

6. The underwritten field of post-Fugitive poetry is evident both in the dearth of criticism and in poetry's marginal place within anthologies of southern literature.

In Rubin's *The History of Southern Literature* (1985), an account that spans over six hundred pages, post–World War II poetry is compressed into James Justus's twenty-page "Poets After Midcentury," plus chapters on Randall Jarrell, James Dickey, and A. R. Ammons, which add up to nine pages total. William Andrews's *The Literature of the American South: A Norton Anthology* (1998) reflects a similar domination by prose writers. There have been only a few anthologies devoted exclusively to contemporary southern poetry, and some of these are out of print. In terms of critical scholarship, the spring 2006 issue of the *Mississippi Quarterly*, which is devoted to southern poetry, provides a start in the right direction. However, a collective interview eliciting responses from a number of current southern poets yielded few productive answers to the question "What critical essays or books would you most recommend to a student of Southern poetry?" Dave Smith's comment is telling:

> In my 11 years at Louisiana State University, English faculty repeatedly affirmed "Southern literature" as the strength of its graduate curriculum. Numerous doctoral degrees were done in that area, all with fiction dissertations. I am not aware of one in Southern poetry. Other than the one I taught, no graduate or undergraduate course in Southern poetry was offered. I can think of very few critical studies of Southern poets younger than Warren. If the source of definition is the academy's measurement, one would have to conclude it regards Southern poetry as an inconvenient cousin, preferable to ignore, and fiction as the true heir. (Quoted in McFee 243)

Furthermore, the fact that contemporary southern poetry requires its own critical reckoning is suggested by R. S. Gwynn's representative response to the same question that acknowledges only dated renascence "classics":

> Well, *I'll Take My Stand,* though maddening in many respects, is still worth looking at, though it's not specifically about poetry (though largely written by poets). Ransom's criticism is still valuable, and Cleanth Brooks was a great critic. *The Mind of the South,* of course, should be read, once. But I think I'd still direct a student to the fiction—Faulkner, O'Connor, Wolfe (who reads him nowadays?), and *Tobacco Road,* which is still a terrifically funny and unsettling novel. (Quoted in McFee 230)

There has been a handful of essays on current southern poetry that offer more critical approaches, such as William Harmon's "Is Southern Poetry Southerner than Southern Fiction?" (1993), David Kirby's "Is There a Southern Poetry?" (1994), and Kate Daniels's "Porch-Sitting and Southern Poetry" (1996). Though these essays go beyond the typical surveys, they do not go far enough in terms of theorizing and contextualizing the larger meanings of this poetry. None offers a theoretically or historically informed sense of the field: current theory is absent from their readings, and history is but a pale backdrop.

7. John Lang's *Six Poets from the Mountain South* (2010) sets forth perceptive and thoroughgoing readings of six Appalachian poets—Jim Wayne Miller, Fred Chappell, Robert Morgan, Jeff Daniel Marion, Kathryn Stripling Byer, and Charles Wright—and thus helps to redress this void; however, Lang's book is more specialized than my study, both in its geographic range (focusing on the mountain South) and in its primary concern with charting the spiritual ethos of these poetries in connection with their depictions of the natural landscape. George B. Handley's *New World Poetics* (2007) envisions the poetics of the hemispheric South, interweaving ecocritical interpretations of Walt Whitman, Pablo Neruda, and Derek Walcott that offer an excellent model for tracing transregional dynamics through the poetries of the global South. Although it is an anthology of poetry, Camille T. Dungy's *Black Nature* (2009) presents a gripping thesis about how African American poets, including many black southern writers, figure nature as an antipastoral force that crosshatches the potential beauty of nature with images of racial violence or of hardship and toil; in black southern poetry, rolling fields often become sites of labor, and trees create metonymic cuts to lynching trees.

8. Bone offers an extensive critique of the Fugitive-Agrarian touting of rurality as foundational to their model of traditional southern exceptionalism, noting that "the Agrarian sense of place was of a rural, self-sufficient and nigh-on precapitalist locus focused upon the small farm, operating largely outside the cash nexus, and absent large-scale land speculation" (5). Conceiving of "southern place as agricultural real property, apotheosized in the subsistence farm," the core members warned that "if subsistence farming fails—if the South's agricultural society capitulates to a money economy, finance-capitalist land speculation, and large-scale real-estate development—then the South's unique sense of 'place' expires too" (viii).

9. In *The Condition of Postmodernity*, David Harvey has defined the economic program of post–World War II capitalism—known by a variety of titles, such as "late capitalism," "consumer culture," "postindustrialism," or "flexible accumulation"—as the integration of the fordist model of mass production and industrial infrastructure with the "postfordist" emphasis on the growth of the service industry, on conditioning consumer habits through advertising and product placement, and on more flexible sites and forms of production and distribution. Such economic transitions can have homogenizing effects on the markers of traditional regional culture, eliding local distinctiveness in the wake of an increasingly standardized market.

10. Thomas F. Haddox provides the following assessment of the critical turn from autochthonous southernism to postsouthernism:

> In this discourse [of traditional southernism] the term *community*
> assumes a position of central importance, for it recalls Ferdinand
> Tönnies's influential distinction between community (*Gemeinschaft*)
> and society (*Gesellschaft*), between "living organism" and "mechanical
> aggregate and artifact." Where Louis D. Rubin, Jr. and Cleanth Brooks

once lauded southern literature as a richly felt, even "sacramental" expression of *Gemeinschaft*, holding it in implicit contrast to the poverty of merely institutional and political existence, postsouthern critics such as Lewis P. Simpson and Michael Kreyling observe that such metaphysical groundings can no longer be assumed. Instead, the community, the South, and the tropes associated with them frequently become targets of irreverence and parody that can be revealed as fabrications rather than as markers of an authentic southern identity. (567)

11. The concept of transouthernism, when considered in an international context, can be seen as consonant with the current theorization of the global South, which has initiated a boom of recent criticism, including such foundational texts as *South to a New Place: Region, Literature, Culture* (2002), edited by Suzanne W. Jones and Sharon Monteith; *Look Away! The U.S. South in New World Studies* (2004), edited by Deborah Cohn and Jon Smith; *The American South in a Global World* (2005), edited by Carrie R. Matthews, James L. Peacock, and Harry L. Watson; and *Globalization and the American South* (2005), edited by James C. Cobb and William Stueck. To these books can be added the December 2006 special issue of *American Literature* titled *Global Contexts, Local Literatures: The New Southern Studies*, edited by Kathryn McKee and Annette Trefzer.

12. Of course, region's continuing significance can carry with it more insidious implications. On an economic level, the crucial persistence of regional difference amid the transnational movement of capital and networks of transportation and communications can involve the flux of capital across regional borders precisely because of imbalances between different areas. The American South remains an attractive site for such exchanges because it has less corporate regulation, it maintains a tradition of boosterism which offers incentives for companies to relocate down South, and it provides a relatively cheap labor source since labor agreements tend to be more beneficial to employers as a result of the region's anti-unionism. Regional association thus provides a means of bordering a "borderless" capitalism, though this is not always a good thing, as localism can become little more than a system of moving money around.

13. For a fuller account of poetry's status as a particular use of language, see Kenneth Koch's *Making Your Own Days: The Pleasures of Reading and Writing Poetry* (1998), which acknowledges and expands French poet Paul Valéry's theory of poetics.

14. The new lyric studies critique "formalist" readings that treat poetry as a distinct genre, instead focusing on the constructedness of definitions of poetry in various historical and ideological contexts. For these critics, what is defined as poetry is purely arbitrary and politically invested. For a fuller account of the study of "historical poetics," see Virginia Jackson's *Dickinson's Misery: A Theory of Lyric Reading* (2005), as well as the January 2008 *PMLA*, which devotes a section of essays to "The New Lyric Studies." Though what counts as poetry shifts according to various periods

and cultures, my analysis coincides with those critics who argue for some continuity in an empirical definition of how language typically (not automatically or absolutely) works as poetry.

15. Although it lacks an account of the ideological implications of meter, Derek Attridge's *Poetic Rhythm* (1995) also makes rhythm the focal point of a working definition of poetry, foregrounding the bodily impulse of rhythm's flow, since "rhythm is what makes a physical medium (the body, the sounds of speech or music) seem to move with deliberateness through *time*, recalling what has happened (by repetition) and projecting itself into the future (by setting up expectations), rather than just letting time pass it by" (4). Susan Stewart's *Poetry and the Fate of the Senses* (2002) also has much to say about the materially connective quality of poetic rhythm; her analysis of the intersubjective power of metered language, however, stops short of linking this idea to sociohistorical practices and is primarily an ahistorical account.

16. The ineffable power of poetic rhythm shares much with the (post-Kantian) sublime as defined by Aviram: "a sense of infinitude, or excess, specifically in relation to language—that which exceeds one's ability to put it into words and thus fills one with a sense of speechless wonder" (19). It signifies a reality that is "transcendental" only insofar as it "transcends the individual in that it is before and beyond the limitations of individual consciousness" (239).

17. Displaying a rather unqualified nostalgia for the Fugitives' supposedly seamless bond with their regional community of rhetoric, Louise Cowan sees their poetry as performing "a communal sacrament" that binds them to their native culture (xxi): "Southern society provided for the Fugitives . . . a code of manners and morals, with its underlying *gentilesse*—that blend of gentility and spirit, honor and humility, sympathy and humor—that made for gracious friendships and called forth intimate though not introspective conversation" (xxii). In "The Gathering of the Fugitives: A Recollection" (1994), Rubin notes the volatile nature of the Fugitive meetings, where "the cultural and spiritual inheritors of the economically threadbare, tradition-bound orthodoxy of the defeated nineteenth-century south were coming into violent intellectual collision with the vanguard of twentieth-century western thought, belief, and culture" (664). Cowan's and Rubin's views of the Fugitives are countered by more recent critics, such as Michael O'Brien, who argues that, far from being "No matter" (Rubin 673), the politics informing the Fugitives' poetics are crucial to understanding their role in southern literary history. O'Brien suggests that "one could with no great difficulty parallel from Southern history the procession of laments for a vanished integrated agrarian society that prefaces Raymond Williams's *The Country and the City*" (163) and that "nothing has been more crucial to traditional Southern literary criticism than the belief that once upon a time there was an undifferentiated Southern society, which is now lost. The demise has been variously dated: at the Civil War, with the rise of the New South, at the First World War. But everyone has agreed that it happened at some moment" (164).

18. In "On the Uses and Disadvantages of History for Life" (1874), Friedrich Nietzsche asserts that the practitioners of monumentalism connect history into an epic chain, believing

that the great moments in the struggle of the human individual consti-
tute a chain, that this chain unites mankind across the millennia like
a range of human mountain peaks, that the summit of such a long-
ago moment shall be for me still living, bright and great—that is the
fundamental idea of the faith in humanity which finds expression in
the demand for a *monumental* history. But it is precisely this demand
that greatness shall be everlasting that sparks off the most fearful of
struggles. For everything else that lives cries No. The monumental shall
not come into existence—that is the counter-word. (68)

The visions of past grandeur constructed by this form of historiography create an
intensive cultural nostalgia for the monumentalized past that is "still living, bright
and great" for those alive who can recognize its greatness. Yet these epic moments—
alas—are always already past, and so monumentalists hold "that he lives best who
has no respect for existence" (69) because our present lives are paltry in themselves,
valuable only insofar as they form a lesser part of the larger, heroic struggle of history.
The Fugitives' practice of historical monumentalism is suggested by John Burt's
argument that "it was a commonplace of the poetry of former Fugitives to claim that
we—both the poet and the reader—do not measure up to our ancestors, be they the
mountain men of Davidson's 'The Tall Men,' or the casualties of Tate's 'Ode to the
Confederate Dead'" (87). True to monumentalist form, "the values that Davidson's
and Tate's narrators recognize but cannot embody are unquestionably good things
which only our weakness keeps us from" (87).

    19. In a letter of March 17, 1930, asking Warren for a contribution to the
Agrarian manifesto that would become *I'll Take My Stand*, Davidson provides "Red"
with a title for his essay by referencing the Uncle Remus tales: "It's up to you, Red,
to prove that Negroes are country ~~animals~~ folks—'bawn and bred in a briar-patch.'
Go to it. Don't let the grass grow under your feet. And don't keep me on the anxious
seat, I pray you. Write promptly, if it's nothing but a note" (Robert Penn Warren
Papers: Box 21, Folder 399). Davidson would later object to Tate that Warren's essay
on the significance of rural black labor to the subsistence of the agrarian South was
too "progressive" in its germinal suggestion of a separate but equal policy. Davidson's
racism comes through in his original letter to Warren with his veiled equation of
"Negroes" to "animals," before striking this word out and deciding on the less offen-
sive "folks." Though "animals" may indeed reference the Brer Rabbit tales, it doubles
as a dehumanizing joke, evoking shades of social Darwinist attitudes that labeled
blacks as a species nearer to animals on the evolutionary chain.

    20. Davidson's "Sequel of Appomattox" (1938) proposes an avowedly racist ac-
count of the Lost Cause mythos. Summoning the ghosts of fallen C.S.A. cavalry, the
poem doubles as a song of praise for the Confederate dead as well as their modern
inheritors of the Lost Cause, the members of the Ku Klux Klan. Given its disturbing
subject matter, the poem's use of a ballad stanza—a form typically reserved for light
verse in the context of twentieth-century poetics—is chilling. The opening stanzas
are fraught with images of things falling apart, centers not holding in the wake of

Appomattox. The cultural equation is clear: modernity is decay. This South is rapidly being, not reconstructed, but deconstructed until the dead rise and gather, effecting a twofold haunting as they are reincarnated as both ghostly Confederates as well as real-life Klansmen on a midnight spree of racial terror. As the fallen Confederate cavalier/Klansman remarks to his racial doppelgänger, "Remember, I was your master / Remember, you were my slave" (42), the response of the former slave/contemporary southern black is whited out, his voice silenced, showing little concern for the very race upon whose labor the capital of the "pastoral" South rested. As in the surreal vision of a whites-only "paradise" at the conclusion of D. W. Griffith's *The Birth of a Nation* (1915), Davidson's alarming nostalgia requires that white-black, master-slave relations hold true in the next world as well—and indeed, in the contemporaneous world of the Jim Crow South—as the poem's grim rallying cry in honor of the Klan makes clear. Though the Confederate legacy will be, Davidson hopes, passed on proudly to its white southern inheritors, the historical inheritance of southern blacks is not so comforting a memory; for them, the sequel of Appomattox was the bleak history of racial oppression under the codes of the lynch-law South.

21. In any project that attempts to survey a field, it is important to defend one's choices for inclusion and exclusion. One might wish to see examined in detail other significant southern poets, such as Randall Jarrell, A. R. Ammons, Allison Hedge Coke, David Bottoms, C. D. Wright, Andrew Hudgins, T. R. Hummer, Brenda Marie Osbey, Dan Albergotti, James Applewhite, Fred Chappell, or Ron Rash, to name a few notables who, besides perhaps a passing reference, have not been included. However, I believe that the poets discussed at length in the present chapters provide a useful spectrum of several of the most important trends and countertrends of the poetic output of the contemporary U.S. South. The chosen poets are therefore both specific and representative, but certainly not all encompassing.

1. Poetic Historiophoty

1. Warren (1905–1989) was born in Guthrie, Kentucky, and raised on his family's tobacco farm. His father was a businessman and his mother a schoolteacher, and the young Warren grew up listening to the stories of his grandfathers who had both fought for the Confederacy during the Civil War. Put simply, Warren was one of the twentieth century's most accomplished men of letters. A highly influential scholar as well as creative writer, he was the author of ten novels, sixteen books of poetry, a biography of John Brown, two books focusing on the civil rights movement, and several works of literary criticism, including coauthoring with Cleanth Brooks the cornerstone texts *Understanding Poetry* (1938) and *Understanding Fiction* (1943). Although Warren had received an appointment to the U.S. Naval Academy, he never enrolled because he lost sight in one eye when his younger brother accidentally struck him with a stone. Thus prevented from attending Annapolis, Warren earned his B.A. from Vanderbilt University (1925), his M.A. from the University of California at Berkeley (1927), and his B.Litt. as a Rhodes Scholar at New College, Oxford (1930).

While an undergraduate at Vanderbilt, he joined the Fugitive group and his first poems were published in *The Fugitive*. He was also associated with the Vanderbilt Agrarians and contributed "The Briar Patch," an essay supporting a separate but equal stance on racial segregation, to *I'll Take My Stand*. Moreover, along with Brooks, Tate, and Ransom, he was one of the central proponents of the style of literary close reading that became known as the New Criticism and took firm root in the academy from the 1940s until the 1960s. Warren held teaching positions at a range of institutions, including Southwestern College, Vanderbilt, Louisiana State University, the University of Minnesota, and Yale University. While at LSU, he cofounded with Brooks the *Southern Review*, which become a nationally known literary journal. A charter member of the Fellowship of Southern Writers, Warren was rewarded with three Pulitzer Prizes for his work; he is the only writer to win for fiction as well as poetry. Named the nation's first official Poet Laureate in 1986, Warren collected nearly every literary honor, including a Bollingen Prize, a Guggenheim Fellowship, a National Book Award, a MacArthur Fellowship, and a Chancellorship of the Academy of American Poets. His first marriage to Emma Brescia, begun in 1930, ended in divorce in 1951; his second marriage to Eleanor Clark in 1952 produced two children, Rosanna and Gabriel. Though he lived for nearly four decades in Fairfield, Connecticut, his literary output is characterized by an abiding concern with exploring the complexities and contradictions of southernness, especially surrounding the history of his home state of Kentucky.

 2. In terms of prosody, Anthony Szczesiul provides a thorough description of Warren's technical shift from the rather strict formalism of his earlier poetry as he began to experiment with looser structures once he returned from his decade-long interruption from writing poetry, which ended with the publication of the original version of *Brother to Dragons* in 1953.

 3. White argues that filmic techniques offer a different kind of historical transmission from traditional historiography, since "the representation of historical events, agents, and processes in visual images presupposes the mastery of a lexicon, grammar, and syntax—in other words, a language and a discursive mode—quite different from that conventionally used for their representation in verbal discourse alone" (1193). Cinema does not merely offer a secluded retreat from history into the pleasures of screened vision but is one of the predominant cultural means of structuring historical sentiment, of conditioning the way we perceive the past. As Mark Goble has asserted, "cinema's spectacle of history possesses the power to affect us out of all proportion to the transparency of its simulation" (80).

 4. My reading of cinematic technique in *Audubon* is original to Warren studies. Only Deborah Wilson has explored in detail the influence of film on Warren's work, and her argument centers almost exclusively on matters of content, not form, reading *All the King's Men* (1946) as a film noir detective story, with Jack Burden as "a 1940s ironic God-Bogart 'brooding on history' and searching for truth" (70).

 5. Scholarship on *Audubon: A Vision* typically defines the poem in one of two ways: 1) as an exemplar of modern primitivism according to which the title character

reconnects with primal nature and, as a result of reawakening his primitive passion, is rejuvenated to walk once again in the abstract world of social existence; or 2) as an expression of a Romantic-humanist ethos according to which Audubon's artistic vision of nature works in conjunction with his search for an authentic identity, his "knowledge" commingling at last with his "love," a transcendent moment often enfolded in the rhetoric of a universalizing liberal humanism. For an interpretation of the primitivist theme in *Audubon*, see Robert S. Koppelman's *Robert Penn Warren's Modernist Spirituality* (1995), which posits that "immersion into primary nature is central" in the poem and that "art is a vital form of experience and not an escape from or artificial construction of experience" (149). Keen Butterworth's "Projections and Reflections in *Audubon: A Vision*" (2003) adeptly examines Jungian archetypes in *Audubon*, arguing that the poem explores the primal territory of "the powerful reservoir of patterns or archetypes which inform our understanding of life that is otherwise nothing more than unrelated events. . . . Here psychology is elevated to the realm of metaphysics and theology" (90). For readings of Warren as a Romantic poet, see Victor Strandberg's *The Poetic Vision of Robert Penn Warren* (1977), James H. Justus's *The Achievement of Robert Penn Warren* (1981), Calvin Bedient's *In the Heart's Last Kingdom* (1984), Lesa Carnes Corrigan's *Poems of Pure Imagination: Robert Penn Warren and the Romantic Tradition* (1999), James A. Grimshaw's *Understanding Robert Penn Warren* (2001), and Anthony Szczesiul's *Racial Politics and Robert Penn Warren's Poetry* (2002). Strandberg asserts Warren's "essentially Romantic sensibility" (190), while Justus touts the poet as a "latter-day Romantic" (113). Bedient suggests that "Warren has a romantic and heroic idea of Audubon," whereas Corrigan contends that Warren's yearning for life as significance "aligns him with the Romantics in their insistence upon the possibilities of joy in a ruined and lost world, transitory and fleeting glimpses of transcendence that are nonetheless rooted in experience and the external world" (5). Szczesiul makes a valuable reassessment of the issue of race in Warren's poetry, analyzing his changing poetics in light of his equally shifting political views on racial issues and focusing part of the discussion on Warren's Romanticism. In *Robert Penn Warren and American Idealism* (1988), John Burt uses the context of American idealism to investigate Warren's postwar poetry but does so in order to deconstruct readings of him as a Romantic-humanistic idealist.

6. One should be mindful of contemporary ethnographer Mary Louis Pratt's important distinction between "frontiers" and what she defines as "contact zones" in terms of describing colonial encounters:

> "Contact zone" in my discussion is often synonymous with "colonial frontier." But while the latter term is grounded within a European expansionist perspective (the frontier is a frontier only with respect to Europe), "contact zone" is an attempt to invoke the spatial and temporal copresence of subjects previously separated by geographic and historical disjunctures, and whose trajectories now intersect. By using the term "contact," I aim to foreground the interactive, improvisational

dimensions of colonial encounters so easily ignored or suppressed by diffusionist accounts of conquest and domination. A "contact" perspective emphasizes how subjects are constituted in and by their relations to each other. It treats the relations among colonizers and colonized, or travelers and "travelees," not in terms of separateness or apartheid, but in terms of copresence, interaction, interlocking understandings and practices, often within radically asymmetrical relations of power. (7)

I use the term "frontier" because it reflects the mythos of westward expansion in operation in Audubon's vision of a wilderness in need of "civilization." However, Warren's text contains a significant undercurrent of "contact zone" transculturation, especially in Audubon's powerful identification with the cultural others he encounters on the prairies—less the injured Native American than the hag-woman and her two sons.

7. For the source behind Warren's poem, see the sections entitled "The Prairie" and "The Regulators" in Audubon's *Delineations of American Scenery and Character*. Warren retains the primary components of Audubon's original version, such as the hag-like frontier woman (whose "voice was gruff, and her attire negligently thrown about her" [15]); the wounded Indian ("the arrow had split upon the cord, and sprung back with such violence into his right eye as to destroy it for ever" [15]); the woman's enraptured response to Audubon's gold watch ("But my watch had struck her fancy, and her curiosity had to be gratified by an immediate sight of it. I took off the gold chain that secured it from around my neck, and presented it to her. She was all ecstasy, spoke of its beauty, asked me its value, and put the chain round her brawny neck, saying how happy the possession of such a watch should make her" [15–16]); the woman and sons' attempt to murder Audubon and the Indian, preempted by the arrival of regulators ("I was several times on the eve of rising and shooting her on the spot:—but she was not to be punished thus. The door was suddenly opened, and there entered two stout travelers, each with a long rifle on his shoulder" [17]); and the summary frontier justice for the condemned ("Day came, fair and rosy, and with it the punishment of our captives. They were now quite sobered. Their feet were unbound, but their arms were still securely tied. We marched them into the woods off the road, and having used them as Regulators were wont to use such delinquents, we set fire to the cabin, gave all the skins and implements to the young Indian warrior, and proceeded, well pleased, towards the settlements" [18]).

8. Vivian Sobchack describes the doubled or "reversible" relation invoked by filmic experience, as a "film presents and represents acts of seeing, hearing, and moving as both the *original structures of existential being* and the *mediating structures of language*" (11). When we go to the movies, we respond viscerally to the sights, sounds, and movements that emanate from the screen, yet cinema offers a sense of both direct and mediated experience.

9. Randolph Paul Runyon examines the way in which many of Warren's postwar poems are interwoven into sequences that establish thematic continuities

between individual poems. My reading of *Audubon* contends that Warren's use of the poetic sequence bears the signposts of cinematic form.

10. Mary Ann Doane explains how cinematic technology created a new experience of temporality in its "apparent ability to transcend time as corruption by paradoxically fixing life and movement, providing their immutable record" (1): "What the new technologies of vision allow one to see is a record of time" but "because time's corruption is 'proper' to it, its fixed representation also poses a threat, produces aesthetic and epistemological anxiety" (3). Indeed, "the very rapidity of the changing images in film is potentially traumatic for the spectator and allows the cinema to *embody* something of the restructuration of modern perception" (15). Susan McCabe offers a further description of how film altered the modern perception of the body's movement in time:

> Cinematic montage and camera work often exposed the body's malleability. Sped up or slowed down, the pacing and piecing of film could recreate the moving "lived" body, while these methods ruptured fantasies of physical self-presence or wholeness. Broadly speaking, film showed that the temporal present could be endlessly repeated; it was mechanical yet created a *felt* immediacy; and consequently, it subordinated the inherited conceit of the Cartesian mind to less aggregated kinesthetic processes. In sum, film crystallized a cultural debate in modernity over the unstable conjunctions between the mind and the sensate body. (3)

11. The fact that Warren was thoroughly familiar with the SOP of the typical Western is made clear in his description of one of his dreams during a 1982 interview with David Farrell:

> Warren: Well, I dream a lot. I love dreams, especially funny dreams, funny, elaborate dreams. I'll tell you one. I'm in a barroom that somehow is like a fake barroom scene in the Far West; but clearly fake—as if it had canvas walls or something. There's a big bar, a lot of high-heeled gunmen around with Stetsons—ranchers and cowhands and so forth—and everybody's drinking. A man leaps on the bar. He's a man of some importance, a rancher, and he has a gun in each hand, and he says, "Everybody knows I know how to use a pistol." He waves them around and he says, "Somebody here's betrayed my daughter. Now, I never shot a man down without warning. I'm going to give him the count of ten to declare himself." And he begins, "One . . ." and he shoots out a light. But it doesn't make a boom; it makes a "ping"! Then, "Two . . . three . . ." He got to nine and then, "Ha, ha, ha!"—a burst of laughter comes in sudden blackness and a big explosion, and offstage a voice says, "And he fell with sixty bullet holes in his body!"

Farrell: What was your role in this dream?

Warren: I'm an observer.

Farrell: Not the man who's betrayed the daughter?

Warren: No. I wish I had been, but I can't say that I was.

Farrell: Is this a recurring dream?

Warren: No; it just happened once. And I often dream poems. (198–99)

It seems that the Western form had infatuated not only Warren's poetic consciousness, but his subconscious as well. This is not surprising, considering the pervasiveness of Westerns on television as well as the big screen during the early post–World War II era; in fact, Westerns "were consistently among the top-rated TV shows for most of the 1955–70 period. . . . No other type of action/adventure show in this period (detective/police, combat, and the like) commanded so consistently high a share of prime time over so many years" (Slotkin 348). It may also be significant that Warren is an observer in the dream sequence, especially when investigating *Audubon's* invocation of a cinematic model of spectatorship; like Warren in the dream, Audubon functions primarily as a viewer, not a performer.

12. That Warren considered the nineteenth-century Kentucky frontier—the setting for both *Audubon* and *Brother to Dragons* (1953; 1979)—part of the original West is suggested in his November 9, 1944, letter to Katherine Anne Porter. He describes his discovery of the source material for *Brother to Dragons* in a journal that held the story of "two sons of Charles Lewis, who was related to Meriwether and married to Thomas Jefferson's sister. The sons became involved in a perverse, violent, and hideous situation, out west in Kentucky" (Blotner 214). Although *Brother to Dragons* contains some elements of the Western form, *Audubon* exploits more fully the generic structure and feeling of being "out west in Kentucky." Sidney Burris also notes the Western's influence on *Audubon*:

> When I read *Audubon*, I feel as if I'm . . . an American. It's a curious reaction, and I don't fully understand it. There are stereotypes in the poem, of course, that offer up their comforting and confining familiarity: the Indian, called "Injun" by the old woman, the long rifle, the lynching—all fairly stock images from the Westerns that I grew up on. So the poem runs partly on the vast powers of homogenization that American popular culture has long made into its version of American history. . . . Yet, against these overwhelming forces of popularity and homogenization, I recognize the man Audubon: passionate, willful, driven, individuated, alone, "only himself," as Warren says in the poem's opening lines. So, another American stereotype: the loner, the high-plains drifter, Shane. (151)

Burris's brief account is part of his paean to the value of taking "deep delight" in lyric poetry against the flux of the Technotronic Age, a world given over to computers. He therefore does not offer a fuller explication of these motifs. Moreover, Burris views the figure of Audubon as a successful embodiment of the Western mythos—another Shane—whereas I place these references in an ironic light. Joseph Millichap also calls attention to Warren's interest in the U.S. West, arguing that "for Warren, the West is a symbolic as well as a geographical distinction: the West is not simply a direction, but a turn of mind, the American mind" (55).

13. Robert H. Brinkmeyer interprets the effects of this peculiarly volatile mix of regional associations in *Remapping Southern Literature: Contemporary Southern Writers and the West* (2000), his analysis of the "southernized" West: "there is no better place from which to witness America's ideological construction—and destruction—at work; and there is no better place from which to critique that ideological enterprise" (32–33). Brinkmeyer examines the ideological functions of Westerns produced by southern writers, such as Cormac McCarthy's unceasingly grim *Blood Meridian, or the Evening Redness in the West* (1985) and Barry Hannah's grotesquely comic *Never Die* (1991), arguing that "in writing Westerns, Southern authors are not seeking refuge from the problems of postmodern (and Southern) life but are instead seeking vantage points for exploring those problems" (32).

14. For detailed discussions of how Westerns explore constructions of masculinity, see Lee Clark Mitchell's *Westerns: Making the Man in Fiction and Film* (1996) and Jane Tompkins's *West of Everything*. Both Mitchell and Tompkins also take up the issue of the Western's cover-up of the genocide of Native Americans. For more on the postwar Western's relation to Cold War ideology, see Richard Slotkin's exhaustive *Gunfighter Nation* (1992), Stanley Corkin's *Cowboys as Cold Warriors* (2004), and John H. Lenihan's *Showdown: Confronting Modern America in the Western Film* (1980). Prime examples of the Cold War Western film include Howard Hawks's *Red River* (1948), Fred Zinnemann's *High Noon* (1952), John Ford's *The Searchers* (1956), and Sergio Leone's "spaghetti Westerns" of the late 1960s, as well as Clint Eastwood's *High Plains Drifter* (1973) and *The Outlaw Josey Wales* (1976). Janet Walker provides a lucid account of the Western's "historiographic function":

> Through the lens of history, we come to realize that westerns incorporate, elide, embellish, mythologize, allegorize, erase, duplicate, and rethink past events that are themselves—as history—fragmented, fuzzy, and striated with fantasy constructions. The relation between the western and the history of the West must be more complex than an "is." (13)

Corkin adds that "Westerns offer a particularly rich object of study for their power to graft discussions of imperialism onto assertions of the power and sanctity of the individual," allowing us "to understand, however speculatively, the powerful devices that promote particular constructions of national identity in a period marked by intense chauvinism and broad acceptance of a kind of economic and cultural hegemony" (5).

15. The opening montage of Audubon gazing at the heron in the dawn sky is tellingly inverted in a later visual alliteration as he sights a trumpeter swan rising in flight against the sunset:

> You saw, from the forest pond, already dark, the great trumpeter swan
> Rise, in clangor, and fight up the steep air where,
> In the height of last light, it glimmered, like white flame. (262)

This vision occurs after Audubon has suffered through the dream he never knew the end of and has discovered a new dimension of beauty in the spectacle of the hag and her sons' hanging. By the time of the sighting of the swan, Audubon's subjectivity has been restored, though the "you" in these lines seems to reference both Audubon and his double, the reader-spectator. This perhaps suggests that Audubon has come to a degree of knowledge. He seems to have recognized his own complicity in the death of the frontier dwellers, and his restored subjectivity is founded on his understanding of his status as a complicit spectator.

16. Perhaps the most memorable of these panoramic sunrises/sunsets occurs in the fifth section of the sequence, "The Sound of That Wind," which incorporates a vision of Audubon that is filled with iconography drawn from the cinematic Western's memorialization of the lost frontier. It reads like a scene treatment for a shot panning across Monument Valley:

> At dusk he stood on a bluff, and the bellowing of buffalo
> Was like distant ocean. He saw
> Bones whiten the plain in the hot daylight.
> He saw the Indian, and felt the splendor of God. (263)

17. Slotkin further elucidates how the cinematic Western is informed by contemporary historical pressures:

> The beginning of the Cold War in 1948 inaugurated the Golden Age of the Western: a 25-year period, regularly punctuated by the appearance of remarkable films, that saw the genre achieve its greatest popularity and that ended with its virtual disappearance from the genre map. The rise and fall of the Western mirrors the development of the Cold War and its sustaining ideological consensus from its seedtime in 1948–54 to its fulfillment in the years of the liberal counteroffensive under Kennedy and Johnson, to its disruption by the failure of the war in Vietnam. During this period there was a more or less continual exchange of symbols, themes, and concerns between the discourses of politics and movie production. The genre provided a frame in which alternative approaches to the political and ideological problems of the Cold War era could be imaginatively entertained. (347)

18. Corkin critiques the Kennedy Administration's coinage of "the New Fron-
tier" for expressing "a longing for the glory days of the age of empire" that "was at the
core of Kennedy and Johnson's ruinous Vietnam policies," for "to view the world as
though it was an extension of the continental United States was to seriously miscon-
strue its features, both geographic and social. The notion that Vietnam could be *lost*
. . . suggests a worldview that has not fully considered the distinction between John
Ford's Southwest and Ho Chi Minh's Hanoi" (247).

19. One could argue that all film displays a latent scopophilic dimension in
manipulating our pleasure in the vision of human bodies in motion, as a person is
mechanically transformed into an actor, into an object on the screen. This sense is
heightened in the Western, whose love of graphic images of violence, maiming, and
death makes the sadomasochistic relation between veiled spectator and screened
performer begin to look like a kind of necrophilia. Mitchell explores in detail the
motif of necrology, which he argues becomes a leading pattern in postwar Westerns.

20. In a letter to Albert Erskine, his editor at Random House, Warren suggests
two other possibilities for this concluding line:

> Dear Albert:
> Here is another possible revision. The version you have of sheet 6 has the line:
> So became aware of his erection.
> This sheet offers two more possibilities, as marked:
> So became aware of his pecker at ready.
> or:
> So became aware that he was in the manly state.
>
> Erection is strictly a 20th century semi-polite, semi-technical term.
>
> Think it over.
> Yrs,
> R
> (Robert Penn Warren Papers: Box 115, Folder 2131)

Thankfully, once Erskine thought it over, he decided against the image of Audubon's
"pecker at ready." Each of the alternate lines points up the pornographic aspect of the
scene.

2. Returning the "Undying Cry of the Void"

1. The son of a lawyer and a homemaker, Dickey (1923–1997) was born in Atlanta,
Georgia, and become one of the most highly visible American literary personalities
during his lifetime. Although he was well known for his fiction (including three pub-
lished novels, *Deliverance* [1970], *Alnilam* [1987], and *To the White Sea* [1993]), literary
criticism, and essays, poetry was at the core of his creative output. He enrolled at Clem-

son University in 1942, where he played football, only to leave after a semester to serve in World War II in the Army Air Corps. He flew missions over Japan and was awarded five Bronze Stars. After the war, Dickey entered Vanderbilt University, where he earned his B.A. in 1949 and his M.A. in 1950. Despite an interruption from 1955 until 1960 to pursue a career in advertising, he held teaching positions at Rice University, the University of Florida, and the University of South Carolina, where he taught from 1968 until his death. Among other honors, Dickey was asked to read his poem "The Strength of Fields" at the 1977 presidential inauguration of fellow Georgian Jimmy Carter. Dickey's descent into alcoholism in the 1970s—not coincidentally following the massive popular and critical success of *Deliverance*—dissipated much of the power of his work while cementing his national reputation as an unruly, tough-talking, hard-drinking southern writer. He made every effort to publicize and celebrate the continuing value and relevance of poetic art. Much of his life was spent as a featured author on the lecture circuit, as he put it, "barnstorming for poetry," and he deeply influenced the course of contemporary poetry, both in terms of those later poets who mined a similar vein and those who reacted against his work. His centrality to post–World War II southern poetics is evidenced in the mass interview with southern poets included in the *Mississippi Quarterly* special issue on southern poetry. When asked to name those poets or writers whose work had impacted their own in positive and/or negative ways, thirteen of the twenty-one poets surveyed invoked Dickey. Ron Rash's response is representative. After praising the early poems, he notes his disappointment in the later work, yet still allows that "at his best [Dickey] is remarkable and has had a huge impact, increasingly unacknowledged, on Southern poetry" (McFee 242).

2. In "'Not as a Leaf': Southern Poetry and the Innovations of Tradition" (1997), Fred Chappell anoints Dickey as the major transitional figure for post–World War II southern poetry. For Chappell, Dickey's regenerative primitivism is different from what went before (namely, what Chappell titles the "Fugitive-Metaphysical" school of modernist southern poetry) and what has come after (the current new formalism and new narrative movements). Chappell's essay, however, does not provide an adequate account of what makes Dickey's poetry such a compelling force in contemporary southern poetry. Dickey's primitivist ethos continues to produce countercurrents among the South's contemporary poets, such as James Seay's ethereal primitivism and Dan Albergotti's (one of Dickey's former students) ironic replication of Dickey's poetics, a parody of a parody.

3. Originally the poems that make up *Falling, May Day Sermon, and Other Poems* were included as a section of new poems in Dickey's *Poems 1957–1967* (1967) and were not published as a separate volume until 1981. The poems were subsequently incorporated into *The Whole Motion* (1992), from which my citations are drawn.

4. Gillian Beer outlines the influence of the emergence of Darwinism on models of memory, both personal and collective:

> Darwinian theory brings into question the value of memory. It high-
> lights the extent of our inevitable ignorance of the lived past, both our
> own past and that of the physical order of the world. . . . It also prepares

for a recovery of the human position through the idea of the unconscious. But for Lyell, for Darwin, and for Huxley, the unconscious was not the guardian of prior memories, but rather a separate domain, relating to the earth's movements, and to "natural" instead of "artificial" selection, genetic as opposed to reasoned continuity. (63)

Beer's thesis is applicable to Dickey's work, since his version of twentieth-century primitivism finds its roots in Darwinian theories of deep memory. Beer assesses Victorian anxiety over the loss of a stable sense of origin in the wake of Darwin's findings. Evolutionary theory undercut religious explanations of human origins, suggesting instead the contingency of the development and survival of the human race and spurring a cultural impulse to reestablish barriers against the loss of a theological essentialism. Emerging theories concerning the unconscious served as one of these safeguards. For the early Darwinists, the unconscious held the link to humanity's instinctual past, whereas with the rise of Freudian theory the unconscious was seen as a means of discovering the origins of one's personal character, a link into the recesses of the individual's buried past.

5. Suarez shifts the meaning of Cash's phrase somewhat. Cash defined the southern savage ideal in an explicit social context as an integral part of the cultural machinery of the South. Indeed, the duel of honor was his primary example. For Cash, the savage ideal represented the southern code of behavior according to which one had to accept and replicate the opinions and assumptions of his fellow southerners, however destructive or biased these may have been, or else be exposed to potentially brutal retribution at the hands of others for the sin of not conforming. Though this sense of the savage ideal is in operation in Suarez's analysis, he also dislocates Cash's term from its social context, using it equally to describe Dickey's use of a poetic primitivism that escapes culture into the primal essence of Darwinian nature. My argument exploits this sense of doubleness in the term, eventually reestablishing the social basis of the term, returning the savage ideal to the realm of southern culture.

6. In "The Strength of James Dickey" (1985), Dave Smith aptly describes Dickey's "beast-vision," his "imaginative attempt to make a true connection to the continuous energy of the phenomenal and animal world" (172). Robert Kirschten provides a succinct account of this critical strain: "Dickey's most spectacular contributions to American poetry consist of lyric dramatization of ritual violence" (105). In *Outbelieving Existence: The Measured Motion of James Dickey* (1992), Gordon Van Ness provides a comprehensive survey of Dickey criticism through the early 1990s, compiling a thorough summary of the myriad critics who have addressed the primitivism theme in Dickey's poetry.

7. Dickey was a radar specialist during World War II, not a pilot, as he often claimed. As a matter of fact, he washed out of flight training. Like Faulkner, Dickey was prone to exaggerate his military achievements, among other things, consciously exploring the creative possibilities of the lie. This is the overriding thesis of Henry Hart's biography of Dickey, which is titled *James Dickey: The World as a Lie* (2000).

8. Although the terms used here invoke the language of Emerson's famous search for an "original relation" of self to universe in *Nature* (1836), Dickey's metaphysics and his poetics diverge significantly from Emerson's in at least two regards: 1) although Dickey focuses on renewal through the individual's heightened awareness of and fuller integration into the workings of the natural realm—even at times extending to the level of mystical transcendence—he emphasizes the importance of patterns of violence inherent in nature to the process of human as well as natural regeneration; and 2) Dickey's definition of the human relation to the universe is original not so much in the sense that it originates with the individual's imaginative consciousness, as for Emerson, but in the sense that immersion of the self into the natural world enables a reconnection to a collective human past, to a form of instinctual memory that reunites the modern individual with his primitive origins.

9. In *Gone Primitive: Savage Intellects, Modern Lives* (1990), Mariana Torgovnick argues that contemporary uses of primitivism reflect two fundamental, yet conflicting aims. On the one hand, references to the primitive can suggest a deep spiritual drive to reach a level of primal transcendence; on the other hand, invoking the discourse of primitivism offers a form of escapism and can degenerate into a set of chauvinistic cultural clichés that "create a never-never-land of false identities and homologies" (11).

10. Pierre Nora draws a pertinent distinction between primitive or archaic culture and modern civilization that reflects primitivism as a form of ultranostalgic longing for a primal past. Nora argues that members of primitive societies existed within living memory, being connected by the bonds of thoroughly ritualized and therefore unconscious collective recall. The citizens of the modern nation, on the other hand, exist in a world lost to deep memory, a transformational society that recycles the platitudes of abstract history as a means of memorializing the loss of ritual memory: "The remnants of experience still lived in the warmth of tradition, in the silence of custom, in the repetition of the ancestral, have been displaced under the pressure of a fundamentally historical sensibility. Self-consciousness emerges under the sign of that which has already happened, as the fulfillment of something always already begun" (7).

11. Concerning Dickey's manipulation of anapestic lines to produce a repetitive, incantatory rhythm, I have found Kirschten's and Smith's discussions the most useful as well as Paul Ramsey's analysis of Dickey's use of "rising trimeter."

12. In *The Immense Journey* (1957), Loren Eiseley offers a literal-minded interpretation of the mythic fall in the Garden. The fall of man was the fall into consciousness, into imagination, into the capacity to dream other realities beyond the present: "The Eden of the eternal present that the animal world had known for ages was shattered at last. Through the human mind, time and darkness, good and evil, would enter and possess the world" (120). Eiseley provides a description of the evolutionary shift in human biology (the enlargement of the brain) that created the mythic fall away from apreconscious integration with the things of the world into the symbolic use of language:

[Man] was becoming something the world had never seen before—a dream animal—living at least partially within a secret universe of his own creation and sharing that secret universe in his head with other, similar heads. Symbolic communication had begun. Man had escaped out of the eternal present of the animal world into a knowledge of past and future. The unseen gods, the powers behind the world of phenomenal appearance, began to stalk through his dreams. (120)

13. In "Too Much Fudge" (1998), his caustic review of Dickey's posthumously released *Selected Poems*, Chappell offers an account of this stylistic watershed in Dickey's poetry, admitting that he strongly prefers "the earlier poems to the later, the poems with short lines to those long-lined flaccid monstrosities that make so much racket" (2–3). Chappell criticizes the immoderation of Dickey's changed poetics as well as his changed persona. Taking particular aim at Dickey's histrionic live performances of "Falling" ("It seemed to go on forever and he took a special pleasure in the irrelevant lines" [1]) and "May Day Sermon" ("surely no one ever thought that even a renegade minister of whatever gender would spout silly rhodomontade like this" [2]), Chappell suggests that Dickey "had become a persona, his true nature in eclipse" as "he sometimes lacked genuine feeling and strove to cover the deficiency with unashamed displays of egotism" (2).

14. In an ironic turn, Bly eventually took over Dickey's role of vital masculinist, authoring *Iron John* (1991), a paean to fundamental masculinity, a call for men to return to the wild to be one with the woods and get in touch with their inner Tarzan. This stark reversal is satirized by Christopher Dickey in *Summer of Deliverance* (1998), his memoir about his father's descent into a self-aggrandizing alcoholic fog after the enormous popular success of *Deliverance*. Christopher Dickey takes a swipe at Bly's conversion, including a degree of reverse regional prejudice: "Another visitor [to the Dickeys' Atlanta home] was Robert Bly, who later made it a point to attack Dickey's supposed politics (which were never very political), and later still made it his profession to be a manly man. My father loved to say that Bly, from Minnesota, had a voice just like Bullwinkle the Moose" (100).

15. In "Hunting Civil War Relics at Nimblewill Creek" (1962), Dickey shows his Vanderbilt roots, offering an ironic allusion to Tate's *The Fathers* (1938). As he hunts for said relics of the "buried battle" at Nimblewill Creek, he feels the Confederate dead regroup. He cries out, as "one who shall lift up the past," not "Father" but "Fathers! Fathers!" (117), yet "No dead cry takes root" (116). He thus lifts up the past only to let it fall into decay.

16. Reading Dickey straight-facedly as a vital essentialist, as so many critics have done, sets up his work as a final outpost against politically correct criticism, immune to the theoretical whims of feminist and cultural studies. Designating Dickey as a total masculinist may not be as easy as it looks. It is important to bring Dickey back into the current prevailing modes of theoretical discussion, so that his poetry is not kept in critical purgatory because of its alleged political import.

17. The contemporaneous critical responses to Dickey's "May Day Sermon" bore out to a degree his mistrust of northern poets and critics. Believing, not without cause, that Bly and his allies were conspiring against him, Dickey tried to enlist critical support for "May Day Sermon" after it was attacked for its portrayal of violent victimage and sado-eroticism. Among others, he wrote Davidson College professor Edward Dwelle: "If you could manage to say some of the same things to Bob Manning, the editor of the *Atlantic,* it would do us a power of good, for both editor and poet are taking a heavy beating from the umbrellas of little old ladies and the candlesticks of preachers" (Hart 363). Dickey's sometime friend and dovish presidential candidate Eugene McCarthy also chimed in with his displeasure. In his poem "James Dickey," published in *Other Things and the Aardvark* (1968), McCarthy, a candidate for the 1968 Democratic presidential nomination, takes Dickey to task for his use of the southernized savage ideal in "May Day Sermon":

> What is your license to drag us
> to the May-day barn scourging,
> we who would rather stand off and listen,
> to hold us, while lasers of light
> from roof board holes
> thin slice our souls? (Hart 371)

The following stanza further indicts Dickey for using the ethos of the southern primitive to take American social consciousness to the end of its writ, this time offering up the shocking grotesquerie of "The Sheep Child" as evidence against him:

> What is your writ to whisper us
> back to dusty shelves
> where man and his animal
> face their beginning and ending
> in a clouded jar of alcohol? (Hart 371)

These initial responses to "May Day Sermon" are ironic, considering more recent critical evaluations, including my own. By the time of the production of a dramatic performance of "May Day Sermon," brought to the stage in 1992, the work was lauded as a clear exemplar of profeminist polemic. T. W. McCulloh, for example, notes in his review of the production that it is "a striking kaleidoscope of curious and commanding images wound through the Preacher's story of a young country woman's release from the pain of bondage by both religious hypocrisy and a male-dominated society that still exists, particularly in the narrow world of Dickey's South" (Hart 713). That the South is still considered a "narrow world" even by 1992 suggests that the mythos of the southern primitive still carries some authority, even after the poem's parodic campaign.

3. Many Returns

1. Nietzsche defines antiquarian history as a means of dutifully preserving the past that "produces one very imminent danger: everything old and past that enters one's field of vision at all is in the end blandly taken to be equally worthy of reverence, while everything that does not approach this antiquity with reverence, that is to say everything new and evolving, is rejected and persecuted" (74). The impulse often leads to a "mummified past," which can have dire effects for the cultural vitality of the present, if, like Nietzsche's antiquarian historians, one knows "only how to *preserve* life, not how to engender it" (75).

2. Arguing that Morgan "follows Emerson in affirming the interpenetration of the physical and spiritual and the revelatory powers of nature" (76), Lang interprets how Morgan and other poets of the mountain South use the pastoral mode, not merely to escape modernity, but to remind readers of humanity's dependence on nature and nature's well-being, a value now widely conceded in our ecologically conscious age.

3. The word was invented in 1688 by Swiss physician Johannes Hofer, who defined this emotion as a disease, coining the term for "the express purpose of translating a particular feeling (*Heimweh, regret, desiderium patriae*) into medical terminology" (Starobinski 84). Medically defined, nostalgia was the desire to return to one's native land, an affliction particularly severe among mercenaries divided from their homeland and rural residents forced to move from the countryside into emerging urban environments. By the nineteenth century, nostalgia was no longer contained in one's home soil, but had become abstracted into the poignant condition of Romantic sublimity, the unbridgeable "separation of man from the ideal" (95).

4. The southern poetics of nostalgia sometimes reflects the "good past/bad present contrast," which holds that, when compared to the past, present circumstances are "invariably felt to be, and often *reasoned* to be as well, more bleak, grim, wretched, ugly, deprivational, unfulfilling, frightening, and so forth" (Davis 15). This, in turn, can reinforce an unthinking acceptance of restorative nostalgia, since "the nostalgic mood is one whose active tendency is to envelop all that may have been painful or unattractive about the past in a kind of fuzzy, redeemingly benign aura" (14).

5. The third of seven children, Scarbrough was the part-Cherokee (on his father's side) son of an Appalachian sharecropping family who grew up in rural eastern Tennessee. Despite his working-class origins, he was an avid reader and attended the University of Tennessee (1935–36) as well as the University of the South (1941–43), eventually earning his B.A. from Lincoln Memorial University (1947) and his M.A. from the University of Tennessee (1954). Scarbrough was the elder statesman of the contemporary southern poets of nostalgia, having been born in 1915 and having published poetry from the 1940s until his death in 2008. In addition to publishing his poems in more than sixty-five literary magazines, he produced five major books of poetry as well as one novel. Reclusive by nature, he lived and wrote in Oak Ridge, Tennessee. Although Scarbrough's poetry has been lauded by a number of major

figures, from Allen Tate to James Dickey, he never earned a solid national following, a fact explained in part by R. T. Smith's assessment that Scarbrough "pledged allegiance to no network, joined no coterie, cultivated no clique" (7).

6. In the author's note from the first edition of *Tellico Blue*, Scarbrough provides the following description of his home territory among the east Tennessee Smokies: "My title, *Tellico Blue*, names the large mountain area of Tellico, sixteen miles from my house, a land of high peaks, ridges, cold blue rivers, ferocious boars, deer, and Indian memories" (x). The ethos of placefulness in Scarbrough's work is aptly described by Ramsey: "actuality of place gives grip, presence, validity, and a kind of mythic vision" (58). Robert Phillips adds that, for Scarbrough, the self "is a persona formed in a starkly romantic sensibility that gathers most of its images and metaphors from rural east Tennessee and that values deeply its agrarian antecedents" (419), while Forrest Gander equally suggests that "both the world of human relationships and the domain of memory are fixed, for him, in a landscape of wild upland groves, vine and stalk, bastard figs, gooseberries and muscadines" (14).

7. Morgan was born in 1944 in the western North Carolina region of the Green River Valley. Though he has published eleven volumes of poetry, he is as famous for his fictional exploits, having produced eight novels, including *Gap Creek* (2000), which was named an Oprah Book Club selection. He has received a number of awards for his verse, including the Hanes Poetry Prize of the Fellowship of Southern Writers (1991) and the North Carolina Award in Literature (1991), as well as Guggenheim (1988–89) and National Endowment for the Arts (1968, 1974, 1982, and 1987) fellowships. He earned a B.A. in English from the University of North Carolina at Chapel Hill (1965), an M.F.A. from the University of North Carolina at Greensboro (1968), and an honorary Doctor of Letters from UNC–Chapel Hill in 2006. Morgan is the Kappa Alpha Professor of English at Cornell University, where he has taught since 1971.

8. Justice (1925–2004) was born in Miami, Florida. He received a B.A. from the University of Miami, an M.A. from the University of North Carolina, and a Ph.D. from the University of Iowa. Even though he, like Scarbrough, was not an overly prolific poet, turning out seven original volumes of poetry over a career than began in 1960, he privileged quality over quantity, and this paid off in a number of poetry's most prestigious awards, including a Lamont Award (1960), a Pulitzer Prize (1980), and a Bollingen Prize (1991). His status in the profession is also reflected in his election as a chancellor of the Academy of American Poets in 1997. He was offered the opportunity to serve as U.S. poet laureate in 2003, but declined because of failing health. Having taught at Syracuse University, the University of California at Irvine, Princeton University, the University of Virginia, and the University of Iowa, Justice had an immeasurable effect on the course of contemporary U.S. poetry, influencing a number of major poets under his tutelage. He returned to his native state in 1982 to conclude his teaching career at the University of Florida, where he stayed until his retirement in 1992. He then returned to Iowa City with his wife, writer Jean Ross, and remained there until his death.

9. Charles Wright describes the influence of Rafael Alberti and Rainer Maria Rilke on Justice's verse: "The nostalgia, sadness, melancholia, and sense of a world lost and a time lost (especially of childhood and adolescence) in both these poets shine like a sunrise, or sunset, over many of Justice's poems, brightening and clarifying, darkening and adumbrating their own singularity and substance" ("Homage to the Thin Man" 741). Lewis Turco notes how, as Justice's poetry returns to childhood scenes, his "original nostalgia . . . was pared to the bone, making its poignance excruciating" (542). David Young defends Justice's longing for *nostos* by showing how formal distance moderates oversentimentality: "Poetic form and poetic tradition make available to us materials that help temper that risk of excess. So Justice's formalism is already at his service as a defense against sentimentality" (81). Mark Jarman calls attention to the mordant quality of Justice's figurative homesickness, suggesting that in his work "we hear the voice of a supremely skeptical romantic, not a cynic, but an ironic elegist who, in his paradoxical largess, can sing not only of your death, mine and his own; he can even sing of the death of his own poetic gift" (108–9).

10. As Rigsbee and Brown suggest, "beauty must make its way by rising through a rubble of clichés, but in some important sense, Justice's poems succeed because the very second- and third-rate quality of the aesthetic soil serves to extend the theme of absence" (153).

11. David Yezzi posits a similar connection between Justice's formal repetitions and the reiterations of memory, asserting that "Justice's career-long innovations with repetitive forms" serve to "mimic memory as it bears the past back to the speaker in successive waves" (22). However, where Yezzi believes that such recurrences work to "fix these memories, however distant or vague they may be initially, by pressing them into a glittering and durable object" (22), I argue that these formal returns tend toward ever more evanescent abstraction, showing memory to be increasingly insubstantial: the repetitions are nonsustaining.

12. Adcock is a native of San Augustine, Texas, a small farming town in east Texas. Much of her professional life has been spent in North Carolina as a faculty member at Meredith College, Warren Wilson College, Lenoir-Rhyne College, Duke University, and North Carolina State University. She has published six volumes of poetry since 1975. Her awards include a Guggenheim Fellowship (2002), the North Carolina Medal for Literature (1996), and the L. E. Phillabaum Award (2008); she was also a finalist for the Lenore Marshall Prize (2002).

13. Taylor was born in Loudon County in rural Virginia in 1942. He grew up as an avid horseman, an experience that enters his verses as a recurrent motif. Loudon County has a strong Quaker heritage, and Taylor is himself descended from this stock. In addition to translations from a variety of modern languages (Bulgarian, French, Hebrew, Italian, and Russian) as well as from classical Greek and Roman sources, he has published eight volumes of poetry and a work of criticism, *Compulsory Figures: Essays on Recent American Poets* (1992). A member of the Fellowship of Southern Writers, he has also earned the Witter Bynner Prize (1984), the Aiken Taylor Award (2004), and a Research Grant from the National Endowment for the Humanities (1980-1981). Taylor received the Pulitzer Prize as a relatively young poet

for only his third volume of poetry, *The Flying Change* (1985). He is Professor Emeritus of Literature at American University, where he taught from 1971 until 2003. He now resides in the Pacific Northwest.

14. George Garrett offers a similar, albeit more detailed, checklist of Taylor's "deliberately, determinedly unfashionable" style (326), which displays the following characteristics: "strong narrative line and structure, the poem as contained story; simple, straightforward, auditory language wrapped in a syntax that is intended to be appropriate to the action and thus may be extremely complex; an emphasis on form, which may manifest itself in a structure of rhymed stanzas or may, also, be shown in and through the subtle use of a clearly defined rhythmic base; a subject matter of country life and matters, often including horses and riders" (325).

15. Smith was born in Portsmouth in the Tidewater region of Virginia in 1942. His verse often integrates autobiographical elements, including family members as characters and referring to their working-class origins (for instance, his grandfather was a foreman and his uncle an engineer for the B&O Railroad). He is the author of twenty-five books, including fourteen volumes of poetry, and has collected numerous awards and fellowships, including a Guggenheim Fellowship (1982), National Endowment for the Arts Poetry Fellowships (1975 and 1982), an American Academy and Institute of Arts and Letters Award (1980), and a Pushcart Prize (1997). The first in his family to earn a college degree, Smith received a B.A. in English from the University of Virginia (1965), an M.A. in English from Southern Illinois University (1969), and a Ph.D. in English from Ohio University (1976). Between his M.A. and Ph.D., he joined the U.S. Air Force for a four-year term. After teaching stints at the University of Utah, SUNY-Binghamton, the University of Florida, and Virginia Commonwealth University, Smith served as a coeditor of the *Southern Review* and as a professor at the Louisiana State University for twelve years until he relocated in 2002 to Johns Hopkins University, where he is the Elliot Coleman Professor of Poetry. In 1996, he was honored with induction into the Fellowship of Southern Writers.

16. In his interview with Suarez, Smith describes his connection to his native Virginia landscape:

> Ultimately I went back to my own region, no matter where I lived. Since I've been here in Louisiana, which is physically, topographically, very like my native part of Virginia, I have written almost consistently of the Virginia landscape I lived in probably up to the age of thirty, off and on. That is not to say I haven't written poems about Louisiana. Maybe there will be more as I grow older, but I suspect that the same coastal landscape which is mine by historic gift will continue to be what I write about. I once had a professor who said, "When are you going to stop writing about these swamp things?" Swamps didn't particularly interest this man from Illinois, but you know, that's what was given to me to write about. Swamps and the character of people made by that place as surely as the tides and winds determine what sort of trees and groves flourish there. I haven't exhausted my swamps yet. (28–29)

Although he does mine the topography of his native part of Virginia, he is careful to avoid falling into an unthinking veneration of its pastoral beauty—he is talking about *swamps* here, not green rolling hills or soft pastures.

4. Lost Highways and Ethereal Landscapes

1. Born in Pickwick Dam, Tennessee, in 1935, Wright spent his youth and early adulthood in eastern Tennessee and western North Carolina. He graduated with a B.A. from Davidson College in 1957, then joined the U.S. Army and was stationed in Verona, Italy, from 1957 to 1961. After the service, Wright earned an M.F.A. at the University of Iowa in 1963 and then was awarded a Fulbright Scholarship at the University of Rome, 1963–65, as well as a Fulbright Lectureship at the University of Padua, 1968–69. He has taught at the University of California at Irvine and now lives in Charlottesville and teaches at the University of Virginia. Wright has published twenty books of poetry as well as translations of Italian poets Eugenio Montale and Dino Campana. He has also produced two collections of nonfictional essays and interviews, *Halflife* (1988) and *Quarter Notes* (1995). His stature in contemporary American poetry is evident in having received numerous prestigious awards for his verse, including a PEN Translation Prize in 1979, an Ingram Merrill Fellowship in 1980, a Lenore Marshall Prize for *Chickamauga* in 1995, a Pulitzer Prize and National Book Critics Circle Award for *Black Zodiac* in 1997, and an Award of Merit Medal from the American Academy of Arts and Letters in 1992. He was elected to the Fellowship of Southern Writers in 1991 and named a chancellor of the Academy of American Poets in 1999.

2. Below is a list of publication dates and abbreviations for those of Wright's poetry collections that I will examine in this chapter. Although all quotations are taken from the collected volumes, except for those drawn from *The Short History of the Shadow* (2002) [SHS], I have included the abbreviations of individual volumes in parenthetical citations to give a greater sense of the development of Wright's themes over the course of his career. Selections from *The Grave of the Right Hand* (1970) [GRH], *Hard Freight* (1973) [HF], *Bloodlines* (1975) [BL], and *China Trace* (1977) [CT] appear in *Country Music: Selected Early Poems* (1982) [CM]. Poems from *The Southern Cross* (1981) [SC], *The Other Side of the River* (1984) [OSR], *Zone Journals* (1988) [ZJ], and *Xionia* (1990) [X] appear in *The World of the Ten Thousand Things: Poems 1980–1990* (1990) [WTT]. Texts from *Chickamauga* (1995) [CH], *Black Zodiac* (1997) [BZ], *Appalachia* (1998) [APP], and *North American Bear* (1999) [NAB] appear in *Negative Blue* (2000) [NB].

3. During our interview, Wright described his poetry as "God-haunted":

The ritual call and response of the American service, the cadences of the King James Bible, early country music, the loony "spiritualism" of the Sky Valley Community in my early teenage years all certainly played a part in the pastiche of my life and poetry. So yes, a tangential

Christianity. I remain, however, a God-fearing non-believer, though
Christ doesn't really enter in to it. (Turner)

4. Lang argues for this idea, proposing that Wright "embraces nature both for
its physical beauty and for its seeming testimony to spiritual presence," although what
the poet discovers is "often only nature's indifference—not evidence of the infinite but
sure knowledge of human finitude" (159). Despite "so gloomy a prognosis regarding
[Wright's] spiritual dis-ease," Lang contends that Wright has nevertheless "continued
to portray himself, throughout his forty-year career, as a religious 'pilgrim,'" even
if he is more compelled by the "energy of absence" rather than that of clear divine
presence (159).

5. In "The Pragmatic Imagination and the Secret of Poetry" (1995), Jarman
provides an apt description of Wright's typical modus operandi: "many of his lines
move in a staggered two-step across the page: a portion of a line, then a descent
to the rest of the line, allowing a fullness to enter without running up against the
margin" (105). Bonnie Costello adds in "Charles Wright, Giorgio Morandi, and the
Metaphysics of the Line" (2002) that "what most attracts Wright is the way the line
both breaks and evokes the emptiness of the page, creating a haunting dialectic of
presence and absence" (153). The white space created by the continual drop and re-
turn of his lines, their staggered enjambments, reminds us that nothing is there, rein-
forcing his thematic concern with the metaphysics of absence: the unwritten space
maps the zone of negative sublimity.

6. In a 1999 interview, Wright notes the surplus of memories that come disem-
bedded from narrative emplotting and loom alone on the horizon, separate and intact
moments-in-themselves trailing off into the abstract distance:

> As I get older, again, I find that I don't write about memory so much. Or
> I write about memory in a different way, which is to say that memory is
> not as count-on-able as I once thought it to be. It is not as all-giving and
> sustaining and nourishing as I once thought it to be. There was a time
> when memory meant everything to me. And what you remembered, if
> you remembered it well, was the basis to all you were able to transfer or
> to translate into your waking current life. But it tends to loom alone on
> the horizon more often now than it tends to engulf me. (Suarez 42–43)

Christopher Miller agrees that memory becomes an increasingly diminished thing in
Wright's later poems, which "create an atmosphere of disconsolate remembrance, a
process rather than a result" (569), while Calvin Bedient provides perhaps the most
concise description of Wright's conceptualization of memory as "the oceanic witless-
ness of random memory. The patternless observations of a lifetime" (26). That Wright's
sense of overaccumulation works at a double remove, memories piled upon simulated
memories, is suggested in Bedient's further comment: "Sick Narcissus, memory finds in
memories metaphors of memory. Everywhere it lingers over its own likenesses" (26).

7. One might also suggest a third major site for cartographic memory in Wright's work: his depictions of metaquotidian yardscapes as he re-creates the sometimes eerily defamiliarizing space of his suburban Charlottesville backyard. Such panoramic yardscapes serve as another form of the abstract and repetitive landscaping of Wright's simulated South: the suburb as simulacrum.

8. Originally conceived as a means of extending the reach of the military-industrial complex, the interstate highway system was "the greatest and the longest engineered structure ever built" (Lewis ix), and it effectively encouraged the movement of capital down South. In the wake of the first wave of fordist production—the assembly-line generation of cheap automobiles for middle America by Henry Ford himself—there was a need for improved roads to cater to this new drive toward automobility. Good-roads movements were created on a local level to aid the repair of older roads and the construction of new routes. However, federal organization and funding were required to plan and build a network of roads that could keep up with the proliferation of mass-produced automobiles. The responsibility for building roads shifted from local good-roads movements to the federally operated Bureau of Public Roads, which was founded to oversee the construction of a federal system of interstate roadways, a project that culminated in the results of the Federal-Aid Highway Act of 1956. The interstate grid contributed to the nationalization of the country, linking up states and regions into a federal system of transportation that, while designed to meet military and industrial needs, also created avenues for recreational trips as well as for the spread of service and tourism industries. The federalist impulse of the interstate system is apparent in the caption on a map of suggested routes put out by the National Highways Association: "Highways will bind the states together in a common brotherhood and thus perpetuate and preserve the union" (Lewis 99). This nationalist project did not come without its costs:

> The system connects American cities and people in a vast web of roads
> that carry the life of the nation; yet to build it, tens of thousands of
> Americans were dispossessed of their land and saw their homes and
> neighborhoods destroyed. It gave Americans almost complete mobility
> and yet endless congestion. . . . It was first conceived of by highway
> planners in the thirties when Americans considered the automobile one
> of the blessings of the modern age; in the eighties, when it was nearly
> complete, many considered the automobile a blight. . . . It enabled us to
> speed across the land into vast stretches of wilderness; yet it distanced
> us from the very land we sought. (Lewis ix-x)

The highways helped lead the national economy into a more flexible program, but one that created imbalances of power as a result of newly constructed spatial relations; as Harvey notes, the production of space entailed by new transport systems meant that "any change in space relations wrought by such investments, after all, affected the profitability of economic activity unevenly, and therefore led to a redistribution of wealth and power" (*The Condition of Postmodernity* 255).

9. Howard Lawrence Preston argues that the post-1956 interstate grid produced "wholesale, predictable sameness" (1) along the highway routes while "Southerners' newfound automobility and improved, well-publicized tourists routes were catalysts for nationalism below the Mason-Dixon line" (7). Preston claims that all but the vestiges of superficial difference (relaxed life, slower speech, religious sentiments, and good manners) were thereby erased from southern living, asserting that the traditional South began to disappear in a haze of homogenization, and "it has done so first along the highway" (1).

10. Adorno notes this relation between automobility and the vanishing American landscape, for "what the hurrying eye has merely seen from the car it cannot retain, and the vanishing landscape leaves no more traces than it bears upon itself" (quoted in Lewis 277). In *America* (1986), Baudrillard similarly suggests that driving is "a spectacular form of Amnesia" and that "All you need to know about American society can be gleaned from an anthropology of its driving behaviour" (54). Although these critics can tend toward the hyperbolic, overstating the amnesiac flux of the interstates, there is some sense that through high-speed travel, geographic realities are abstracted to the level of simulacra; as Lewis notes, "we drive faster and cover more of the landscape but have the disturbing thought that we are seeing and feeling less of what we pass" (xiii).

11. William Kaszynski notes the economic evisceration wrought by the new interstate system on bypassed spaces:

> As construction of the [1956] interstate highways bypassed some of the old U.S. system, areas adjacent to the new highways were immediately affected. . . . In rural areas, cities and towns on federal aid routes saw a sharp decline in traffic and tourism. Merchants in bypassed areas saw their business drop to a trickle the day following the opening of a new section of interstate. Some businesses relocated to the nearest freeway interchange to survive; those that didn't often were forced to close. Many of the smaller hamlets withered away, becoming little more than ghost towns. (175)

12. In addition to this side trip to Idaho, "Lonesome Pine Special" also contains a couple of Montana roadscapes. This switching back from South to West lends the poem an even greater sense of transregionality, of Wright's identifications with territories beyond the South.

13. The maps and driving directions provided in the WPA guidebooks also served to reinforce the sense of a national imagined community created by the interstate grid: "as contributors to the shaping of a national citizenry, the WPA guidebooks carried a double authority: the truth claims of an informational genre and the official sponsorship of the federal government" (Bold 3). The guidebook's "objective" mapping of the cultural landmarks and places of interest for a given state conceals its deeper ideological function to condition the flow of recreational travel down the highways and, by extension, the flow of capital into the tourist industry along such routes.

14. Holiday Inn was the first major hotel chain to originate in the South. Named after a 1942 Bing Crosby movie, it was founded along U.S. 70 in Memphis in 1952 by Kemmons Wilson. Taking advantage of the postwar boom, it soon became the model of not just the southern, but of the American hospitality industry, presenting a microcosm of how the South was integrated into larger networks of capital exchange (Jakle, Sculle, and Rogers 261).

15. In the wake of federal funding and construction, several locally named highways were drained of regional associations, as a standardized numbering system took precedence over such titles as the Lee Highway, the Dixie Highway, and the Jefferson Davis Highway.

16. Wright's vision of the South shares much with Stevens's. Though in a late poem Stevens claims that "a mythology reflects its region," his poems that investigate both the value and limits of regionalism typically proffer a vision of region dressed, if at all, only in the thin rags of its own threadbare mythology. This dynamic is true of his many poems that invoke particular southern places but hardly seem to touch these at all: the mythos of the South is little more than a watermark impressed lightly behind the words of the poem. In interviews, Wright is careful to distance himself from Stevens, not wishing to be categorized as merely a post-Stevensonian—and rightly so, since his style certainly stands on its own.

17. In his interview at Oberlin College, Wright spoke about his role as a contemporary landscape poet:

> I did grow up in east Tennessee and western North Carolina, which had a
> lot to do with my poems. Place has a lot to do with everyone's poems. . . .
> My biography is pretty much the biography of almost everyone here. I
> happened to be in that place and you were probably somewhere else. We
> all went through more or less the same things. (60)

Wright exhibits self-consciousness about how the standardization of place is related to the sharedness of experience. Landscape is a staple of everyone's poems, and his memories are interchangeable with everyone else's. We (i.e., well-educated, white, middle-class suburbanites) "all went through more or less the same things." He describes the region he grew up in as "a type of back wilderness that is very lush and large and that encroaches on you continually" (60). However, little of the lushness and largeness of the wilderness is reenacted in his poetic cartographies of the Tennessee–North Carolina landscape.

18. Rodger Cunningham argues that "Appalachia exists in a blank created by a double otherness—a *doubly* double otherness. For the region is not only an internal Other to the South as the South is the internal Other of America, but it is also the occupier of a simultaneous gap and overlap *between* North and South" (45).

19. During our interview, Wright explained his choice of the title for *Chickamauga*: "I always wanted to have a book with a Southern title, so I picked *Chickamauga* and on the front of the book there's a picture my wife took of me saying 'Chickamauga.'"

Thus Wright invokes the sanctified place-name of Chickamauga in order to empty it of its narrative history, reducing this storied past down to a mere four syllables.

20. The epigraph to two sections of Wright's *China Trace* is drawn from Italo Calvino's *Invisible Cities*:

> "On the day when I know all the emblems," Kublai Khan asked Marco, "shall I be able to possess my empire, at last?"
> And the Venetian answered: "Sire, do not believe it. On that day you will be an emblem among emblems."

5. Ghostwriting the Claims of the Dead

1. Born James William Brown Jr., the son of a carpenter, in Bogalusa, Louisiana, in 1947, Komunyakaa changed his name to honor his grandfather, a stowaway from Trinidad. After high school, he joined the U.S. Army and fulfilled a tour of duty in Vietnam from 1969 to 1970 as an information specialist, where he saw combat and received a Bronze Star. Between 1975 and 1980, he earned a B.A. in English and sociology at the University of Colorado, an M.A. in creative writing at Colorado State University, and an M.F.A. in creative writing at the University of California at Irvine. After teaching at the University of New Orleans and Indiana University, in 1997, he became a professor at Princeton University until accepting a position in 2006 as the Distinguished Senior Poet for the Creative Writing Program at New York University. He has published more than a dozen volumes of poetry, adapted the ancient Sumerian epic *Gilgamesh* into a verse play, recorded three CDs of lyrical compilations with jazz musicians, authored the lyrics for two operas in collaboration with composer T. J. Anderson (*Slip Knot* and *The Reincarnated Beethoven*), and coedited with Sasha Feinstein two editions of *The Jazz Poetry Anthology*. In addition to winning the 1994 Pulitzer Prize and serving as a Chancellor for the Academy of American Poets from 1999 to 2005, he has garnered a range of poetry's most coveted awards, including the Kingsley-Tufts Poetry Award, the Ruth Lilly Poetry Prize, the William Faulkner Prize from the Université de Rennes, and the Hanes Poetry Prize, as well as fellowships from the National Endowment for the Arts. His importance to contemporary American literature is further underscored by the fact that *Callaloo*, a premiere journal of African American criticism, devoted an entire volume to Komunyakaa's work in 2005.

2. In his interview with Michael Collins, Komunyakaa expands on his earlier assertion that poetry "has always been political," insisting on the interwoven strands of poetics and politics:

> Human beings are social and political animals, so how can one of our oldest artistic expressions not reflect that? Language itself is political, but what troubles me about many so-called political poems is that the politics are on the surface, that one is told how to exist and what to think. How can any beauty and celebration survive in such contention?

I'm not suggesting that the poem should be a verbal sucker punch, but I am saying that, for me, the ideal poem is layered with numerous nuances, that it even risks beauty. (633)

He further asserts that a true political poetry should contain "some gut and deep singing inside the language. I believe that the poetry of evasion cannot live beside this other more substantial work, because what doesn't have life cannot give life, even if it fattens itself on illusion and pretense" (633).

3. Although it is one of his main themes, traumatic memory is not the only subject that characterizes Komunyakaa's verse. His overall canon proves that he is a remarkably versatile poet, taking on a spectrum of materials from jazz and blues to the aboriginal peoples of Australia to ancient history to homages to some of his poetic influences. *Talking Dirty to the Gods* (2000) in particular reflects Komunyakaa's exceptional range. The volume creates an ironic form of mythopoesis, a multicultural synergy of the proliferating gods flooding the contemporary era, from the more traditional myth-making machinery of religion to the new mythologies of science, film/television, politics, and consumer capitalism, producing a brilliant pastiche of nearly everything under the sun—and above it too.

4. For a detailed account of some of the telling intersections of southern literature and the Vietnam War, including Komunyakaa and ranging from Bobbie Ann Mason to James Dickey and Barry Hannah, see Owen W. Gilman's *Vietnam and the Southern Imagination* (1992).

5. In explaining the divide between Heidegger's incarnative poetics and Derrida's disembodied linguistics, Karen Mills-Courts invokes Emily Dickinson's sentiment that "Nature is a haunted house—but Art—a house that tries to be haunted" (16). While experience is traumatic, art is post-traumatic. Although her analysis focuses on poetry as a haunted form marked by "the ghost-like ambiguity of being both dead and alive" (13), Mills-Courts does not provide an adequate justification for poetry's specific relation to a sense of hauntedness. My interpretation of Komunyakaa's work contends that it is poetic rhythm that evokes "the emptiness of a nothing that seems, somehow, to signify something. It is the nothingness of a haunting" (13).

6. While there remains critical debate about whether Adorno intended to single out lyric poetry as a barbaric form in the wake of the Holocaust, locating his critique in the context of this genre adds further force and complexity to Komunyakaa's pointed revisions of lyric form.

7. Mieke Bal provides the following explanation of paraleptical doubling as a result of trauma:

> In narratological terms, repression results in ellipsis—the omission of important elements in the narrative—whereas dissociation doubles the strand of the narrative series of events by splitting off a sideline. In contrast to ellipsis, this sideline is called paralepsis in narrative theory. In other words, repression interrupts the flow of narrative that shapes

memory; dissociation splits off material that cannot then be reincorporated into the main narrative (ix).

8. According to Cathy Caruth, "trauma is not locatable in the simple violent or original event in an individual's past, but rather in the way that its very unassimilated nature—the way it was precisely not known in the first instance—returns to haunt the survivor later on" (4), for what reemerges to disrupt a stable notion of self and time for the victim is "not only the reality of the violent event but also the reality of the way that its violence has not yet been fully known" (6). This definition of trauma follows Freud's observations on the recurrent nightmares experienced by shell-shocked World War I veterans in *Beyond the Pleasure Principle* (1920): "Now dreams occurring in traumatic neuroses have the characteristic of repeatedly bringing the patient back into the situation of his accident, a situation from which he wakes up in another fright. This astonishes people far too little" (7). Freud suggests that such paraleptical nightmares—dreams that place the sufferer back into the moment of trauma without any self-awareness that he is engaged in a separate or divergent reality—are endeavoring to "master the stimulus retrospectively, by developing the anxiety whose omission was the cause of the traumatic neurosis" (26). Trauma patients undergoing paraleptical recyclings of the moment of accident, which literally become alternate performances of reality, parallel histories, suffer a precise reenactment that, because literal, has no meaning. This understanding of trauma has been elaborated by contemporary critics, such as Caruth, Shoshana Felman, Dominick LaCapra, Kalí Tal, Marita Sturken, Kirby Farrell, and Gregg Horowitz, who represent a range of disciplines, including psychology, literary analysis, history, cultural studies, and philosophy. In terms of trauma's effects on an individual sufferer, Tal offers the following account of the medical definition of post-traumatic stress disorder (PTSD), which was not formally acknowledged by the American Psychiatric Association until 1980:

> The characteristic symptoms include autonomic arousal, which is often manifest in panic attacks or startle reactions; a preoccupation with the traumatic event in the form of nightmares, flashbacks, or persistent thoughts about the trauma that intrude into everyday affairs; and a general dysphoria, a numbness that takes the meaning out of life and makes it hard to relate to other people. [Often] the symptoms manifest themselves after a latency period of several years or . . . alternate with apparently asymptomatic periods that, on closer inspection, turned out to be periods of denial. (135)

9. Farrell describes how traumatic experience is encoded on inextricable personal and cultural levels, asserting that "whatever the physical distress . . . trauma is also psychocultural, because *the injury entails interpretation of the injury*" (7), and "those interpretations are profoundly influenced by the particular cultural context" (7) that

"registers the dissonance—the shock—of meeting long-denied realities that threaten our individual and collective self-esteem" (15).

10. African American combatants in Vietnam died in disproportionately high numbers. James William Gibson notes that while blacks represented 11 percent of the general U.S. population, "twenty-four percent of army deaths in Vietnam in 1965 were black men's deaths" (215). According to Gibson, "originally the Army had made a special effort to draft minorities" (215), since "Technowar needed an ever-increasing labor supply at the point of production. Standards were changed so that those at the bottom of the racial and economic system of power could fight and die in Vietnam" (217).

11. Focusing on the black cultural legacy of jazz and blues, Keith Leonard provides a perceptive reading of "Blue Light Lounge Sutra," exploring the poem's representation of the interweaving complexities of individual consciousness and communal tradition. Leonard argues that Komunyakaa uses "the musical or poetic representation of introspection" to prevent "conceptions of aesthetic effect and communal unity from being rendered static parts of the commodified cultural order that delimits the black self and that maintains the various modes of cultural hierarchy that subordinates and alienates black people" (832–33).

12. Komunyakaa further expresses how deeply this atmosphere of social violence was embedded in the symbolic structures of southern culture:

> James Baldwin says a black boy can't survive if he doesn't know the score
> by fourteen. Of course, this is doubly true in the South I knew in the
> '50s. This was near the time Emmett Till was murdered in Mississippi.
> But the South was also a mecca of language and images. I learned about
> the naming of things there. The wrong word could get a man killed.
> ("More Than a State of Mind" 164)

Although he does not engage in writing what he has dismissed as an obsolete and limiting brand of African American "service literature" (Mitrano 529), Komunyakaa's southern poetry reflects an abiding claim for a black southern presence in the "acute competition for the symbolic materials of subjectivity, the markers of status and autonomy that prevent social death" (Farrell 30).

13. As psychologist John Dollard put it succinctly in 1937, "Every Negro in the South knows that he is under a kind of sentence of death; he does not know when his turn will come, it may never come, but it may also be at any time" (359). For more on the concept of social death in the context of African American history, see Patterson's landmark study *Slavery and Social Death* (1982), as well as Abdul R. JanMohamed's *The Death-Bound-Subject: Richard Wright's Archaeology of Death* (2005).

14. To give some perspective on the scale of violence exercised against African Americans in the Jim Crow South, Stewart Tolnay and E. M. Beck identify

> 2,805 victims of lynch mobs killed between 1882 and 1930 in ten
> southern states. Although mobs murdered almost 300 white men and

women, the vast majority—almost 2,500—of lynching victims were African-American. Of these black victims, 94 percent died in the hands of white lynch mobs. The scale of this carnage means that, on the average, a black man, woman, or child was murdered nearly once a week, every week, between 1882 and 1930 by a hate-driven white mob. (ix)

Neil R. McMillen offers the following description of the ritualistic procedures of southern spectacle lynchings, grotesquely termed "Negro Barbeques":

Savage as the statistical record was, postbellum mob violence did not turn truly sadistic until after 1890. Until late in the century, hanging and shooting were the customary forms of lynching; in the twentieth century, however, as the number of victims gradually declined, mobs grew more barbarous. Once comparatively rare, some form of mutilation became commonplace, either preceding or following an execution; lynchers and spectators frequently gathered souvenirs—small bones, ears, toes, and fingers—for use sometimes as watch fobs or for display as curiosities in service stations or general stores. Even the methods of execution changed as the noose increasingly gave way to the faggot and to varied and often highly inventive forms of torture. (233)

Recent critical studies, such as *Violence, the Body, and "The South"* (2001), edited by Baker and Dana Nelson, assert the South's continuing status as America's racialized core where past and present mutilations and killings of blacks—from fourteen-year-old Emmett Till's lynching in Mississippi in 1955 to James Byrd Jr.'s dragging and decapitation in Jasper, Texas, in 1998—in conjunction with more "subtle" institutionalized forms of racist intimidation and de facto segregation provide a living synonym for American cultural trauma. Even while the South has been marked as the place where racial violence seems "always in ascendance" (232), Baker and Nelson note that the region should not be allowed to symbolically contain all elements of white American racism.

15. The South depicted in Komunyakaa's verse represents a series of what Yi-fu Tuan defines as "landscapes of fear," spaces pervaded with "a diffuse sense of dread" (5), where anticipatory horror is an ever-present state of being. Landscapes of fear embody "almost infinite manifestations of the forces for chaos" (6) that induce a "fear of the imminent collapse of [the] world and the approach of death—that final surrender of integrity to chaos" (7).

16. Baker's *Turning South Again* (2001) understands race as fundamental to defining and punishing criminal behaviors in the South, where the history of the prison structure is entangled inextricably with the history of slavery and racism. Under the auspices of a "humane" judicial system, blacks are profiled for punishment in a way that seems only a marginal improvement over lynch law: as the prison work camp replaces the plantation, so the hanging tree and the electric chair come to one and the same. The number of executions of southern blacks—especially men—during the Jim Crow period shows that African American males were particularly marked

for criminal punishment: "Between 1882 and 1930, 1,977 African-Americans were executed in . . . ten southern states . . . an average of forty executions a year," which means that "an African-American was put to death somewhere in the South on the average of every four days" (Tolnay and Beck 100); in the same period only 451 whites were executed, leaving an indefensible disparity.

17. Black southerners not only were subjected to extralegal violence, but also found little protection under the law during the Jim Crow era. As McMillen suggests, "black defendants in Mississippi courts in the half century after 1890 may have enjoyed relatively less procedural fairness than did slaves" (201), since as ostensibly free citizens, blacks had to confront the thinly veiled double standards of the unwritten statutes of "negro law."

18. Although Komunyakaa has noted clearly that the speakers of his Vietnam poems should not be equated to the poet himself, some of the events described in these works are based on moments he witnessed while on duty in Vietnam. In an interview with Toi Derricotte, he gives the following account of his military service:

> I had gone to infantry OCS and at that particular time they were searching for lieutenants who could perform as platoon leaders and somewhere along the line I heard that in a combat situation a second lieutenant only lasts for ten seconds. I said, "Well, why didn't I know that before?" [laughter] What happened is that I went off to jungle warfare training afterwards, and I applied for a branch transfer in the information field. And people were telling me, "Well, the army spent $10,000 on your training; you won't get a branch transfer into Information." And I thought, once the branch transfer came through, that I was lucky—until I got there. Because then I was in the field every day for six months, pursuing stories that happened in the area of operation. I was in the Americal Division, the largest in Vietnam, about twenty-four or twenty-five-thousand soldiers. (516)

19. The title of *Dien Cai Dau* reveals Komunyakaa's efforts to incorporate an awareness of how the Vietnamese viewed their nation and their war. Recent Vietnamese authors, such as Le Ly Hayslip and Christian Nguyen Langworthy, have also challenged American assimilationist writing and films about Vietnam, redressing the status of Vietnam as U.S. cultural fetish.

20. As Angela Salas asserts, *Dien Cai Dau* counters "the popular-cultural tendency to homogenize or lighten the aggregate complexion of American soldiers in Vietnam (à la television's *China Beach* and the statuary additions to Maya Lin's Vietnam Veterans Memorial)" in order to "subtly, yet incisively, [inform] readers that African American soldiers and their white counterparts often experienced the war in quite different ways" (69).

21. In addition to his poetry about Vietnam, a transsouthern dynamic is also present in Komunyakaa's poetry that connects the American South to the Caribbean, which further relates his work to theories of the global South. For more on the trans-

national impulse in Komunyakaa's verse, see my "Modern Metamorphoses and the Primal Sublime: The Southern/Caribbean Poetry of Yusef Komunyakaa and Derek Walcott" (2011) as well as my "Dying Objects/Living Things: The Thingness of Poetry in Yusef Komunyakaa's *Talking Dirty to the Gods*" (2012). Komunyakaa discussed with me his poetic concern with the transnational, fluid space of the Atlantic basin in our interview, "Remaking Myth in Yusef Komunyakaa's *Talking Dirty to the Gods, Taboo*, and *Gilgamesh*: An Interview" (2009). Keith Cartwright's "Weave a Circle Round Him Thrice: Komunyakaa's Hoodoo Balancing Act" (2005) also offers an important reading of the Afro-Caribbean influence on Komunyakaa's poetics, using the Haitian Creole notion of "balanse" (the Vodou ritualistic process of energizing by rhythmically evoking contradiction) as a telling framework.

22. Arthur Danto makes a relevant distinction between monuments and memorials:

> We erect monuments so that we shall always remember, and build memorials so that we shall never forget. Thus we have the Washington Monument, but the Lincoln Memorial. Monuments commemorate the memorable and embody the myths of beginnings. Memorials ritualize remembrance and mark the reality of ends. . . . The memorial is a special precinct, extruded from life, a segregated enclave where we honor the dead. With monuments we honor ourselves. (152)

23. Salas points out that Andrew Johnson's name also serves as a literal referent that binds the Wall's history to Komunyakaa's individual memory:

> In the many times I have visited the Vietnam Veterans Memorial since the 1996 Modern Languages Association Convention in Washington, D.C., I have always made it my ritual to find the name Andrew Johnson in one of the directories at the site of the memorial. I know by this point that I will find him on the 62nd line of panel 22E, but I check anyway, reminding myself that Johnson was, indeed, a young man raised in Bogalusa, Louisiana and killed before his twentieth birthday. Komunyakaa has given me the ambiguous gift of "the booby trap's white flash," and I see this flash as I furtively run my fingers across his name and wonder how the world might be different had Johnson, a man I never met, not died a teenaged soldier in Vietnam. (86)

24. Identifying this ideologically invested tendency to rewrite trauma into nostalgia, Lorrie Smith exposes the hypermediation of American collective memory of the war, arguing that "understanding the war's significance is harder than ever because of the media blitz which has helped jog but also clog our memories" (49) since "popular perceptions of Vietnam have coalesced around patriarchal, patriotic myths which Hollywood, the mainstream media, and the political establishment work hard to reinforce" (49). Smith posits the brunt of poetry produced by Vietnam veterans as

an antidote to such a cover-up of the deeper injuries of the war, a view that coincides with Gotera's argument in *Radical Visions: Poetry by Vietnam Veterans* (1994) that ex-soldiers' work "shows how the uniqueness of that war affected our basic ways of seeing and interpreting the world" (xi) in an effort to effect a "countercultural politicization" (xi) against prevalent political and popular media discourse about the war.

25. Renny Christopher both praises and critiques Komunyakaa's relative self-consciousness about trying to view the Vietnam War from a Vietnamese perspective. Admitting that *Dien Cai Dau* "often turns its point of view toward Vietnamese—poems attempt to see a rape from the standpoint of the victim, to see the lives of bar girls" (253), she grants the author some credit, for "it is unusual for an American writer or filmmaker to stretch far enough to see a Vietnamese woman's point of view at all" (254), but "these attempts mostly remain outside, though, and the Vietnamese remain mysterious" (253–54). Komunyakaa attempts to imagine more deeply the Vietnamese perspective in *Thieves of Paradise*, which contains his most sustained efforts to understand Vietnam as an autonomous culture with its own political and socioeconomic complexities.

26. Michelle Satterlee's work also attempts to broaden the definition of trauma from a pathological model (the traumatic event viewed as necessarily shattering and denying the possibility of representation) to a sociocultural one that holds some potential for trauma to be conceived as not merely repressive, but even productive within a particular historical context. Using the research of psychiatrist Judith Herman, Satterlee contends that literary representations of trauma can produce "a reformulation of previous conceptions of self and relations to the world" (239) that can lead to a reorganization of social reality and reclamation of the self through connection to a communal geographic/cultural space, for "the place of trauma is significant insofar as that place highlights the ways cultural values and mythic stories are connected to specific lands and communities that influence the remembrance and recital of trauma and healing" (155). Drawing on Maurice Blanchot's theory of disaster, Michael Dowdy also sees something for hope in Komunyakaa's poems, since "disaster pushes individuals and communities to the point of destruction but leaves them space to rebuild relationships and exercise responsibility" (813).

6. Transouthern Hybridities

1. There are a number of other living poets who explore transouthern transformations in their verse, such as Brenda Marie Osbey, Allison Hedge Coke, Kwame Dawes, Afaa Michael Weaver, Dan Albergotti, and Jake Adam York.

2. Foucault defines countermemory in "Nietzsche, Genealogy, History" (1971) as "a use of history that severs its connection to memory, its metaphysical and anthropological model, and constructs a counter-memory—a transformation of history into a totally different form of time" (160). The dissociative use of countermemory is "directed against identity, and opposes history given as continuity or representative of a tradition" (160) and conceives of the self as "a complex system of distinct and multiple

elements, unable to be mastered by the powers of synthesis" (161). Dissociative countermemory "does not seek to define our unique threshold of emergence, the homeland to which metaphysicians promise a return; it seeks to make visible all of those discontinuities that cross us" (162).

3. Lest I be charged with utopianism in describing the work of countermemory in current southern poetics, I should reiterate that these writers record the effects of an often hostile and conflicted cultural landscape.

4. Daniels was born in a working-class neighborhood on the south side of Richmond, Virginia, in 1953. She is the daughter of a British war bride who divorced her American serviceman husband after two years and then married Daniels's father in 1952. The first member of her family to attend college, Daniels earned a B.A. and an M.A. from the University of Virginia (1975, 1977), and an M.F.A. from Columbia University (1980). She served as a Fellow at Harvard University's Bunting Institute and has taught creative writing at Wake Forest University, Bennington College, and Vanderbilt University. Her poetry has earned the Pushcart Prize, the Crazyhorse Prize for Poetry, the Louisiana Literature Poetry Prize, and the James Dickey Prize. She has published four volumes of original verse and is currently an associate professor of English and an associate dean of arts and science at Vanderbilt. Daniels challenges the venerated codes of the Fugitives while walking the same halls that Ransom, Davidson, Tate, and Warren once walked.

5. In "Porch-Sitting and Southern Poetry," Daniels grants the Fugitives credit for seeking "a rare and daring compromise with modernity" on both political and poetic levels (64). While her assessment does not dwell on the more unsavory aspects of the Fugitives' politics, especially their implicit racial condescension, Daniels shares with them a mistrust of technology run amok, a sense of the value of a rural lifestyle, and a desire for poetic experimentation.

6. "Rebel Yell" shares the counternostalgic sentiment of Noel Polk's description of the failure of the Lost Cause ideology in *Outside the Southern Myth* (1997):

> Thus we romanticize and spiritualize defeat; we tell stories of the
> doomed charge against overwhelming odds, of our brave boys dying in
> and for a Cause lost from the beginning not because we were wrong but
> because we were finally outnumbered by the soulless Yankees. We stress
> the tales of gallantry, of heroism, of courage and character; of ex-slaves
> who loved ol' Miss and ol' Massa so much they stayed around, even
> helping to fight the Yankees; of women at home sewing the flags, being
> beautiful and faithful, tending the wounded. . . . We are still tending
> the wounded, still constructing a past that will let us be both right and
> defeated, that will permit us to transcend our shabby and problematic
> present, which falls far short of what a righteous people deserve. (39)

7. A child of sharecroppers who lived on a small farm near the border between North and South Carolina, Jordan was born in 1961 near the town of Marshville, North Carolina. Her parents, who experienced the hardships of the Depression-era

South, eventually worked their way up from sharecroppers to tenant farmers to small landowners. After her mother's death when Jordan was seven years old, she was left in the care of her father and her four older brothers. She was the first member of her family to attend college, earning a B.A. in women's studies (1990) and an M.F.A. in poetry (1995) from the University of Virginia, as well as an M.F.A. in fiction (1999) from the University of Utah. Before her first volume of poetry was published, she had a long work history, being employed in an ice cream factory, greenhouses, a farmer's market, restaurants, pizza delivery, and as a writing instructor. Jordan currently teaches creative writing at California State University at San Marcos. Her debut volume of poetry, *Carolina Ghost Woods*, collected two highly touted prizes, the 1999 Walt Whitman Award of the Academy of American Poets and a National Book Critics Circle Award.

8. In his preface to *The Order of Things* (1966), Foucault defines heterotopias as against utopias, which reinforce existing social conditions:

> Utopias afford consolation: although they have no real locality there is nevertheless a fantastic, untroubled region in which they are able to unfold. . . . Heterotopias are disturbing, probably because they secretly undermine language, because they make it impossible to name this and that, because they shatter or tangle common names, because they destroy "syntax" in advance, and not only the syntax with which we construct sentences but also that less apparent syntax which causes words and things (next to and also opposite one another) to "hold together." This is why utopias permit fables and discourse: they run with the very grain of language and are part of the fundamental dimension of the fabula; heterotopias . . . desiccate speech, stop words in their tracks, contest the very possibility of grammar at its source; they dissolve our myths and sterilize the lyricism of our sentences. (xvii–xviii)

These spaces of otherness are "linked with all the others" but "contradict all the other sites" ("Of Other Spaces" 24) and reflect "real places . . . which are something like counter-sites, a kind of effectively enacted utopia in which the real sites . . . are simultaneously represented, contested, and inverted" (24).

9. For a further illustration of how heterotopic space functions in contemporary southern poetry, see my account of counternostalgia in Andrew Hudgins's work, "Heterotopic Space in Andrew Hudgins' *After the Lost War*" (2007).

10. Rodney Jones (1950–) was born in Falkville, Alabama, and raised in this rural section of northern Alabama. He earned his B.A. from the University of Alabama in 1971 and his M.F.A. in creative writing at the University of North Carolina at Greensboro in 1973. He has produced eight books of poetry, which have garnered him a National Book Critics Circle Award (1989), the Lavan Younger Poet Award from the Academy of American Poets (1986), and the Kingsley Tufts Award (2007). He also received a National Endowment for the Arts Fellowship (1984) as well as a Guggenheim Fellowship (1985). *Elegy for the Southern Drawl* was short-listed as a

finalist for the Pulitzer Prize (2000). He is a professor at the University of Southern Illinois at Carbondale, where he has taught since 1984.

11. Mullen was born in Florence, Alabama, in 1953 and raised in Fort Worth, Texas. She has produced six volumes of original poetry as well as one critical study, *Freeing the Soul: Race, Subjectivity, and Difference in Slave Narratives* (1999). She earned her B.A. in English from the University of Texas at Austin (1975) and her M.A. (1987) and Ph.D. (1990) in literature from the University of California at Santa Cruz. Having taught at Cornell University, she is now a professor in the English Department at the University of California at Los Angeles. She has been honored with the Gertrude Stein Award for innovative poetry as well as a Guggenheim Fellowship, and her fifth volume of poetry, *Sleeping with the Dictionary* (2002), was a finalist for the National Book Award, the National Book Critics Circle Award, and the Los Angeles Times Book Prize.

12. In a 1996 interview, Mullen describes her multiple identifications in terms of region, defining Texas as a hybrid space, simultaneously southern and not southern:

> [M]y notion of who I was had to do with being in a southern state—but in another way, Texas isn't southern: it's southwestern or western. So it's being in and actually on the edge of a southern black culture. Texas, when I was young, was a segregated state. I remember the colored and white signs on the rest rooms and water fountains, and I remember the first time we tested integration by going to a drive-in restaurant where they refused to serve us, and we left after waiting there for about thirty minutes for our hamburgers that never arrived. We were the first black family in our neighborhood, and our neighbors moved out; the next door neighbors packed overnight bags and went to a motel so that they would not have to spend a single night next to us. . . . So that's part of what growing up in Texas meant to me. (Bedient 651)

13. A native of Gulfport, Mississippi, who was born in 1966, Trethewey has published three volumes of poetry, *Domestic Work* (2000), *Bellocq's Ophelia* (2002), and *Native Guard* (2006), as well as *Beyond Katrina: A Meditation on the Mississippi Gulf Coast* (2010), a creative nonfiction response to the impact of Hurricane Katrina on her native Gulf Coast region that interweaves her own personal and familial memories of the area. *Domestic Work* won the 1999 Cave Canem Poetry Prize as well as the 2001 Lillian Smith Book Award. Trethewey has been awarded a Pushcart Prize and the Grolier Poetry Prize and has earned fellowships from the Bunting Fellowship Program and the National Endowment for the Arts. Her work achieved national attention when *Native Guard* won the 2007 Pulitzer Prize for poetry. Trethewey earned her B.A. in English from the University of Georgia, an M.A. in English and creative writing at Hollins University (where her father, Eric Trethewey, a poet himself, is a professor of creative writing), and an M.F.A. from the University of Massachusetts at Amherst. Having taught at Auburn University, the University of North Carolina at Chapel Hill, and Duke University, she is currently a professor of creative writing

at Emory University, where she holds the Phillis Wheatley Distinguished Chair in Poetry.

14. During an interview with Jill Petty, Trethewey was asked about the things that play the largest roles in what she writes about:

> Well, certainly being black, but also I think being mixed, having had a biracial experience, that's also important. The fact that I come from a very matrilineal family is very significant and influences what things get played out in the work. And I've talked about growing up with chickens and all that, but at the same time my grandmother's house sits right on Highway 49—*the* Highway 49 of all the blues songs—so we've got this big highway running right through this neighborhood that has been rural for the longest time. And some big company talked her into allowing them to put in a billboard, so the billboard is half in our yard and half on government property. My father is a poet who comes from a rural atmosphere, and he writes about that a lot; but anything that's rural for me is always undercut by a highway, undercut by this other world being smashed right up against it. In many ways, I guess this understanding hearkens back to being a mixed person. There are pieces of identity that you know fit together and everything's fine, but at the same time you know there might occasionally be some opposition going on, and so opposition is probably something really important in my work. One of the ways it's physical for me is my parents having a mixed marriage and living right there, straddling, you know, this rural community and a highway at the same time. (368)

15. Trethewey describes the absence latent in photographic representation:

> Every photograph represents a moment that is no longer, passed, as well as ways of being that have disappeared. I've always been a little obsessed with the way photographs hold and create an object out of that moment. And I've often thought if you look at a photograph, if you really study the gestures and expressions that the people have in the photograph, you could see the rest of their lives, everything that's to come. (Petty 364)

16. From one perspective, as Sontag asserts, "a photograph—any photograph—seems to have a more innocent, and therefore more accurate, relation to visible reality than do other mimetic objects" (*On Photography* 6), since "photographed images do not seem to be statements about the world so much as pieces of it, miniatures of reality that anyone can make or acquire" (4). Yet far from simply recording an "innocent" view of a past reality, photographs "give evidence—often spurious, always incomplete—in support of dominant ideologies and existing social arrangements. They fabricate and confirm these myths and arrangements. . . . Photographs tell us how things ought to look, what their subjects should reveal about themselves" (*Where the Stress Falls* 220).

17. Katherine Henninger includes Trethewey among a cadre of current southern women writers who use fictive representations of photography to wage "an openly visible, visual contest to determine who and what will represent 'the South,' what and who can be included (acknowledged, accommodated) within the canon of southernness" (157). These authors place "cameras in the hands of their female protagonists" to recontextualize "formal ethics in an explicitly gendered (as well as raced and classed) frame" (158).

18. The portraits have been reproduced in *Bellocq: Photographs from Storyville, the Red-Light District of New Orleans* (1996). In her essay "Bellocq" (1996), Sontag gives a perceptive introduction to the Storyville sequence:

> So much about these pictures affirms current taste: the low-life material; the near-mythic provenance (Storyville); the informal, anti-art look, which accords with the virtual anonymity of the photographer and the real anonymity of his sitters; their status as *objets trouvés*, and a gift from the past. Add to this what is decidedly unfashionable about the pictures: the plausibility and friendliness of their version of the photographer's troubling, highly conventional subject. And because the subject is so conventional, the photographer's relaxed way of looking seems that much more distinctive. If there had once been more than eighty-nine glass negatives and one day a few others turned up, no one would fail to recognize a Bellocq. (*Where the Stress Falls* 223)

She further credits Bellocq for avoiding the salaciousness typically involved with photographing such quasi-pornographic subject matter: "Clearly, no one was being spied on, everyone was a willing subject. And Bellocq couldn't have dictated to them how they should pose—whether to exhibit themselves as they might for a customer or, absent the customers, as the wholesome-looking country women most of them undoubtedly were" (226). Because of this unique perspective on a conventional subject, Sontag is able to take some pleasure in the series: "That part of the subject I do take pleasure in is the beauty and forthright presence of many of the women, photographed in homely circumstances that affirm both sensuality and domestic ease, and the tangibleness of their vanished world. How touching and good-natured the pictures are" (226).

19. Trethewey's Ophelia intertwines cultural with personal memory: "I found Ophelia . . . because I was searching for a persona through whom I might investigate aspects of my own mixed-race experience growing up in the Deep South" (Rowell 1027). She identifies the barriers on Ophelia's identity that the volume hopes to expose and pass beyond, for Ophelia's "sense of self has always run up against what someone else perceived her to be based on her color, class, gender" (Rowell 1029). As for the character of the artist, she claims that "Bellocq functions as a kind of disembodied eye that is always looking at her, training the camera on her" (1030), although she is careful not to "indict Bellocq as someone who is objectifying her because I did not want to see her simply as some victim of objectification" (1030).

20. Trethewey's Pulitzer Prize-winning *Native Guard* (2006) also provides a brilliant record of the workings of transouthernism and grounded globalism, especially in its account of the natural and artificial structures of the Mississippi Gulf Coast, where seemingly permanent boundaries, geographic and social, are recast as permeable shadings.

Bibliography

Adcock, Betty. *Intervale: New and Selected Poems.* Baton Rouge: Louisiana State UP, 2001.

Adorno, Theodor. "After Auschwitz." 1949. *Negative Dialectics.* Trans. E. B. Ashton. New York: Continuum, 1973. 361–64.

Attridge, Derek. *Poetic Rhythm: An Introduction.* New York: Cambridge UP, 1995.

Audubon, John James. *Delineations of American Scenery and Character.* New York: Baker, 1926.

Aviram, Amittai F. *Telling Rhythm: Body and Meaning in Poetry.* Ann Arbor: U of Michigan P, 1994.

Ayers, Edward L. "What We Talk about When We Talk about the South." *All Over the Map: Rethinking American Regions.* Ed. Edward L. Ayers, Patricia Nelson Limerick, Stephen Nissenbaum, and Peter S. Onuf. Baltimore: Johns Hopkins UP, 1996. 62–82.

Baker, Houston A., Jr., *Turning South Again: Re-thinking Modernism/Re-reading Booker T.* Durham, NC: Duke UP, 2001.

Baker, Houston A., Jr., and Dana D. Nelson, eds. *Violence, the Body, and "The South."* Special issue of *American Literature* 73.2 (2001).

Bal, Mieke, Jonathan Crewe, and Leo Spitzer, eds. *Acts of Memory: Cultural Recall in the Present.* Hanover, NH: UP of New England, 1999.

Barthes, Roland. "The Photographic Message." 1961. *The Responsibility of Forms: Critical Essays on Music, Art, and Representation.* Trans. Richard Howard. Berkeley: U of California P, 1991. 3–20.

———. *Camera Lucida: Reflections on Photography.* New York: Hill & Wang, 1980.

Baudrillard, Jean. *America.* 1986. Trans. Chris Turner. London: Verso, 1988.

———. *Simulacra and Simulation.* 1981. Trans. Sheila Faria Glaser. Ann Arbor: U of Michigan P, 1994.

Bedient, Calvin. *In the Heart's Last Kingdom: Robert Penn Warren's Major Poetry.* Cambridge, MA: Harvard UP, 1984.

———. "The Solo Mysterious Blues: An Interview with Harryette Mullen." *Callaloo* 19.3 (1996): 651–69.

——. "Tracing Charles Wright." 1982. *The Point Where All Things Meet*. Ed. Tom Andrews. Oberlin, OH: Oberlin College P, 1995. 21–38.

Beer, Gillian. "Origins and Oblivion in Victorian Narrative." *Sex, Politics, and Science in the Nineteenth-Century Novel*. Ed. Ruth Bernard Yeazell. Baltimore: Johns Hopkins UP, 1986. 63–87.

Bellocq, E. J. *Bellocq: Photographs from Storyville, the Red-Light District of New Orleans*. New York: Random, 1996.

Bernstein, Charles. "Artifice of Absorption." *A Poetics*. Cambridge, MA: Harvard UP, 1992. 9–89.

——, ed. *Close Listening: Poetry and the Performed Word*. New York: Oxford UP, 1998.

Bhabha, Homi K. *The Location of Culture*. New York: Routledge, 1994.

Blotner, Joseph. *Robert Penn Warren: A Biography*. New York: Random, 1997.

Bly, Robert. "The Collapse of James Dickey." *Sixties* 9 (1967): 70–79.

Bold, Christine. *The WPA Guides: Mapping America*. Jackson: UP of Mississippi, 1999.

Bone, Martyn. *The Postsouthern Sense of Place in Contemporary Fiction*. Baton Rouge: Louisiana State UP, 2005.

Bordwell, David, Janet Staiger, and Kristin Thompson. *The Classical Hollywood Cinema: Film Style and Mode of Production to 1960*. New York: Columbia UP, 1985.

Bottoms, David. *Armored Hearts: Selected and New Poems*. Port Townsend, WA: Copper Canyon, 1995.

Boym, Svetlana. *The Future of Nostalgia*. New York: Basic, 2001.

Brinkmeyer, Robert H., Jr. *Remapping Southern Literature: Contemporary Southern Writers and the West*. Athens: U of Georgia P, 2000.

Bruccoli, Matthew J., and Judith S. Baughman, eds. *Crux: The Letters of James Dickey*. New York: Knopf, 1999.

Burris, Sidney. "Mega-Processors, Advanced Peripherals, and Robert Penn Warren's *Audubon*." *Studies in the Literary Imagination* 35.1 (2002): 137–64.

Burt, John. *Robert Penn Warren and American Idealism*. New Haven, CT: Yale UP, 1988.

Butterworth, Keen. "Projections and Reflections in *Audubon: A Vision*." *Southern Literary Journal* 36 (2003): 90–103.

Campbell, Joseph, with Bill Moyers. *The Power of Myth*. Ed. Betty Sue Flowers. New York: Doubleday, 1988.

Cartwright, Keith. "Weave a Circle Round Him Thrice: Komunyakaa's Hoodoo Balancing Act." *Callaloo* 28.3 (2005): 851–63.

Caruth, Cathy. *Unclaimed Experience: Trauma, Narrative, and History*. Baltimore: Johns Hopkins UP, 1996.

Cash, W. J. *The Mind of the South*. 1941. New York: Vintage, 1969.

Chappell, Fred. "'Not as a Leaf': Southern Poetry and the Innovation of Tradition." *Georgia Review* 51.3 (1997): 477–89.

——. "Too Much Fudge: How James Dickey's Posturing Buried the Genius Beneath." *Brightleaf*. 1998. 6 Oct. 2000 <http://www.brightleaf-review.com/Winter98/chappell.html>.

Christopher, Renny. *The Viet Nam War/The American War: Images and Representations in Euro-American and Vietnamese Exile Narratives.* Amherst: U of Massachusetts P, 1995.

Clabough, Casey Howard. *Elements: The Novels of James Dickey.* Macon, GA: Mercer UP, 2002.

Clark, Thomas D. *The Emerging South.* New York: Oxford UP, 1968.

Cobb, James C., and William Stueck, eds. *Globalization and the American South.* Athens: U of Georgia P, 2005.

Cohn, Deborah. *History and Memory in the Two Souths.* Nashville: Vanderbilt UP, 1999.

Cohn, Deborah, and Jon Smith, eds. *Look Away! The U.S. South in New World Studies.* Durham, NC: Duke UP, 2004.

Collins, Michael. "Komunyakaa, Collaboration, and the Wishbone: An Interview." *Callaloo* 28.3 (2005): 620-34.

Corkin, Stanley. *Cowboys as Cold Warriors: The Western and U.S. History.* Philadelphia: Temple UP, 2004.

Corrigan, Lesa Carnes. *Poems of Pure Imagination: Robert Penn Warren and the Romantic Tradition.* Baton Rouge: Louisiana State UP, 1999.

Costello, Bonnie. "Charles Wright, Giorgio Morandi, and the Metaphysics of the Line." *Mosaic* 35.1 (2002): 149-71.

———. "Charles Wright's *Via Negativa*: Language, Landscape, and the Idea of God." *Contemporary Literature* 42.2 (2001): 325-46.

Cowan, Louise. *The Fugitive Group: A Literary History.* Baton Rouge: Louisiana State UP, 1959.

Culler, Jonathan. "Why Lyric?" *PMLA* 123.1 (2008): 201-6.

Cunningham, Rodger. "Writing on the Cusp: Double Alterity and Minority Discourse in Appalachia." *The Future of Southern Letters.* Ed. Jefferson Humphries and John Lowe. New York: Oxford UP, 1996. 41-53.

Current, Richard N. *Northernizing the South.* Athens: U of Georgia P, 1983.

Daniels, Kate. "Porch-Sitting and Southern Poetry." *The Future of Southern Letters.* Ed. Jefferson Humphries and John Lowe. New York: Oxford UP, 1996. 61-71.

———. "Rebel Yell." *Five Points* 4.3 (1999): 49-50.

———. *A Walk in Victoria's Secret.* Baton Rouge: Louisiana State UP, 2010.

Danto, Arthur. "The Vietnam Veterans Memorial." *The Nation* 31 Aug. 1985: 152.

Davidson, Donald. *Lee in the Mountains and Other Poems Including The Tall Men.* Boston: Houghton, 1938.

———. Letter to R. P. Warren. 17 March 1930. Robert Penn Warren Papers. Box 21, Folder 399. Yale Collection of American Literature. Beinecke Rare Book and Manuscript Library, Yale U.

———. *Southern Writers in the Modern World.* Athens: U of Georgia P, 1958.

Davis, Fred. *Yearning for Yesterday: A Sociology of Nostalgia.* New York: Free Press, 1979.

Davis, Natalie Zemon, and Randolph Starn. "Introduction." *Memory and Counter-Memory.* Special issue of *Representations* 26 (1989): 1-6.

Davis, Thadious M. "Expanding the Limits: The Intersection of Race and Region." *Southern Literary Journal* 20.2 (1988): 3–11.

Derricotte, Toi. "Seeing and Re-Seeing: An Exchange between Yusef Komunyakaa and Toi Derricotte." *Callaloo* 28.3 (2005): 513–18.

Dickey, Christopher. *Summer of Deliverance: A Memoir of Father and Son.* New York: Simon & Schuster, 1998.

Dickey, James. *Alnilam.* New York: Doubleday, 1987.

——. *Babel to Byzantium: Poets and Poetry Now.* New York: Farrar, 1968.

——. Papers. Robert W. Woodruff Library, Emory U.

——. *Self-Interviews.* Garden City, NY: Doubleday, 1970.

——. *The Suspect in Poetry.* Madison, MN: Sixties Press, 1964.

——. *The Whole Motion: Collected Poems, 1945–1992.* Middletown, CT: Wesleyan UP, 1992.

Doane, Mary Ann. *The Emergence of Cinematic Time: Modernity, Contingency, the Archive.* Cambridge, MA: Harvard UP, 2002.

Dollard, John. *Class and Caste in a Southern Town.* New Haven, CT: Yale UP, 1937.

Dowdy, Michael C. "Working in the Space of Disaster: Yusef Komunyakaa's Dialogues with America." *Callaloo* 28.3 (2005): 812–23.

Dungy, Camille T. *Black Nature: Four Centuries of African American Nature Poetry.* Athens: U of Georgia P, 2009.

Edmundson, Mark. "James Dickey: Learning from Others." *Raritan* 15.3 (1996): 47–63.

Eiseley, Loren. *The Immense Journey.* New York: Vintage, 1957.

Farrell, David. "Poetry as a Way of Life: An Interview with Robert Penn Warren." *Conversations with Robert Penn Warren.* Ed. Gloria L. Cronin and Ben Siegel. UP of Mississippi, 2005. 189–203.

Farrell, Kirby. *Post-Traumatic Culture: Injury and Interpretation in the Nineties.* Baltimore: Johns Hopkins UP, 1998.

Felman, Shoshana, and Dori Laub. *Testimony: Crises of Witnessing in Literature, Psychoanalysis, and History.* New York: Routledge, 1991.

Fenin, George N., and William K. Everson. *The Western: From Silents to the Seventies.* New York: Grossman, 1973.

Foucault, Michel. "Nietzsche, Genealogy, History." 1971. *Language, Counter-Memory, Practice: Selected Essays and Interviews.* Ed. and trans. Donald F. Bouchard. Ithaca, NY: Cornell UP, 1977. 139–64.

——. "Preface." *The Order of Things: An Archaeology of the Human Sciences.* 1966. New York: Vintage, 1970. xvi–xxvi.

——. "Of Other Spaces." *Diacritics* 16.1 (1986): 22–27.

Freud, Sigmund. *Beyond the Pleasure Principle.* 1920. Trans. James Strachey. New York: Norton, 1961.

Frow, John. "Tourism and the Semiotics of Nostalgia." *October* 57 (1991): 123–51.

Gander, Forrest. "The Inflorescence of Variety: An Iconoclastic Southern Poet." *Shenandoah* 51.1 (2001): 12–16.

Garrett, George. "Henry Taylor." *American Poets Since World War II.* Detroit: Gale, 1980. 322–27.

Gibson, James William. *The Perfect War: Technowar in Vietnam.* Boston: Atlantic Monthly P, 1986.

Gilman, Owen W., Jr. *Vietnam and the Southern Imagination.* Jackson: UP of Mississippi, 1992.

Goble, Mark. "'Our Country's Black and White Past': Film and the Figures of History in Frank O'Hara." *American Literature* 71.1 (1999): 57–92.

Gotera, Vince. "'Lines of Tempered Steel': An Interview with Yusef Komunyakaa." *Callaloo* 13.2 (1990): 215–29.

——. *Radical Visions: Poetry by Vietnam Veterans.* Athens: U of Georgia P, 1994.

Graham, Allison. "History, Nostalgia, and the Criminality of Popular Culture." *Georgia Review* 38.2 (1984): 348–64.

Grainge, Paul. *Monochrome Memories: Nostalgia and Style in Retro America.* Westport, CT: Praeger, 2002.

Greeson, Jennifer Rae. *Our South: Geographic Fantasy and the Rise of National Literature.* Cambridge, MA: Harvard UP, 2010.

Griffin, Larry J. "Southern Distinctiveness, Yet Again, or, Why America Still Needs the South." *Southern Cultures* 6.3 (2000): 47–72.

Grimshaw, James A., Jr. *Understanding Robert Penn Warren.* Columbia: U of South Carolina P, 2001.

Gunn, Thom. "Things, Voices, Minds." *"Struggling for Wings": The Art of James Dickey.* Ed. Robert Kirschten. Columbia: U of South Carolina P, 1997. 13–15.

Haddox, Thomas F. "Elizabeth Spencer, the White Civil Rights Novel, and the Postsouthern." *Modern Language Quarterly* 65.4 (2004): 561–81.

Handley, George B. *New World Poetics: Nature and the Adamic Imagination of Whitman, Neruda, and Walcott.* Athens: U of Georgia P, 2007.

Harmon, William. "Is Southern Poetry Southerner than Southern Fiction?" *Mississippi Quarterly* 46.2 (1993): 273–78.

Hart, Henry. *James Dickey: The World as a Lie.* New York: Picador, 2000.

Harvey, David. *The Condition of Postmodernity: An Enquiry into the Origins of Cultural Change.* Cambridge, MA: Blackwell, 1989.

——. "The Geopolitics of Capitalism." *Social Relations and Spatial Structures.* Ed. Derek Gregory and John Urry. New York: St. Martin's, 1985. 128–163.

Henninger, Katherine. *Ordering the Facade: Photography and Contemporary Southern Women's Writing.* Chapel Hill: U of North Carolina P, 2007.

Hobson, Fred. *The Southern Writer in the Postmodern World.* Athens: U of Georgia P, 1991.

Horowitz, Gregg M. *Sustaining Loss: Art and Mournful Life.* Stanford, CA: Stanford UP, 2001.

Jackson, Virginia. *Dickinson's Misery: A Theory of Lyric Reading.* Princeton, NJ: Princeton UP, 2005.

Jakle, John A., Keith A. Sculle, and Jefferson S. Rogers. *The Motel in America.* Baltimore: Johns Hopkins UP, 1996.

Jameson, Fredric. *Postmodernism; or, The Cultural Logic of Late Capitalism.* Durham, NC: Duke UP, 1991.

JanMohamed, Abdul R. *The Death-Bound-Subject: Richard Wright's Archaeology of Death.* Durham, NC: Duke UP, 2005.

Jarman, Mark. "Ironic Elegies: The Poetry of Donald Justice." *Pequod* 16–17 (1984): 104–9.

——. "The Pragmatic Imagination and the Secret of Poetry." *The Point Where All Things Meet.* Ed. Tom Andrews. Oberlin, OH: Oberlin College P, 1995. 96–104.

——. "The Trace of a Story Line." 1986. *The Point Where All Things Meet.* Ed. Tom Andrews. Oberlin, OH: Oberlin College P, 1995. 105–9.

Jarvis, Brian. *Postmodern Cartographies: The Geographical Imagination in Contemporary American Culture.* London: Pluto, 1998.

Jarvis, Simon. "For a Poetics of Verse." *PMLA* 125.4 (2010): 931–35.

Jones, Rodney. *Elegy for the Southern Drawl.* Boston: Houghton, 1999.

Jones, Suzanne W., and Sharon Monteith, eds. *South to a New Place: Region, Literature, Culture.* Baton Rouge: Louisiana State UP, 2002.

Jordan, Judy. *Carolina Ghost Woods.* Baton Rouge: Louisiana State UP, 2000.

Justice, Donald. *New and Selected Poems.* New York: Knopf, 1997.

Justus, James H. *The Achievement of Robert Penn Warren.* Baton Rouge: Louisiana State UP, 1981.

Kammen, Michael. *Mystic Chords of Memory: The Transformation of Tradition in American Culture.* New York: Knopf, 1991.

Kaszynski, William. *The American Highway: The History and Culture of Roads in the United States.* Jefferson, NC: McFarland, 2000.

Kirby, David. "Is There a Southern Poetry?" *Southern Review* 30.4 (1994): 869–80.

Kirschten, Robert. *James Dickey and the Gentle Ecstasy of Earth.* Baton Rouge: Louisiana State UP, 1988.

Koch, Kenneth. *Making Your Own Days: The Pleasures of Reading and Writing Poetry.* New York: Knopf, 1988.

Komunyakaa, Yusef. *Pleasure Dome: New and Collected Poems.* Middletown, CT: Wesleyan UP, 2001.

——. "More Than a State of Mind." *Studies in the Literary Imagination* 35.1 (2002): 163–64.

Koppelman, Robert S. *Robert Penn Warren's Modernist Spirituality.* Columbia: U of Missouri P, 1995.

Kreyling, Michael. "Fee, Fie, Faux Faulkner: Parody and Postmodernism in Southern Literature." *Southern Review* 29.1 (1993): 1–15.

——. *Inventing Southern Literature.* Jackson: UP of Mississippi, 1998.

Kristeva, Julia. *Powers of Horror: An Essay on Abjection.* Trans. Leon S. Roudiez. New York: Columbia UP, 1982.

LaCapra, Dominick. *Writing History, Writing Trauma.* Baltimore: Johns Hopkins UP, 2001.

Lang, John. *Six Poets from the Mountain South.* Baton Rouge: Louisiana State UP, 2010.

Lenihan, John H. *Showdown: Confronting Modern America in the Western Film.* Urbana: U of Illinois P, 1980.

Leonard, Keith. "Yusef Komunyakaa's Blues: The Postmodern Music of *Neon Vernacular*." *Callaloo* 28.3 (2005): 825–49.

Lewis, Tom. *Divided Highways: Building the Interstate Highways, Transforming American Life*. New York: Viking, 1977.

Matthews, Carrie R., James L. Peacock, and Harry L. Watson, eds. *The American South in a Global World*. Chapel Hill: U of North Carolina P, 2005.

McCabe, Susan. *Cinematic Modernism: Modernist Poetry and Film*. New York: Cambridge UP, 2005.

McFee, Michael. "Seven Questions about Southern Poetry." *Mississippi Quarterly* 58:2 (2005): 217–53.

McKee, Kathryn, and Annette Trefzer, eds. *Global Contexts, Local Literatures: The New Southern Studies*. Special issue of *American Literature* 78:4 (2006).

McMillen, Neil R. *Dark Journey: Black Mississippians in the Age of Jim Crow*. Urbana: U of Illinois P, 1989.

Miller, Christopher R. "Poetic Standard Time: The Zones of Charles Wright." *Southern Review* 34.3 (1998): 566–86.

Millichap, Joseph R. "Robert Penn Warren's West." *Southern Literary Journal* 26.1 (1993): 54–63.

Mills-Court, Karen. *Poetry as Epitaph: Representation and Poetic Language*. Baton Rouge: Louisiana State UP, 1990.

Mitchell, Lee Clark. *Westerns: Making the Man in Fiction and Film*. Chicago: U of Chicago P, 1996.

Mitrano, G. F. "A Conversation with Yusef Komunyakaa." *Callaloo* 28.3 (2005): 521–30.

Morgan, Robert. *Topsoil Road*. Baton Rouge: Louisiana State UP, 2000.

Mullen, Harryette. *Muse & Drudge*. Philadelphia: Singing Horse, 1995.

Nietzsche, Friedrich. "On the Uses and Disadvantages of History for Life." 1874. *Untimely Meditations*. Trans. R. J. Hollingdale. New York: Cambridge UP, 1983. 57–124.

Nora, Pierre. "Between Memory and History: *Les Lieux de Mémoire*." *Representations* 26 (Spring 1989): 7–24.

O'Brien, Michael. *Rethinking the South: Essays in Intellectual History*. Baltimore: Johns Hopkins UP, 1988.

Patterson, Orlando. *Slavery and Social Death: A Comparative Study*. Cambridge, MA: Harvard UP, 1982.

Peacock, James L. *Grounded Globalism: How the U.S. South Embraces the World*. Athens: U of Georgia P, 2007.

Perloff, Marjorie. "What We Don't Talk about When We Talk about Poetry." *Poetry On and Off the Page: Essays for Emergent Occasions*. Evanston, IL: Northwestern UP, 1998. 168–91.

Perloff, Marjorie, and Craig Dworkin. "The Sound of Poetry / The Poetry of Sound: The 2006 MLA Presidential Forum." *PMLA* 123.3 (2008): 749–61.

Petty, Jill. "An Interview with Natasha Trethewey." *Callaloo* 19.2 (1996): 364–75.

Phillips, Robert L. "George Addison Scarbrough (1915–)." *Contemporary Poets, Drama-tists, Essayists, and Novelists of the South: A Bio-Bibliographical Sourcebook.* Ed. Robert Bain and Joseph M. Flora. Westport, CT: Greenwood, 1994. 418–22.

Poe, Edgar Allan. "The Poetic Principle." 1850. *The Collected Works of Edgar Allan Poe.* Vol. 1. Cambridge, MA: Belknap, 1969. 164–97.

Polk, Noel. *Outside the Southern Myth.* Jackson: UP of Mississippi, 1997.

Pratt, Mary Louise. *Imperial Eyes: Travel Writing and Transculturation.* New York: Rout-ledge, 1992.

Preston, Howard Lawrence. *Dirt Roads to Dixie: Accessibility and Modernization in the South, 1885–1935.* Knoxville: U of Tennessee P, 1991.

Prunty, Wyatt. "At Home and Abroad: Southern Poets with Passports and Memory." *Southern Review* 30.4 (1994): 745–50.

Ramazani, Jahan. *The Hybrid Muse: Postcolonial Poetry in English.* Chicago: U of Chi-cago P, 2001.

Ramsey, Paul. "James Dickey: Meter and Structure." *James Dickey: The Expansive Imagination; A Collection of Critical Essays.* Ed. Richard J. Calhoun. Deland, FL: Everett/Edwards, 1973. 177–94.

——. "The Truth at the Door: The Poems of George Scarbrough." *Appalachian Journal* 6 (1978): 55–61.

Ransom, John Crowe. *Selected Poems.* New York: Knopf, 1969.

Rigsbee, David, and Steven Ford Brown, eds. *Invited Guest: An Anthology of Twentieth-Century Southern Poetry.* Charlottesville: UP of Virginia, 2001.

Ritivoi, Andreea Deciu. *Yesterday's Self: Nostalgia and the Immigrant Identity.* New York: Rowan, 2002.

Romine, Scott. *The Narrative Forms of Southern Community.* Baton Rouge: Louisiana State UP, 1999.

——. *The Real South: Southern Narrative in the Age of Cultural Reproduction.* Baton Rouge: Louisiana State UP, 2008.

Rowell, Charles Henry. "Inscriptive Restorations: An Interview with Natasha Trethewey." *Callaloo* 27.4 (2004): 1021–34.

Rubin, Louis D., Jr. "The Gathering of the Fugitives: A Recollection." *Southern Review* 30.4 (1994): 658–73.

Runyon, Randolph Paul. *The Braided Dream: Robert Penn Warren's Late Poetry.* Lexington: UP of Kentucky, 1990.

Salas, Angela M. *Flashback through the Heart: The Poetry of Yusef Komunyakaa.* Selins-grove, PA: Susquehanna UP, 2004.

Satterlee, Michelle. "How Memory Haunts: The Impact of Trauma on Vietnamese Immigrant Identity in Lan Cao's *Monkey Bridge.*" *Studies in the Humanities* 31.2 (2004): 138–62.

Scarbrough, George. *New and Selected Poems.* Ed. Patricia Wilcox. Binghamton, NY: Iris, 1977.

——. *Tellico Blue.* 1949. Oak Ridge, TN: Iris, 1999.

Sharp, Nicholas A. "Taylor's 'One Morning, Shoeing Horses.'" *Explicator* 57.1 (1998): 62–64.

Simpson, Lewis P. *The Fable of the Southern Writer.* Baton Rouge: Louisiana State UP, 1994.

Slotkin, Richard. *Gunfighter Nation: The Myth of the Frontier in Twentieth-Century America.* New York: Atheneum, 1992.

Smith, Dave. "The Strength of James Dickey." *Local Assays: On Contemporary American Poetry.* Urbana: U of Illinois P, 1985. 170–86.

———. *The Wick of Memory: New and Selected Poems, 1970–2000.* Baton Rouge: Louisiana State UP, 2000.

Smith, Lorrie. "Resistance and Revision in Poetry by Vietnam War Veterans." *Fourteen Landing Zones: Approaches to Vietnam War Literature.* Ed. Philip K. Jason. Iowa City: U of Iowa P, 1991. 49–66.

Smith, R. T. "'Lusher Materia Medica I Have Not Seen.'" *Shenandoah* 51.1 (2001): 7–11.

Sobchack, Vivian. *The Address of the Eye: A Phenomenology of Film Experience.* Princeton, NJ: Princeton UP, 1992.

Soja, Edward W. *Postmodern Geographies: The Reassertion of Space in Critical Social Theory.* New York: Verso, 1989.

Sontag, Susan. *On Photography.* New York: Farrar, 1977.

———. *Where the Stress Falls: Essays.* New York: Farrar, 2001.

Starobinski, Jean. "The Idea of Nostalgia." *Diogenes* 54 (1966): 81–103.

Stewart, Susan. *On Longing: Narratives of the Miniature, the Gigantic, the Souvenir, the Collection.* Baltimore: John Hopkins UP, 1984.

———. *Poetry and the Fate of the Senses.* Chicago: U of Chicago P, 2002.

Strandberg, Victor. *The Poetic Vision of Robert Penn Warren.* Lexington: UP of Kentucky, 1977.

Sturken, Marita. *Tangled Memories: The Vietnam War, the AIDS Epidemic, and the Politics of Remembering.* Berkeley: U of California P, 1997.

Suarez, Ernest. *James Dickey and the Politics of Canon: Assessing the Savage Ideal.* Columbia: U of Missouri P, 1993.

Suarez, Ernest, with T. W. Stanford III and Amy Verner. *Southbound: Interviews with Southern Poets.* Columbia: U of Missouri P, 1999.

Szczesiul, Anthony. *Racial Politics and Robert Penn Warren's Poetry.* Gainesville: UP of Florida, 2002.

Tate, Allen. *Collected Poems, 1919–1976.* New York: Farrar, 1977.

Tal, Kali. *Worlds of Hurt: Reading the Literatures of Trauma.* New York: Cambridge UP, 1996.

Taylor, Henry. *The Flying Change.* Baton Rouge: Louisiana State UP, 1985.

Tichi, Cecelia. *Embodiment of a Nation: Human Form in American Places.* Cambridge, MA: Harvard UP, 2001.

Tolnay, Stewart, and E. M. Beck. *A Festival of Violence: An Analysis of Southern Lynchings, 1882–1930.* Urbana: U of Illinois P, 1995.

Tompkins, Jane. *West of Everything: The Inner Life of Westerns.* New York: Oxford UP, 1992.

Torgovnick, Mariana. *Gone Primitive: Savage Intellects, Modern Lives.* Chicago: U of Chicago P, 1990.

Trethewey, Natasha. *Bellocq's Ophelia*. Saint Paul, MN: Graywolf, 2002.

Tuan, Yi-fu. *Landscapes of Fear*. New York: Pantheon, 1979.

Turco, Lewis. "Donald Justice." *The Twayne Companion to Contemporary Literature in English*. Ed. R. H. W. Dillard and Amanda Cockrell. New York: Twayne, 2003. 540–45.

Turner, Daniel Cross. "Dying Objects/Living Things: The Thingness of Poetry in Yusef Komunyakaa's *Talking Dirty to the Gods*." *Mosaic* 45:1 (Spring 2012): 137–54.

——. "Heterotopic Space in Andrew Hudgins' *After the Lost War*." *Southern Quarterly* 44.4 (2007): 175–95.

——. "Modern Metamorphoses and the Primal Sublime: The Southern/Caribbean Poetry of Yusef Komunyakaa and Derek Walcott." *The South and the Sublime*. Ed. Thomas F. Haddox. Special issue of *Southern Quarterly* 48.3 (2011): 52–69.

——. "Oblivion's Glow: The (Post)Southern Sides of Charles Wright: An Interview." 2005. *Charles Wright in Conversation: Interviews, 1979–2006*. Ed. Robert D. Denham. Jefferson, NC: McFarland, 2008. 133–42.

——. "Remaking Myth in Yusef Komunyakaa's *Talking Dirty to the Gods, Taboo,* and *Gilgamesh*: An Interview." *Mississippi Quarterly* 62.2 (2009): 335–50.

——. "Southern Crossings: An Interview with Natasha Trethewey." *Waccamaw* 6 (Fall 2010). 12 July 2011 <http://www.waccamawjournal.com/pages.html?x=324>

Van Ness, Gordon. *Outbelieving Existence: The Measured Motion of James Dickey*. Columbia, SC: Camden, 1992.

Vendler, Helen. "Catching a Pig on the Farm." Review of *The Wick of Memory: New and Selected Poems 1970–2000* by Dave Smith. *New York Review of Books* 48.4 (2001): 44–46.

——. "Charles Wright." 1988. *The Point Where All Things Meet*. Ed. Tom Andrews. Oberlin, OH: Oberlin College P, 1995. 13–20.

——. "The Transcendent 'I'." 1980. *The Point Where All Things Meet*. Ed. Tom Andrews. Oberlin, OH: Oberlin College P, 1995. 1–12.

Walker, Janet, ed. *Westerns: Films through History*. New York: Routledge, 2001.

Warren, Robert Penn. *Audubon: A Vision*. 1969. *The Collected Poems of Robert Penn Warren*. Ed. John Burt. Baton Rouge: Louisiana State UP, 1998. 251–67.

——. *Brother to Dragons: A Tale in Verse and Voices*. A New Version. 1979. Baton Rouge: Louisiana State UP, 1996.

——. Papers. Yale Collection of American Literature. Beinecke Rare Book and Manuscript Library, Yale U.

——. *A Plea in Mitigation: Modern Poetry and the End of an Era*. Macon, GA: Wesleyan College, 1966.

West, Robert. "A Study in Sharpening Contrast: Robert Morgan and the Distinction between Prose and Poetry." *Pembroke Magazine* 35 (2003): 77–81.

White, Hayden, "Historiography and Historiophoty." *American Historical Review* 93.5 (1988): 1193–99.

——. "The Modernist Event." *The Persistence of History: Cinema, Television, and the Modern Event*. Ed. Vivian Sobchack. New York: Routledge, 1996. 17–38.

Wilson, Deborah. "Medusa, the Movies, and the King's Men." *The Legacy of Robert Penn Warren.* Ed. David Madden. Baton Rouge: Louisiana State UP, 2000. 70–83.

Wright, Charles. *Country Music: Selected Early Poems.* Middletown, CT: Wesleyan UP, 1982.

——. *Hard Freight.* Middletown, CT: Wesleyan UP, 1973.

——. "Homage to the Thin Man." *Southern Review* 30.4 (1994): 741–44.

——. "Interview at Oberlin College." 1977. *Halflife: Improvisations and Interviews, 1977–87.* Ann Arbor: U of Michigan P, 1988. 59–88.

——. "'Metaphysics of the Quotidian': A Conversation with Charles Wright." *The Post-Confessionals: Conversations with American Poets of the Eighties.* Ed. Earl G. Ingersoll, Judith Kitchen, and Stan Sanvel Rubin. Cranbury, NJ: Associated UPs, 1989. 37–48.

——. *Negative Blue: Selected Later Poems.* New York: Farrar, 2000.

——. *A Short History of the Shadow.* New York: Farrar, 2002.

——. *The World of the Ten Thousand Things: Poems 1980–1990.* New York: Farrar, 1990.

Wright, Richard. *12 Million Black Voices.* 1941. New York: Thunder's Mouth, 2002.

Yaeger, Patricia, ed. "The New Lyric Studies." *PMLA* 123.1 (2008): 181–234.

Yezzi, David. "The Memory of Donald Justice." *New Criterion* 23.3 (2004): 21–25.

Young, David. "Translating America." *Field* 72 (2005): 74–83.

Index

Brinkmeyer, Robert H., 202n13

Brooks, Cleanth, 191n6, 192n10, 196n1

Caruth, Cathy, 138, 221n8

cartographic memory, xiv, 60, 87, 97–119,
137–38, 216n7, 218n17; definition of,
xxx, 90–96

Chappell, Fred, 192n7, 196n21, 205n2,
208n13

Christianity. *See* religious imagery

cinematic memory. *See* filmic memory

civil rights movement, xiii–xiv, 23, 127,
131, 196n1

Civil War, xiii, xxii–xxiii, xxiv–xxviii,
19, 47, 50, 80–85, 93, 110–11, 135,
143, 151, 158–59, 161, 168, 194n17,
195n18, 195n20, 196n1, 208n15; and
Cult of the Lost Cause, xv, xxiii, xxv-
xxviii, 47, 80–85, 106, 111, 151, 157,
159, 169, 195n20, 227n6; and Old
South, xxv, 83, 152, 159, 161; and
Robert E. Lee, xxiv, xxvi–xxviii, 50,
53, 85, 105–7, 159, 218n15

Clabough, Casey, 26

Clark, Thomas D., 93

class divisions, xviii, xxxi, 7, 12, 19, 35,
37, 56, 62, 119, 121, 127–29, 150–51,
157–67, 177–86, 190n5, 210n5,
213n15, 218n17, 227n4, 231n17,
231n19

Cobb, James C., 193n11

Cohn, Deborah, 190n4, 193n11

community, xv, xxvi, 46, 50, 57, 66,
74, 83, 112, 114, 152, 154, 190n3,
192n10, 194n17, 217n13, 230n14

"confessional" poetry, 23, 35–41

consumerism. *See* flexible accumulation

contact zone, 187, 198n6

contrapposto, 12–13

Cold War, xiv, xxviii, xxix, 4–6, 12–13,
17, 202n14, 203n17

Confederate States of America. *See* Civil
War

Costello, Bonnie, 90, 215n5

countermemory, xiv, 73,–74, 149–51,
159–62, 166–67, 171–72, 176–77,
181–87, 226n2, 227n3; and counter-
nostalgia, 151–57, 227n6, 228n9

critical memory, xxx, 51, 73, 86

Culler, Jonathan, xix–xx, 88

cultural memory, xiii–xiv, xviii, xxviii,
xxx, 19, 46, 48, 91, 95, 118, 142,
150–53, 160, 162–63, 176–77, 188;
definition of, xxii–xxiii

Current, Richard, 48, 94

Daniels, Kate, xiv, xxxi, 149, 150–59,
186, 191n6, 227n4, 227n5

Davidson, Donald, xv, xxiv–xxviii, 50,
53, 158–59, 189n2, 195n18, 195n19,
195n20, 227n4

Davis, Fred, 50, 210n4

Davis, Thadious, 173

Dawes, Kwame, 226n1

Deacons for Defense and Justice, 130–
31

dialect, xv, xxii, xxxi, 31, 46, 57, 65, 71,
74, 88, 114, 125, 152, 164–69, 171–
75

Dickey, Christopher, 208n14

Dickey, James, xiv, xvi, xxix, 19–21,
23–46, 87, 191n6, 204n1, 205n2,

205n3, 205n4, 206n5, 206n6, 206n7, 207n8, 207n11, 208n13, 208n14, 208n15, 208n16, 209n17, 211n5, 220n4, 227n4

Dove, Rita, 177

Dungy, Camille T., 192n7

Edmundson, Mark, 27

Eiseley, Loren, 207n12

ekphrasis, xxxi, 2, 150, 184, 186

Eliot, T. S., 172

Emerson, Ralph Waldo, 207n8, 210n2

exceptionalism, xvii, xix, xxiii, 35, 46, 68, 93, 169, 187, 192n8

Farrell, Kirby, 221n8, 221n9, 222n12

Faulkner, William, xvii, 171, 191n6, 206n7, 219n1

filmic memory, xxviii–xxix, 7–19, 141, 197n3, 197n4, 199n8, 200n10, 204n19; definition of, 1–6; and kinesis, xxix, 2, 4–5, 7, 10–11, 16–19, 141, 200n10; and seriality, xxix, 2–9, 11–12, 16, 18, 199n9; and spectacle, xxviii–xxix, 2–11, 14–15, 18, 197n3, 203n15; and temporality, 2–3, 10–11, 14–16, 200n10

flexible accumulation, xiv, xvi–xvii, xxx, 17, 24, 83–86, 91–96, 98, 101–6, 110, 119, 143, 145, 149, 174, 183, 192n8, 192n9, 193n12, 216n8, 217n13, 218n14, 220n3

fordism, xiv, xxix, 24, 91, 93–96, 101–2, 105, 155, 166, 190n4, 192n9, 193n12, 216n8

Foucault, Michel, 92, 150-51, 171, 226n2, 228n8

Freud, Sigmund, xxi, 134, 183, 206n4, 221n8

Frow, John, 62

gender identity, xviii, 5, 35, 37, 41, 150, 174, 177, 179–83, 190n5, 208n13, 231n17, 231n19

Ginsberg, Allen, xxix, 24, 38–41

global capitalism. See flexible accumulation

global South. See transouthernism

Gotera, Vince, 121, 124, 226n24

Graham, Allison, 86

Grainge, Paul, 49

Great Depression, 160, 227n7

Greeson, Jennifer Rae, xvi

Griffin, Larry J., xxii–xxiii, 189n1

Griffith, D. W., 196n20

grotesque, xvi, xxx, 4–5, 9–11, 14, 36, 41, 43–44, 77–78, 103, 119, 128, 158, 163, 202n13, 209n17, 223n14

grounded globalism, xviii, xxxi, 149–50, 180, 232n20

Haddox, Thomas F., 192n10

Halbwachs, Maurice, xxii

Handley, George B., 192n7

Hannah, Barry, 202n13, 220n4

Harvey, David, 83, 110, 187, 192n9, 216n8

Hedge Coke, Allison, 196n21, 226n1

Henninger, Katherine, 231n17

heterotopic space, 160–62, 228n8, 228n9

historical prosody. *See* new lyric studies
historiophoty, xiv, xxviii, 1–3, 13, 18
Hudgins, Andrew, 196n21, 228n9
Hummer, T. R., 196n21

industrial capitalism. See *fordism*
interstate highway system, xxx, 60, 87,
    92–109, 119, 158, 177, 216n8, 217n9,
    217n10, 217n11, 217n12, 217n13,
    218n14, 218n15, 230n14

Jameson, Fredric, 30, 49, 50
Jarman, Mark, 87–88, 212n9, 215n5
Jarrell, Randall, 191n6, 196n21
Jarvis, Brian, 92, 110
Jarvis, Simon, xx, 88
Johnson, Robert, 175
Jones, Rodney, xiv, xxxi, 51, 149, 150,
    164–72, 186, 228n10
Jones, Suzanne W., 193n11
Jordan, Judy, xiv, xxxi, 149, 150, 159–
    164, 186, 227n7
Justice, Donald, xiv, xxix, 48, 61–68, 73,
    211n8, 212n9, 212n10, 212n11

Kammen, Michael, 48
kenosis, 88
kinship, 42, 57, 66, 68, 85, 106
Kirschten, Robert, 26, 206n6, 207n11
Komunyakaa, Yusef, xiv, xvi, xxx–xxxi,
    58, 116, 119, 121–47, 177, 219n1,
    219n2, 220n3, 220n4, 220n5, 220n6,
    222n11, 222n12, 223n15, 224n18,

224n19, 224n21, 225n23, 226n25,
    226n26
Kreyling, Michael, xvii–xviii, xxxii, 24,
    114, 187, 190n5, 192n10
Kristeva, Julia, xxi, 125
Ku Klux Klan, xxviii, 127, 195, 195n20

Lacan, Jacques, xxi, 169
Lang, John, 48, 192n7, 210n2, 215n4
L=A=N=G=U=A=G=E poetry, 172
Lanier, Sidney, 158
late capitalism. *See* flexible accumulation
Lewis, Tom, 216n8, 217n10
lynching, 8, 13–15, 123–40, 172, 192n7,
    196n20, 201n12, 222n14, 223n16
Lyotard, Jean-François, 125
Lytle, Andrew, 20, 96

Matthews, Carrie R., 193n11
McCarthy, Cormac, 202n13
McKee, Kathryn, 193n11
Mencken, H. L., 44, 157
metanostalgia, xxx, 51, 61–73
meter. *See* poetic rhythm
metonymy, 4, 81, 92, 95, 99, 112, 176,
    192n7
mode nostalgia, 49–50, 62–64, 67, 82;
    and mood nostalgia, 49–50, 56, 58,
    62, 67, 72, 74, 79, 82, 210n4
modernism, xxiii, xxv, 1, 190n4, 198n5,
    205n2
modernity, xv, xxiv–xxv, xxvii, 25, 49,
    50, 165, 195n20, 200n10, 210n2,
    227n5

Monteith, Sharon, 193n11

monumentalism, xvi, xxiv–xxvii, 60, 73, 80, 84, 110–11, 142, 151, 160, 194n18

Morgan, Robert, xiv, xxix, 48, 51, 56–61, 192n7, 210n2, 211n7

Mullen, Harryette, xiv, xxxi, 149, 150, 172–76, 177, 186, 229n11, 229n12

mythopoesis, xv, xxiii–xxv, xxviii, 1, 8, 16–19, 29, 37, 43–45, 80, 85, 95, 110, 134, 149, 165, 190n4, 195n20, 198n6, 201n12, 202n14, 207n12, 209n17, 211n6, 218n16, 220n3, 224n21, 225n22, 225n24, 225n26, 227n6, 228n8, 230n16, 230n18,

narrative poetry, xxxi, 1, 3, 4, 8, 52, 56, 73–74, 79, 87, 150, 151–54, 160, 164, 172, 177–78, 205n2, 213n14; and non-narrative poetry, 72, 87, 90, 91, 100, 103, 110, 115, 118, 123–24, 128, 134, 139–41, 143, 145–47, 172, 174, 215n6, 218n19

Native Americans, xvii, 2, 5, 9–11, 13, 57, 105, 111, 198n6, 199n7, 201n12, 202n14, 203n16, 211n6

Nelson, Dana D., 121, 222n14

new lyric studies, xx–xxi, 193n14

New Southern Studies. *See* transouthernism

Nietzsche, Friedrich, xxi, 46, 90, 198n18, 210n1, 226n2

Nora, Pierre, 25, 91, 207n10

nostalgia, xiv, xvi, xxiii, xxv–xxvi, xxix–xxx, 17–19, 20, 25, 36, 44–46, 47–86; and *algia*, xxix, 48, 49, 51, 54, 61, 62, 70; and *nostos*, xxix, 48, 49, 51, 61, 62, 68, 212n9

Osbey, Brenda Marie, 196n21, 226n1

pastoralism, xv, xxiii–xxiv, 8, 17, 19, 42–45, 48, 51, 59, 74–77, 80, 97, 164–65, 185, 195n20, 210n2, 213n16; and antipastoralism, 18–19, 41, 74–75, 77, 156, 164, 166, 192n7

Peacock, James L., xviii, xxxi, 149, 188, 193n11

Perloff, Marjorie, xix–xx, xxx–xxxi, 88

Poe, Edgar Allan, xxi

poetic rhythm, xix, xxxi, 2–3, 6–7, 11, 15–18, 25–32, 36, 40–42, 53–55, 64, 77, 80, 83, 88–90, 99–103, 108, 112, 114–17, 122–28, 130–33, 139–46, 152, 154–55, 159, 161, 173–76, 181, 194n15, 194n16, 207n11, 213n14, 220n5, 224n21; theories of, xix–xxii

Polk, Noel, 159, 227n6

Porter, Katherine Anne, 201n12

postmodernism, 25, 30, 49, 83, 174, 187, 192n9, 202n13, 216n8

postsouthernism, xvii–xviii, 25, 31, 42, 45–46, 82, 85, 192n10; and parody, xvii, xxix, 21, 23–25, 30–31, 34–46, 63, 74, 77, 80, 84–85, 92, 114, 164, 167, 170, 192n10, 205n2, 209n17

Preston, Howard Lawrence, 95, 217n9

primal memory, xiv, xvi, xxix, 20–21, 23–45, 197n5, 206n5, 207n8, 207n9, 207n10; and Darwinism, 24–26, 29,

primal memory (cont.)
205n4, 206n5; and essentialism, 23,
28–30, 33, 35, 41, 45, 205n4, 208n16;
and Freudianism, 205n4
primitivism. *See* primal memory
prison system, 127–28, 223n16
Pulitzer Prize, xiv, 19, 196n1, 211n8,
212n13, 214n1, 219n1, 228n10,
229n13, 232n20
punctum, 179–81, 184

Quentin Compson complex, xxvii

race, xiii, xxv–xxvi, xxx, 77–79, 80, 121–
147, 150, 152–54, 172–86, 190n5,
196n20, 198n5, 222n14, 223n16,
229n11, 231n19; and legal segrega-
tion and desegregation, xiv, xxx, 19,
135, 140, 153, 175, 183–84, 197n1,
222n14, 229n12
Ramazani, Jahan, xix
Ramsey, Paul, 51–52, 207n11, 211n6
Ransom, John Crowe, xv, xxiv–xxv, 60,
121, 154, 161, 191n6, 197n1, 227n4
Rash, Ron, 196n21, 205n1
religious imagery, xiii, xv, xxviii, 31, 36–
37, 42, 45, 88, 103, 112, 164, 173,
206n4, 209n17, 215n3, 215n4, 217n9,
220n3
restorative nostalgia, xxx, 48–63, 66–67,
71, 73–74, 80, 83, 86, 210n4; and
reflective nostalgia, 49–51, 55, 66,
74, 87
Ritivoi, Andreea Deciu, 79
Romine, Scott, xv, xviii, 190n3

Rowell, Charles Henry, 177, 179, 231n19
Rubin, Louis D., xxiii, 190n5, 191n6,
192n10, 194n17
rurality. *See* agrarianism

Salas, Angela, 134, 224n20, 225n23
savage ideal, 24, 30, 35–37, 41, 158,
206n5, 209n17
Scarbrough, George, xiv, xxix, 48, 51–55,
61, 210n5, 211n6, 211n8
sexuality, 14–15, 20, 23, 33, 36–37,
40–44, 103, 190n5, 209n17
Sharp, Nicholas, 77
Simpson, Lewis, xv, 193n10
simulacrum, xxx, 32, 35, 83, 90–92,
95–96, 112, 119, 216n7, 217n10
slavery, xxv, xxvi–xxvii, 36, 38, 127–29,
162, 169, 196n20, 222n13, 223n16,
224n17, 227n6, 229n11
Slotkin, Richard, 11–12, 201n11, 202n14,
203n17
Smith, Dave, xiv, xxix, 32, 48, 73, 79–
86, 191n6, 206n6, 207n11, 213n15,
213n16
Smith, Jon, 193n11
Sobchack, Vivian, 3, 199n8
social death, 127–29, 134, 160–61,
222n12, 222n13
Soja, Edward, 92
Sontag, Susan, 178–79, 186, 230n16,
231n18
southern renascence, xv–xvi, 46, 149,
171, 191n6
Spitzer, Leo, 73
Starobinski, Jean, 48–49, 210n3
Stevens, Wallace, 90, 110, 128n16

Stewart, Susan, xx, 49, 61, 140, 194n15

Suarez, Ernest, 20, 24, 30, 96, 206n5, 213n16, 215n6

sublime, xxi–xxii, xxx, 30, 31, 64, 122–27, 135, 145–46, 194n16, 210n3, 225n21; and negative sublime, xxx, 88–90, 101, 115, 119, 215n5

surrealism, xvi, xxx, 10, 35–36, 42, 124–27, 128, 134, 173, 196n20

synesthesia, 129

Tal, Kalí, 134, 221n8

Tate, Allen, xv, xxiii–xxvi, 19, 50, 53, 121, 158, 161, 195n18, 195n19, 197n1, 208n15, 211n5, 227n4

Taylor, Henry, xiv, xxix, 48, 73–79, 212n13, 213n14

Tichi, Cecelia, 102

Till, Emmett, 133, 222n12, 223n14

Timrod, Henry, 158

Tompkins, Jane, 7–8, 202n14

Torgovnick, Mariana, 25, 207n9

Tuan, Yi-fu, 136, 138, 223n15

traditional southernism, xvii, xviii, xxii–xxiii, xxiv, xxix, xxx, 19, 31, 42, 45, 46, 47–48, 59, 65, 66–68, 73–74, 80–81, 91, 93, 105, 113, 115, 119, 121, 128, 149–51, 152, 154–56, 164, 172–173, 178, 186–187, 192n8, 192n9, 194n17, 217n9

transregionalism. See transouthernism

transnational South. See transouthernism

transouthernism, xiv, xvi–xviii, xxxi–xxxii, 17, 24, 46, 48, 69, 86, 91, 96, 106, 119, 124–25, 134, 142, 144–47, 149–51, 169–70, 172–73, 176, 178, 186–88, 192n7, 193n11, 193n12, 217n12, 224n21, 226n1, 232n20

trauma, xiv, xvi, xxxi, 24, 46, 58, 78, 82, 199, 121, 123–25, 127–46, 162, 200n10, 220n3, 220n7, 221n8, 221n9, 223n14, 225n24, 226n26; and poetic rhythm, xxxi, 122–23, 125, 127, 141, 220n5

Trefzer, Annette, 193n11

Trethewey, Natasha, xiv, xxxi, 149, 150, 177–86, 229n13, 230n14, 230n15, 231n17, 231n19, 232n20

Turner, Daniel Cross, 178, 215n3, 224n21, 228n9

urbanization, xiv, xv, xxix, 24, 43–44, 61, 67, 91, 93, 105, 151, 210n3; and sub-urbanization, xiv, 61, 66, 68, 93–94, 117, 216n7, 218n17

Vanderbilt Fugitives, xv, xvii, xxiii, xxv, xxxi, 18, 190n4, 192n8; and neo-Fugitives, 19, 84, 121; and New Criticism, xxiii; and Vanderbilt Agrarians, xxiii, 18–19, 37, 41, 96, 190n4, 192n8, 195n19, 197n1

Vendler, Helen, 80, 86, 114

vernacular. See dialect

Vietnam, xiv, xxix, xxx–xxxi, 6, 12–13, 23–24, 41, 122–27, 133–46, 189n1, 203n17, 204n18, 219n1, 220n4, 222n10, 224n18, 224n19, 224n20, 224n21, 225n23, 225n24, 226n25

voice. See dialect